OTHERWISE

FARLEY MOWAT

OTHERWISE

McCLELLAND & STEWART

Library and Archives Canada Cataloguing in Publication

Mowat, Farley, 1921–
    Otherwise / Farley Mowat.

ISBN 978-0-7710-6489-0

1. Mowat, Farley, 1921–. 2. Authors, Canadian (English) – 20th century – Biography. I. Title.

PS8526.089Z473 2008   C818'.5409   C2008-901950-4

We acknowledge the financial support of the Government of Canada through the Book Publishing Industry Development Program and that of the Government of Ontario through the Ontario Media Development Corporation's Ontario Book Initiative. We further acknowledge the support of the Canada Council for the Arts and the Ontario Arts Council for our publishing program.

Typeset in Berkley Book by M&S, Toronto
Printed and bound in Canada

ANCIENT FOREST
FRIENDLY

This book is printed on acid-free paper that is 100% recycled, ancient-forest friendly (100% post-consumer recycled).

McClelland & Stewart Ltd.
75 Sherbourne Street
Toronto, Ontario
M5A 2P9
www.mcclelland.com

1 2 3 4 5   12 .11 10 09 08

This book is for all the the Others I have known. It is also for the Sea Shepherd Society, and its leader, Captain Paul Watson, the most indomitable defender of the Others I have ever known.

CONTENTS

AUTHOR'S NOTE

This book is a memoir of my life between early 1937 and the autumn of 1948, excluding my descent into the black horror of the Second World War. Essentially it is a story of discovery that goes to the heart of who, and what I am. It may well be my last hurrah.

Because I've always written books drawn from my own life and experiences, some sections of *Otherwise* inevitably revisit parts of my life that have appeared in greater detail in earlier works, notably *And No Birds Sang*, *Never Cry Wolf*, *No Man's River*, *The Dog Who Wouldn't Be*, and *Born Naked*. I make no apologies. This book overlaps these in time, and seminal incidents in one's life inconveniently remain so.

Part One

BEFORE THE STORM

1937–42

· 1 ·

THE LAST BEST WEST

Born in mid-May 1921 – lilac time in the small town of Trenton on the northern shore of Lake Ontario's Bay of Quinte – I spent my early years messing about in swamps, woods, and farmyards; falling in and out of boats; and surviving in various decrepit houses while establishing fundamental relationships with such disparate beings as snapping turtles, portly spiders, rapier-billed herons, honeybees, a bear who visited me in dreams, Charlie Haultain's silver foxes, crayfish and eels, water snakes along the Murray Canal, a passel of mongrel dogs, and Beatrix – an enormous earthworm who lived through an entire winter in a tin can by my bedside.

When I was eight we moved to Windsor, a grungy industrial city given over to the manufacture of cars and rye whiskey. This move brought about a severe disruption of my universe; never-theless I was able to find natural companions even here. These included a black squirrel named Jitters; a toothy but chummy baby crocodile (gift of a relative in Florida); an enormous and complacent toad who lived under our back porch; gorgeous luna and cecropia moths as large as a human hand whose caterpillars I reared in glass jars until they metamorphosed and I could let them fly to freedom; and Hughie, son of a vagrant victim of the Great Depression, who was so enamoured of grass snakes that he got himself expelled from school for carrying writhing knots of them in his pockets.

Some people felt that Helen, my raven-haired, dark-eyed beauty of a mother, and Angus, my dapper, sinewy father, were recklessly permissive in letting me consort so freely with creatures of such questionable status. But because she possessed infinite faith in a protective providence Helen did not fear for my safety. And Angus was of the opinion that broadening one's associations with animate creation and taking chances were essential to a well-rounded life.

He was so convinced of this that in 1933, just when the worldwide economic meltdown known as the Dirty Thirties was at its worst, he abandoned a secure position as Windsor's chief librarian to accept a similar job at half the pay in distant Saskatoon, Saskatchewan. Similar, but by no means *equivalent*, for the desiccated prairie town had been so battered by the Depression and by several years of blistering drought that many of its residents were on relief and the town was all but bankrupt.

Years later, when I inquired why he made the move, my father seemed surprised.

"Well, you see, Saskatchewan was a dust bowl by then, barely able to afford to feed its human inhabitants. Nothing much left over for the mind, you understand. Library services had all but collapsed just when people needed books as never before. I couldn't bring them bread but, by Heaven, I could at least help them get books to ease the misery a bit. . . . And then too, what an opportunity it was for the three of us to explore new horizons and perhaps learn a little something about how others lived. . . ."

A generation earlier the Great Plains had been devastated by steel-shod plows in the hands of modern men, but had not as yet been utterly laid waste. Although most of the larger natural inhabitants, including bison, grizzly bears, antelope, wolves, whooping cranes, trumpeter swans, and aboriginal people, had been exterminated or reduced to vestigial remnants, a wealth of life still survived even within Saskatoon's city limits. And where the city gave way to the remnant prairies the world of the Others remained in full and vital ferment. This was my entire world during the years between 1933 and 1937, although I did make one singularly exhilarating foray beyond it – one which was of crucial importance in shaping my future.

My passion for the Others had brought me to the notice of Frank Farley, a great-uncle on my mother's side. In 1882, at the age of twenty, Frank had left his family's farm in Ontario and gone homesteading in the Golden West, where he broke several hundred acres near Camrose, Alberta, and farmed them to such good effect that when he retired almost fifty years later, he was wealthy enough to indulge his lifelong fascination with birds. A self-made naturalist in a tradition that sanctioned and encouraged killing wild animals with such avidity that many species were literally pursued to extinction, Frank's specialty was birds' eggs. By the 1930s, he had amassed such an enormous and varied collection that he was accounted one of Canada's outstanding scientists.

Although he and I had never actually met, the far-flung family net had informed him of my fascination with wild creatures. In January of 1935, he wrote my parents proposing that, come spring, I accompany him on an expedition to Hudson Bay to collect the eggs of arctic birds, a project in which "a quick young fellow could be of great assistance." This proposal was as entrancing to me as the offer of a trip to the moon might be to a youngster of today. My parents, bless them, acquiesced without demur and so it was arranged that Frank would pick me up on June 5, a little more than three weeks after my fifteenth birthday.

My mother's diary for that date notes: "Bunje [my nickname] up at 3:00 a.m. No peace for any of us until 7:30, when Uncle Frank's train arrived from Calgary and we went to meet it. Bunje terribly excited."

When Frank Farley swung down from the step of the parlour car, I could hardly have been more agitated if God himself had alighted. My great-uncle seemed so much bigger than life. He stood well over six feet and wore knee-length, lace-up boots. His head was a huge bald dome dominated by the large family nose. His eyes were hooded and had the unnerving stare of a turkey vulture. He was the most awe-inspiring human being I had yet encountered.

But, thankfully, he was smiling. One hand clamped my shoulder so powerfully I almost squealed.

"This is the bird-boy, eh?" he boomed as he shook my slight frame none too gently. "Not much bigger than a bird at that."

He let me go and turned to introduce his companion – Albert Wilks was slight and dark-haired, a young school teacher who had also been enlisted to my uncle's expedition.

Frank explained what he had in mind for us. We would camp on the tundra near Churchill until the pack ice covering the inland sea known as Hudson Bay had slackened enough to permit travel in a boat belonging to someone called Husky Harris. Who would take us north along the coast to Seal River, where we would spend a month making the first scientific collection of animal life from that region. Frank said our collection might include white wolves, arctic foxes, perhaps even a walrus.

I was so bewitched by heroic fantasies of this northern summer that I hardly felt the train pull out of the station. By dinner time the train had left the "big prairie" behind and was trundling north and east through poplar and birch parkland. At midnight it drew to a halt beside the small Hudson Bay Junction station. Here we disembarked to await the arrival of a northbound train that would take us to the enigmatically named town of The Pas.

I dropped into a broken sleep on a station bench until a baleful whistle roused me and we stumbled aboard our train, a colonist car built in the 1800s to ferry European immigrants west from Montreal. It was constructed mainly of wood. The seats were hardwood slats without upholstery of any kind. Lighting was provided by oil lamps whose chimneys were dark with age and soot. It was heated by a wood stove upon which passengers could make tea, cook, and heat water for washing. The toilet was a tiny cubicle with a simple hole in the floor through which one could see the ties rush past – an experience that gave me vertigo, and constipation.

Our fellow passengers were mostly trappers of European, native, or mixed blood. I was fascinated by a trio of middle-aged Inuit (the first I had ever met) on their way back to their homes in the High Arctic after having spent many months in a tuberculosis sanatorium in southern Manitoba. They spoke no English and, since nobody else in the car spoke Inuktitut, I could not begin to satisfy my enormous curiosity about them.

At the ramshackle frontier village of The Pas, our car was shunted onto the recently completed Hudson Bay Railway to become part of a train pulled by a steam locomotive that would in its own good time haul us to Churchill. The train consisted of a long string of boxcars filled with wheat to be shipped from Churchill to Europe, with our solitary colonist car, a baggage car, and a caboose attached to the back end.

Entering the boreal forest, we bumped along at a lethargic twenty miles an hour through a seemingly endless shroud of black spruce trees and peat-filled quagmires. Frank joined me at one of the dirt-streaked windows as I peered out at a seemingly endless sweep of scraggly forest dotted with saturated "moose meadows."

"That's muskeg, me boy. Goes all the way to Churchill, which is why they call this train the Muskeg Express."

Whatever it might be called, it was vigorously alive. The stove was well fed with billets of birch, and the aroma of bannocks fried in pork fat mingled with the burnt molasses reek of the "twist" tobacco most trappers smoked. Those who did not smoke chewed "snouse" (snuff). There were no cuspidors, and few addicts could resist spitting on the hot flanks of the stove in passing.

Tea billies came to the boil and were passed from seat to seat so everyone could have a swig. Bert heated us up a pan of pork and beans. I watched, fascinated, as a Cree matron across the aisle breast-fed her youngest while an older child sucked condensed milk out of a beer bottle.

The first night aboard the Express was given over to celebration. There was lively singing in Cree, French, English, and tongues unidentifiable to me. Bottles were freely passed around. Some men played poker and there was a fight during which I thought I saw the flash of a knife blade.

At this juncture, one of the trainmen came along and leaned down to yell something in Frank's ear. My uncle nodded and pulled me to my feet, bellowing, "Grab your bedroll and follow me!" We swayed out of our car and to the rear through the baggage car, which contained several canoes and a line of Indian dogs chained to a cable along one wall. Beyond it was the caboose, where the crew had its quarters.

"You'll sleep here, Farley me boy. Keep you out of trouble, and it'll be a damn sight quieter."

The crew gave me a bunk and next morning shared breakfast with me. The brakeman allowed me up into the cupola. Reached by a short ladder, this small tower on the back of the caboose provided a stunning view of the country we were passing through. It was rather like having one's own observation car. I was also free to step out onto a porch at the rear of the caboose and I was having a pee from this vantage point when something flipped up from the roadbed and spun viciously past my head. When another followed, I jumped back inside and told one of the crew about it. He laughed.

"That's spikes popping out. You see, kid, the roadbed over the muskeg is so spongy the tracks sink down with the weight of the train, and when they spring back up they flip the spikes out of the ties like stones out of a slingshot."

Thereafter I used the indoor facilities, intimidating as they might be.

I spent a lot of time in the cupola watching for wolves, moose, deer, but saw disappointingly few of these others. Occasionally the Express would ooze to a stop in the midst of nowhere and a couple of people would emerge from the forest to take delivery of packages tossed out of the baggage car. Sometimes a canoe would be offloaded at a river crossing and a Cree family would go paddling away in it. Civilization was limited to the section points, spaced about fifty miles apart, where two or three men charged with track maintenance lived in tiny shanties that bore enigmatic station signs such as WETUKSO . . . WABODEN . . . LA PEROUSE . . . SIPIWESK.

During the morning of our second day out from The Pas, we crossed the mighty Nelson River flowing eastward into Hudson Bay. Then the right-of-way headed due north and the train crawled over a roadbed floating on muskeg, which in turn floated on permafrost. Even in these first days of June the land was still half-buried under snowdrifts and its major lakes and rivers were icebound. Uncle Frank worried that spring seemed to be exceptionally late this year and grew increasingly gloomy about the prospects of travel on Hudson Bay.

The trembling roadbed slowed the train to a virtual crawl. There was little to interest me in the snow-streaked country beyond, and

I was reduced to entertaining myself by clocking the distance we had travelled from The Pas by counting the black-and-white mile-boards nailed to telegraph poles. I had just watched mile-board 410 slide past when the rusty whistle of our engine disturbed the quiet. At its first blast I looked forward from the cupola over the humped backs of the grain cars and beheld what appeared to be a tawny brown river surging out of the thin forest to the eastward and pouring across the track in front of us.

The French-Canadian brakeman scrambled up into the cupola beside me.

"*C'est la foule!*" he shouted. It is the throng! This was the name early French explorers had given to one of the most spectacular displays of animate creation to be found upon our continent or, perhaps, anywhere on earth: the annual mass migration of Barren Land caribou, wild reindeer of the Canadian north.

Although the train's whistle rasped with increasing exasperation, the caribou did not deviate and at length the engineer gave up his attempt to intimidate the multitude and the train drew to a halt with a resigned huff.

For an hour a living river flowed unhurriedly across the track. When the last stragglers had passed, the engine gathered its strength again and we continued north.

At 11 in the evening we rolled sluggishly into Churchill in broad daylight. We had arrived in the Land of the Long Day at a latitude not far short of the southern tip of Greenland. Winter still held Churchill in thrall, its unpainted clapboard shacks and shanties half-buried in dirty grey drifts. The vast sweep of Hudson Bay extending to the northern and eastern horizons was still ice-bound. The tidal estuary of the Churchill River was a frigid mix of open water and break-up ice. The treeless waste of frozen mosses, peat bogs, and ponds surrounding the townsite was smeared with dirty snow. It all made for a singularly desolate scene, one that was not made any more welcoming by a colossal man-made object at its centre – a gargantuan concrete grain elevator. Fifteen storeys high, and looming monstrously over the surrounds of Churchill, this behemoth with its adjacent storage silos and docks for ocean-going vessels was the reason the Hudson Bay Railway and Churchill existed.

Discovered by a Dane, Jens Munk, in 1619, Churchill became and remained a linchpin of the Hudson's Bay Company's empire until the early 1930s, when it was reinvented as a subarctic port from which to ship prairie grain to Europe. When I first saw it on that grey day in 1936, its massive structures seemed to rival the pyramids. However, before I had been many days in their shadow, they lost their appeal for I became enchanted by the wonders of another world, one in which man's works played no significant role.

Soon after our arrival we loaded all our gear aboard a little jigger – a hand-propelled rail trolley – then with Uncle Frank and Bert pumping its handles, we rattled out of Churchill on a narrow-gauge spur line to an abandoned shack some eight miles southeast of the townsite. Not much more than a shanty with tarpapered walls, it contained a barrel stove, double-tiered bunks, a broken table, and the desiccated corpse of an arctic fox that had apparently jumped in through a broken window and been unable to find a way out.

We intended to remain here only until the pack ice withdrew from the coastal waters of Hudson Bay. But the ice remained implacable so we stayed on at the Black Shack for the duration.

We may have stayed *at* the shack but were seldom in it because Frank was not one to waste time.

"Look about you," he lectured me as I tried to linger in bed one shivering morning when our water pails were skimmed with ice. "The birds out on the tundra haven't slept a wink. Too darned busy! And here it is 4:00 a.m. and *you* want more sleep! Up and at 'em, sonny boy!"

I had thought we would be "living off the land" but neither caribou nor seals were procurable so Bert, who acted as our cook, fed us oatmeal porridge, bannocks, boiled beans, and, on special occasions, cornmeal mush. What protein we got came from Uncle Frank's double-barrelled shotgun with which he vigorously slaughtered ducks, ptarmigan, and shorebirds. Bert added some of the corpses to a thin concoction he called Mulligan stew, but many more ended up in the ditch that served as our garbage dump.

When I agonized about these wanton killings, Uncle Frank put me straight.

"Don't be so soft, boy. There's millions of birds out there and if we don't get them something else will. It's honest sport. Besides, we're doing it for science. I measure every specimen I shoot and note the condition of its plumage. Science needs all the information it can get."

My duties, as specified by Frank, were to "find every nest you can. The rarer the bird the better. If she hasn't finished laying her full clutch of eggs, leave the nest alone until she has. If you aren't sure what species she is, shoot her and bring her back along with the eggs."

Mine not to question why – especially when orders came from such an Olympian as my great-uncle. I set about doing as I was told feeling no qualms of conscience.

The subarctic nesting season was short so Bert and I were out roaming the tundra almost every day, even in fog or freezing rain, relentlessly searching for nests, especially those of waterfowl and shorebirds. I was a good finder and loved the work. To flush such a rarity as a Hudsonian godwit from her four eggs elated me as much as if I had uncovered treasure. Between us Bert and I took a heavy toll from the plover, curlews, sandpipers, ducks, geese, and loons who thronged the morass of water and mossy tussocks intent on reproducing during the all-too-brief summer season.

"The pair of you will make first-rate scientists if you keep up the good work," Frank told us encouragingly.

We emptied the eggs of their contents by blowing air through a pipette into a small hole bored with the business end of a dentist's drill in the side of the shell. If fresh, the contents would come bubbling out. If the egg was incubated, we would have to delicately fish the embryo out, using a needle with a bent tip. We saved the contents of fresh and slightly incubated eggs for omelettes. As the incubation season advanced, these omelettes acquired an increasingly pink tinge and meaty flavour.

Lemmings abounded. This was a peak year in their cycle and they were making the most of it. Friendly little rodents somewhat resembling hamsters, they ran around the cabin floor paying little heed to us unless we tried to sweep them out the door.

One morning we three went "collecting" along a high granite ridge fringing the still-frozen bay. We were after the eggs of rough-legged hawks (famed lemming hunters) who occupied a chain of nests spaced at intervals of a mile or so along the seaward face of the cliffs. Bert and I were delegated to do the climbing while Frank supervised from below. Rough-legs are large soaring hawks who normally avoid humans. Bert and I had stolen the clutches from two nests and delivered the eggs to Uncle Frank, waiting below, when the owners of a third nest decided enough was enough.

As I began ascending, they both stooped upon me with talons outstretched and beaks gaping wide. Missing me by inches, the first attacker made me cower against the cliff. The second hit home.

My head was buffeted against the rock by fiercely beating wings. When I raised an arm to protect myself, it was raked from wrist to elbow by sharp talons. I thought I was going to fall, then Frank's shotgun bellowed and my attacker soared away, still screaming defiance.

I slid down the face of the cliff to land on the beach, scared and shaken. Bert bound up my arm with his handkerchief, but Uncle Frank had scant sympathy for me.

"You must have done something to upset them," he said crossly and completely without irony.

To do him justice, he did try to make amends. When next he went into town for supplies and to see if any possibility yet existed for the proposed voyage to Seal River, he took me along.

We went to "Ma" Riddoch's tavern, in whose dark depths we met the redoubtable Husky Harris, a former trapper renowned for having had numerous Inuit wives. He was equally notorious for his addiction to the use of one particular adjective. I listened in awe as he told us there was no effing hope of effingly well getting to the effing Seal River, but he would be effing happy to effing well take us hunting effing white whales in the effing estuary (where the whales were gathering to calve).

Later that day I went alone to the docks to watch several hundred beluga (another name for white whales) feeding in the estuary shallows. When a pair of motorboats put out from shore and their crews began shooting at the whales with heavy-calibre rifles, a marine version of shooting goldfish in a bowl ensued. The whales churned the shoal water in their efforts to escape, and I could see splashes of crimson appearing on the backs and flanks of many.

When I later told my uncle about this, he was mildly disapproving. "That'll be some of the men employed at the grain elevator having their sport. Bit of a waste. The natives can use a couple for dog feed but most of the ones hit will roll up on the beach dead and stink the place up with no profit to anyone."

The natives were mostly Chipewyans from the interior of northern Manitoba who made their way out to Churchill each spring to trade pelts at the Hudson's Bay Company post. They were of interest to Frank as a possible source of specimens so we visited their tent camp on the flats by the river. While he dickered with them for some white fox pelts, I looked about with awe.

They were unlike any people I had ever seen. Small, dark, and solemn (at least around strangers), they spoke a language full of rustling sibilants. Partly dressed in caribou skins, they lived in teepees made of soot-blackened canvas full of rips and tears. When I approached one teepee too closely, an old woman shook a gnarled fist at me. But a much younger woman – hardly more than a girl – smiled and beckoned while at the same time opening the front of her shirt. Unsure whether she was being seductive or mocking, I concentrated on what my uncle was doing.

He was being offered something so exotic I could barely contain my excitement. A live wolf pup! When Frank shook his head and turned away from the little creature straining at the end of a dog chain, I could not contain myself.

"*I'll* buy it!" I cried urgently. "I'll take it home and tame it! Please, Uncle Frank, tell them I'll buy it!"

He continued to shake his head. "You can't afford it. They want its bounty value."

"Lend me the money," I pleaded. "I'll pay it back, I promise!"

"You're talking foolishness, boy. Come along now."

Summer finally arrived during the last week in June and temperatures soared into the sixties. Except for hordes of mosquitoes emerging from the ponds, we could have gone around half-naked. The last of the ice and snow vanished magically. The egg-laying season was ending and all too soon it would be time for both the birds and us to go south.

But first I felt I had to collect one more set of rough-legged hawk's eggs to make up for the clutch I had failed to get. Although Frank had said no more about this failure, memory of it rankled, so one warm and sunny morning I set off alone for the coastal cliffs. I did not go to the stretch we had already robbed but went farther east, where nests turned out to be few and far between. Finally finding one, I climbed down to it and its three eggs from above, keeping a wary eye on the parent birds wheeling overhead.

Although I knew that this late in the season the eggs would be ready to hatch, I collected them anyway, wrapped them in cotton wool, and packed them into my haversack. Then I took the opportunity to look around from my high vantage point.

The waters of the great bay sucked and seethed at stranded floes below me. Open-water leads crisscrossed the decaying ice to seaward. A mile to the east along the coast a strange object loomed. Field glasses revealed it to be the remains of a wrecked ship.

It was irresistible. Sliding down the cliff I hurried off to examine the wreck. It proved to be the forward section of a small freighter that had driven ashore many years earlier. I climbed into it through a maze of twisted, rusty plates and girders until I found myself standing high on the angled rise of the bow. Only then did I discover I was not alone.

Three ivory-coloured bears were ambling along the beach toward me. Two were not much larger than spaniels but the leader was enormous.

"Stay the hell away from a sow bear with cubs!" was a maxim that had been drilled into me in southern climes where relatively small black bears were to be found. I assumed it would apply in spades to the monstrous apparition padding toward me now with such fluid and lethal grace.

Briefly I thought of trying to flee, but to move at all would have meant revealing myself – and I had no stomach for a confrontation. And since the light breeze was in my favour, blowing from the bears toward me, there was a possibility they might pass the wreck without ever realizing I was crouching in it only a few feet above them.

They were within a dozen yards when, for no apparent reason, the female stopped and reared back on her ample haunches. She extended her forelegs for balance, displaying immense paws and long, curved claws. Her pink tongue protruded from between a gleaming palisade of teeth. Perhaps she heard my heart pounding. She looked up and our glances met. Her black nose wrinkled. She sniffed explosively then, with a litheness astonishing in so huge a creature, turned and was off at a gallop in the direction from which she had come, the cubs bounding along behind her.

My departure in the opposite direction was as precipitate. By the time I regained the haven of the Black Shack, I was winded and the hawk's eggs had been churned into a bloody mess in the bottom of my haversack.

I enjoyed a triumphal return to Saskatoon where my tales of Inuit, Indians, and polar bears, together with a cracked walrus tusk found on the beach, a carton of arctic birds' eggs, a pair of friendly lemmings, and a crippled but ferociously lively jaeger – a species of gull possessed of the attitudes and attributes of a bird of prey – provided me with considerable status among my peers.

Through the long winter that followed I was haunted by dreams of the Arctic. Just before Christmas Uncle Frank had written to ask if I would be interested in going north with him again come spring. This time, he assured me, we would certainly reach Seal River and might even travel farther north to the legendary Thlewiaza River, where a trapper had reported freshwater seals of a kind not to be found elsewhere.

Again my parents agreed to let me go, and perhaps they were relieved for they were preoccupied with other problems: my mother with despair at what she referred to in her diary as "this ghastly exile from everything I've ever known"; and Angus because he was at war with his library board over his efforts to provide books to impoverished farmers far beyond the city limits.

Angus was also preoccupied by what to do about a new job offer – that of inspector of public libraries for Ontario, a job that carried with it the prospect of his eventually becoming director of library services for that province. He did not tell either Helen or me about the offer until he had accepted it, so it was not until April that I learned instead of accompanying Uncle Frank back to Hudson Bay I would soon be moving to a new home in Ontario.

I was stunned by the decision, which came as close to breaking my heart as anything I had ever experienced. Being deprived of my arctic adventure was bad enough. The realization that I was also to lose the plains, sloughs, poplar bluffs, and open skies of the prairies and be robbed of the companionship of the creatures, human and otherwise, I had found there, was almost more than I could bear.

I retreated into sullen rebellion. Helen noted in her diary: "This decision has changed poor Bunje into a horrid little boy!"

She at least was aware of my anguish. Angus was not, or if he was chose to hide the knowledge beneath parental bluster.

"Taking you back east where you belong is the best thing that could happen to you. So chin up and take it like a man."

But I was *not* a man, and I found the prospect of leaving the west intolerable. In the privacy of my bedroom, I raged and wept and made desperate plans to run away. My closest friend, Bruce Billings (a farm boy so attuned to the prairie that he proudly called him*self* a gopher), volunteered to join me as did Murray Robb, my next-best friend. It was no use. My time in Saskatoon was inexorably drawing to a close.

May arrived and with it my sixteenth birthday. One morning Helen asked how I would like to celebrate it. I knew exactly what I wanted.

One of the few surviving expanses of aboriginal shortgrass prairie still survived to the southeast of Saskatoon. Waved with small hills, furrowed by coulees, studded with poplar bluffs, and pocked with sloughs, it had escaped the devastation visited on the plains country by homesteaders. It still belonged to the Others. For me it was the last best west, and it held my heart.

"I'd like to spend a week camping out with Brucie and Murray at the big slough near Dundurn. Just the three of us and Rex and Mutt."

Helen smiled. "I'll talk to your father, dear. I think he's feeling a teeny bit guilty about taking you away from all this. . . ." She waved her hand as if to encompass the whole of Saskatchewan. "I'll try to make him feel a little more so."

She was as good as her word.

Early on the morning of May 11, we three loaded ourselves, dogs, and camping gear into my father's Model A, and he drove us over rutted dirt roads across the greening plains to a spreading poplar bluff south of the dour little village of Dundurn. Angus did not linger, nor did I encourage him to do so. It would be a long time before I fully forgave him for having so abruptly altered the tenor of my life.

Spring had come early to the prairies. The sky was clear and the sun beat down brilliantly. There had been little rain but the new grass was vividly, lusciously green and richly alive. The floor of the bluff was dusted by silky seed parachutes drifting down from the cottonwood trees. This snowy stuff kept getting into the dogs' noses and making them sneeze as they snuffled at the burrows made by wood gophers.

We three felt so good we played like little kids, lying on our backs waving our arms and legs to make angels in the cottonwood snow. We gathered piles of it to serve as mattresses beneath our bedrolls. We pitched the tent and cleared a place for a firepit, then went off to visit the slough where, in past years, I had hunted ducks with my father in the autumn and searched for the nests of water-birds in spring.

Big Slough, as it was known locally, was really a lake about six miles long and a mile wide. Although the prolonged drought had turned much of the surrounding country into a dust bowl and reduced the slough itself to little more than a huge alkaline puddle, its murky water still stood knee-deep even among the broad beds of reeds and cattails fringing its shores.

And it was overflowing with life.

Out in the middle, several hundred whistling swans formed a raft so dense it looked like an ice floe. The swans were surrounded by milling multitudes of ducks, geese, grebes, coots, and other waterfowl, some swimming, some diving, others in free flight. We stood at the edge of the rushes and marvelled at the spectacle.

In the southern sky, a heavy-flying wedge of massive white birds with huge heads and jet-black wings was descending like a ghostly phalanx of pterodactyls from Jurassic times. They were white pelicans – fliers whose antiquity stretches back to the age of dinosaurs. There was a wild flurry on the slough as lesser birds scattered to get out of the way and the pelicans planed grandly down to obscure the surface in a curtain of spray.

We worked our way around the slough's perimeter to a stretch of muddy foreshore almost hidden beneath a horde of godwits, curlews, avocets, and smaller shorebirds.

The Others were everywhere in such abundance and variety that I gave up trying to keep track of their kinds and numbers. Our ears were filled with the rush of wings and the cacophony of avian voices gabbling about food, sex, travel, and whatever else birds talk about. With Mutt and Rex plunging after us, we waded out into the reed beds, where we were assailed by mobs of red-winged and yellow-headed blackbirds defending nesting territories. Muskrat houses covered with fresh layers of swamp muck stood among the rushes. Each mound seemed to have a pair of grebes or coots nesting upon it. Marsh wrens were weaving their delicate hanging nests on cattail stems while unseen sora rails yammered at us for trespassing on their watery turf.

On our way back to camp, we had to wait while Rex and Mutt excavated hillocks of soft mud pushed up by pocket gophers.

Although the dogs did not uncover any of these secretive little mammals, they did unearth scores of yellow-spotted tiger salamanders who were using the gopher burrows as covered ways through which to travel to the slough where they would spawn.

When we got back to camp the emerald-leafed poplars were alive with waves of warblers and other small songbirds. Branches overhead were illuminated by the azure flash of mountain bluebirds, the orange challenge of orioles, and the flame of rose-breasted grosbeaks.

We were too tired to pay them much attention. When a skein of sandhill cranes flew low overhead trumpeting their sonorous calls, I looked up only briefly before falling back in a drift of cotton snow to wonder aloud if we would ever again see such a multitude of living creatures as we had seen this day. Bruce was lying near me chewing on a twig. He spat it out to say, "Dunno. Maybe. If we was awful lucky."

Six days later the Model A came puttering back to the campsite, and it was then – at that hour and in that place – that I really bade farewell to the prairie world – to Bruce and Murray and to all the Others with whom I had lived some of the best years of my life.

GO EAST YOUNG MAN

Angus was born at about the same time as the gasoline engine was invented but he nourished the conviction that the fates had chosen the wind as Man's prime mover. Though circumstances forced him to accept the machine age, he never rejected the old gods. When, in 1919, he felt compelled to buy a motor vehicle he chose a topless Model T Ford truck completely open to the weather. This was succeeded in 1934 by an almost equally breezy Model A roadster with a folding canvas hood over the front seat and no shelter of any kind for the occupants of the "rumble seat" in rear.

The canvas hood was seldom used. Angus preferred driving with the wind in his hair and the sun (or, as the case might be, the rain) in his eyes. Since he was indisputably the captain, his passengers had no choice but to follow suit. Once, when Helen remonstrated with him, he told her flatly:

"We'd all be far healthier if we still travelled under sail. We can't always do that now, more's the pity, but *no*, I will *not* put up the top!"

When, in April of 1937, he celebrated his new job by buying a spiffy new Dodge, he again chose a convertible with a folding roof and no provision for sheltering the occupants of the rear seat.

Mutt and I generally occupied the rumble seat but for the journey back to Ontario we had to share it with Annie, an uninhibited nineteen-year-old farm girl who had come to Saskatoon looking for a job and found one as the Mowat family's housemaid.

One vibrant mid-June morning we departed from Saskatoon towing our homemade caravan. Angus and Helen had the car's front seat to themselves, which left the rest of us to squeeze into the rumble. I tried to make Mutt sit between Annie and me but he insisted on occupying the outer edge of the seat where he could balance himself with his forepaws on a back fender while thrusting his head far out into the slipstream. Perhaps he felt he was doing me a favour by forcing Annie and me into one another's laps, but I was intimidated by her, and especially by her forthright approach to sex, for I was still very much a virgin, and a somewhat priggish one to boot. Although Annie did her best to make a man out of me during the long journey east, I was unable to cooperate because I was terrified my parents would twig to what was going on in the rumble seat.

Our first day's travel ended abruptly about a hundred miles south of Saskatoon when both of the caravan's wooden-spoked wheels disintegrated, dropping it onto the gravel road as heavily as if it had been felled by a bullet through its heart.

Angus unhitched the Dodge and drove back to Saskatoon for a new set of wheels, leaving the rest of us to amuse ourselves watching legions of gophers at play in the rippling sea of newly sprouted wheat surrounding us.

There was little evidence of human life except for a grain elevator looming on the distant horizon. Usually two or three of those stark wooden structures presided over a one-room railway station, a shabby false-front café, a garage-cum-blacksmith's shop, a general store, a farm implement agent, and a few unpainted, weather-worn wooden houses that together formed one of the forlorn little hamlets scattered disconsolately across the immensity of the Great Plains.

Next day Angus returned with new wheels, and we set off again. Since no Trans-Canada Highway then existed we had to make a huge semicirclular sweep through the northern tier of the United States, swinging back into Canada at Sault Ste. Marie. The roads were mostly gravel- or dirt-surfaced so we seldom managed to cover even as much as a hundred miles a day. Each evening we would camp, preferably beside a lake or river. Angus and I would erect a bell tent for Annie and Mutt. Sometimes the two women cooked supper on the caravan's kerosene stove; more often they did so over an open fire.

Since no hordes of summer trippers clogged roads and camp-sites in those times, we seldom had human neighbours. We did, however, encounter many of the Others. Deer, black bears, skunks, and foxes checked out our camps, as did innumerable birds, squir-rels, gophers, and rabbits. Once an inquisitive coyote snuffled his way through the door flap of the tent and gave Annie "conniptions," until he was chased off by Mutt.

Unable to resist the lure of the road least travelled, Angus was forever taking shortcuts. These sometimes stranded us miles from anywhere until a friendly farmer with a team of Percherons or, rarely, a tractor might come along to haul us out of a ditch or a pothole in the road.

Our passage through the United States was enlivened by sequences of advertising signs nailed to roadside fence posts at inter-vals of three or four hundred yards. Their message was delivered one line at a time. Thus:

BURMA SHAVE
WON'T MAKE YOU RICH
BUT BURMA SHAVE
WON'T MAKE YOU ITCH

Angus was inspired by these to compose a jingle that he proposed to offer to the manufacturers of a health drink called Ovaltine. Alas, he never got around to sending it to them. Had he done so Ovaltine might have become the Viagra of its time and the Mowats might have become filthy rich.

UNCLE JAMES
AND AUNTIE MABLE
FAINTED AT
THE BREAKFAST TABLE
[*long* linear pause – at least a thousand yards]
BUT OVALTINE
SOON PUT THEM RIGHT
NOW THEY DO IT
NOON AND NIGHT

After re-entering Canada, we headed directly for our penultimate destination: my maternal grandparents' summer cottage in Quebec. The route took us to Sudbury and North Bay then southeastward to the Ottawa River, over which we made a precarious crossing on a wooden ferry barely capable of carrying two cars at a time. Having reached the Quebec side, Angus embarked on another of his shortcuts – this one across the forested mountains separating the Ottawa and Gatineau river valleys. The dirt road quickly degenerated into a muddy creek bed that eventually became a beaver pond in which the immobilized Dodge and caravan became two small islands.

It seemed we would have to swim for it, but we were rescued by a jovial group of lumberjacks who, having carried the "women and children" to safety on their broad backs, hauled our vehicles out with a snorting tractor. Then they pulled car and caravan ten miles over a bush trail to a navigable road running beside the Gatineau River.

This adventure made my father happy as a clam.

"Splendid ending to a voyage!" he crowed. "Almost as good as if these fine chaps were *coureurs de bois* from Champlain's time!"

Helen's aside to me was cogent.

"Your father's *such* a *hopeless* romantic," she whispered in my ear. "Do try and *not* grow up like him."

My grandparents' cottage was on Hawk Lake not far from the village of Kazabazua – a name that, before I saw the place, conjured up visions of Africa or somewhere equally exotic. Hawk Lake was shrouded by forests, its shores still virginal except for the Thomson cottage, a barely weatherproof wooden shell redolent with the aroma of pine, and bereft of indoor plumbing, electricity, or telephone.

My parents' plan was that Mutt, Helen, Annie, and I would remain here while Angus drove to Toronto, his new workplace, to find a house for us to live in – one that my mother hoped might be the first home we had ever actually owned.

Angus intended that we be settled in Toronto before school reopened that autumn. This was not to be. A heat wave in early August drove multitudes of Toronto children to public swimming pools, triggering an outbreak of polio. So many children and young adults became infected that panic gripped the city. Parents able to do so sent their offspring out of town, and children already away at camps or cottages were kept there until the epidemic subsided. I was among those blessed in this way and greatly appreciated the extra month's holiday, which I used to canoe adjacent lakes and rivers and to roam obscure trails through the surrounding forests, getting to know the local inhabitants, human and otherwise.

Among them were French-speaking *habitants* living in snug little log cabins set in small clearings in the "bush." For generations these people had made their livings felling logs, hunting, trapping, and fishing. Hospitable to a fault, they seemed little different from the prairie settlers who had made me feel at home in Saskatchewan. They were my sort of people. They were also Annie's. Within a week of our arrival she had discovered (and been discovered by) a strapping young man who proved to be everything I wasn't. Before long Annie became pregnant and engaged and, as the ancient Norse saga men were prone to say, "was out of our story."

This was a wonderful time for my mother. Her western exile lay behind her and she was home with her own family. Her father, Harry (Hal) Thomson, who had been a bank manager until "given early retirement" for refusing to foreclose on hapless debtors, was a storyteller par excellence who also played a ukulele. He sang narrative songs, one of which was an exciting ballad about a young and amorous but short-sighted whale who unwisely tried to make love to a submarine and got himself torpedoed.

Hal was a fine companion but his wife, George (Georgina), intimidated me, as she did most people. Rangy and raunchy, she brooked no nonsense from lesser beings. At seventy, and despite the fact she had never driven a car, she decided to buy one. She acquired a second-hand Packard and after impatiently undergoing three or four days of instruction set off without benefit of either a companion (Hal wisely chose to stay home) or a licence, to drive from Montreal to Florida. Having miraculously avoided any serious disasters en route, she then went on to make a solo tour of much of the southern United States.

When, upon her return to Canada, my father complimented her on this achievement, she replied nonchalantly:

"Poof, my dear boy. It was as easy as filing off a lug."

George was famous for her malapropisms and inscrutable aphorisms.

At that time Toronto was only the *second* largest city in Canada; however, on the wet October day in 1937 when we drove into its outskirts I knew it was too big for me. My distress mounted as we threaded through miles and miles of crowded streets to our new residence – a crabbed little rental at 90 Lonsdale Avenue. Our woeful expressions on first seeing the place prompted Angus to explain that this was only a stopgap until he could find and buy a *real* home for us.

Although deeply disappointed not to have the house she yearned for, my mother was pleased to be in Toronto, which was familiar turf for her. For me, it was as alien as any place I could imagine. The day after our arrival, I was sent off to register at North Toronto Collegiate Institute, a huge education factory where I knew nobody and nobody knew me. The indifferent woman who took my "particulars" dourly informed me that, though I had apparently graduated into Grade 11 in Saskatoon, I would have to repeat Grade 10 in Toronto because Saskatchewan's educational standards were inferior to those of Ontario. So I found myself sentenced to a dismal repetition of all the Latin, algebra, geometry, physics, and chemistry that had bored me silly the previous year.

The one ray of light in Toronto's gloom was cast by Frank Farley who had provided me with a written introduction to Jim Baillie, assistant curator of the department of ornithology at Toronto's Royal Ontario Museum. With some trepidation, I mailed Baillie the letter, and he responded by inviting me to visit him. One grey Saturday in mid-November I rode the Yonge Street trolley south to the museum, made my way to a cluttered little office, and diffidently introduced myself.

Baillie, a fair-haired youngish man, beckoned me to a chair. "Aha!" he said. "The prairie meadowlark comes to the big city. Tell me about yourself."

This was the friendliest greeting anyone in Toronto had yet given me. Baillie improved upon it by offering to "take me under his wing" (a big wink to make sure I got the joke), which he subsequently did by enlisting me in the Toronto Ornithological Field Group.

The formidable-sounding TOFG consisted of about a dozen boys and three girls, all more or less my own age and all ardent bird-watchers. This little group provided what I then needed most – a tribe of my own kind. Andy Lawrie, "Duke" Boisseneau, Alan Helmsley, and Doug Millar were chiefly responsible for introducing me to the surprising variety of Others who co-existed and even thrived in Toronto's urban sprawl. Mutt and I eventually became familiar with almost every wooded ravine, golf course, municipal park, cemetery, and piece of so-called wasteland in and around the city – places where foxes pranced, owls hooted, fish swam, snakes slithered, frogs shrilled, and birds sang.

On weekends, come rain or shine, we of the TOFG would be abroad, equipped with battered old binoculars, field glasses, and even brass telescopes, searching for the wild ones. When travelling through regions occupied principally by human beings, we used streetcars or bicycles. Elsewhere we went on foot. We thought nothing of trekking ten or fifteen miles to prime localities like Ashbridges Bay to the eastward, Sunnyside and High Park to the west, Thornhill to the north, and Toronto Island to the south.

My journals record that between January 1 and May 7, 1938, alone or with other members of the TOFG, I made eighteen day-long birding excursions, plus fourteen shorter ones. On one February day Andy Lawrie, Mutt, and I covered twenty-six miles – twelve by streetcar (in those times dogs were allowed on public transit) and the rest on foot – and spotted twenty-six species of birds during ten hours "in the field."

It was pretty cold – 10 below zero for a while and it snowed quite a bit. We bivouacked in a ravine at Sunnybrook and brewed tea with molasses and toasted sandwiches for lunch. Mutt just about caught a rabbit and Andy and I saw an Iceland gull at the harbour, my first ever.

I am astonished now by the latitude our parents allowed us. Not only were we permitted to go as far afield as we could manage, we were free to investigate the underbelly of the city. We could and did explore deserted factories, the railroad yards, junk-filled ravines, ruined wharves, bosky swamps – even hobo jungles. Our elders evidently assumed we were competent to look after ourselves and, for the most part, so we were.

In Saskatchewan I had spent my Christmas and Easter holidays as far from town as I could get. Now, in Toronto, I preached the virtues of such excursions to the mostly city-bred members of the TOFG.

They were receptive. As Christmas of 1937 approached, Andy Lawrie, Al Helmsley, and Elgin Annette agreed to accompany me on a week-long expedition to the wilderness of Holland Marsh some thirty miles north of Toronto. Elgin even talked his father into driving us to the edge of this great swamp, where we camped in a dilapidated shack used in the spring for making maple syrup. It had a roof, glass in its one window, a door of sorts, and a huge stove backed by a small mountain of firewood. We spent the next six days here and in the vicinity snowshoeing through frosted woods and across frozen swamps searching for the Others.

One day while we were wandering deep in the swamps we were caught in a blinding blizzard and would have been in trouble had not Mutt led us out of the white maze and back to the shack. That night we were too exhausted to stay awake and stoke the fire, which consequently burned itself out. The temperature inside the cabin fell so low our pail of water turned to ice and my hair froze to the wall while I was trying to sleep. On succeeding nights we zealously kept the big stove roaring and crouched around it, sleeping bags pulled about our shoulders, keeping ourselves awake by telling stories.

Although surrounded by Toronto, I never became enmeshed in it. At the end of each school day I would jump on my bike and pedal home as fast as possible. I would be greeted by Mutt and, regardless of what the weather might be, the pair of us would set off to spend time with the Others.

A favourite haunt was the Mount Pleasant Cemetery, a vast and well-wooded burying ground relatively unencumbered by living human beings. Here I would commune with birds while Mutt checked out the Others.

One spring afternoon in the cemetery I heard an unfamiliar bird song and stopped to search for its owner. Mutt, who had found an interesting trail to follow, raced off among the headstones, his white rump flashing. I assumed he was after a rabbit and in no danger of getting into trouble until, to my dismay, I saw a cluster of soberly clad people directly ahead of him. Urgently I called him back but he paid me no heed.

The people in the funeral party appeared unaware of Mutt's swift approach – except for the undertaker's assistant, a tall young man who, alerted by my shouts, spun about in time to see Mutt bearing down, his queer, lopsided gallop giving him the appearance of drifting off to starboard, whereas in reality he was dead on target.

The skunk Mutt had been homing in upon now became visible trotting nervously among the tombstones, veering from side to side as if uncertain whether Mutt or the large man with the top hat waving his arms in the air posed the more serious threat. The skunk would probably have preferred to avoid the gaggle of human beings gathered around an open grave, for his kind are generally pacific. But Mutt was fast. The skunk nervously ducked its head and broke into a trot.

Dog and skunk and mourners came together with impeccable timing.

There was a great deal of screaming and shouting from the black-clad multitude, out of which Mutt appeared and lurched toward me seeking help and comfort. To my shame I have to admit I turned my back on him and fled the scene as fast as I could. He never did catch up with me because, blinded by skunk spray, he kept bumping into things. Why he was not killed while crossing busy Yonge Street I do not know. He eventually found his own way home, only to be banished to the backyard for the next several days.

At 90 Lonsdale I spent a lot of the time in my bedroom. Its shelves were weighted with books, including Ernest Thompson Seton's *Two Little Savages* and *Wild Animals I Have Known*; a lasciviously illustrated edition of *Gargantua and Pantagruel* by François Rabelais; and *The Wind in the Willows* by Kenneth Grahame. Being a librarian's son, my taste in literature covered a lot of territory.

The remaining space was occupied by my bed; by a desk upon which stood an old-fashioned microscope; and by a clutter of boxes containing birds' nests and eggs, a stuffed gopher, a rattlesnake's skin, and various animal bones.

Cages housed a variety of living creatures, including injured animals picked up during my rambles, and one that was sent to me from New Mexico by my uncle Geddes Thomson. It was a tarantula, a formidable creature, whose hairy legs spread almost as wide as the fingers of my hand. It had an insatiable yen for exploration and, since it also possessed the skills of a Houdini, was more often out of its cage than in it. The tarantula and Helen were not on friendly terms. One evening Angus and I, drawn to the kitchen by my mother's cries, found her perched on a stool, the spider eyeing her beadily from below while she lamented her brother Geddes's "perfectly fiendish sense of humour."

When not in my bedroom, I was often down in the cellar – not banished there in disgrace but because I had things to do in the dark and dusty space that housed a sprawling coal-fired furnace, an enormous coal bin, a concrete cistern for storing rainwater, and a pair of washtubs. In one corner Angus had built me a crude but serviceable darkroom. Here, under the eerie glow of a red safety lamp I developed film and made contact prints. I even made enlargements using a piece of equipment I constructed out of a wooden butter box, an old magic lantern, a sheet of ground glass, and a 100-watt bulb.

Although most of my camera gear was makeshift, the camera was not. It was a Graflex – one of the most expensive and prestigious cameras of its time. A big, black, leather-covered box weighing several pounds, it contained a complex system of springs and mirrors which enabled the operator to compose a picture on a ground-glass screen viewed through a folding hood. My camera had come to me as a munificent gift from a wealthy Saskatoon bachelor who claimed he wanted to further my interest in nature but was perhaps more interested in my vivacious mother.

Possession of the Graflex brought me considerable prestige, even though film for it was so expensive I could afford to take only the occasional picture. Those I did take were mostly of the Others – with one notable exception.

Though Toronto was called the Good, it was by no means as prissy and puritanical as it was made out to be. It had its shady attractions, among which was the Casino, a live theatre in one of the seedier districts. The Casino was notorious for its striptease acts, and I doubt if there was a pubescent male in all of Toronto who had not visited or dreamed of visiting the Casino. I was no exception, but one had to be nineteen to get in. Furthermore I could not afford the one dollar ticket price.

Then Dave Solomon, a schoolmate, offered to pay my way in to a Saturday matinee – *if* I would take a photo of a particularly celebrated stripper named Peekaboo.

"You got the camera to do it, Farl. And you can develop the neg and print off a bunch of pictures without nobody being the wiser. I bet I can sell a hundred of 'em – and we split the profits!"

I did not leap at the bait, not because I had moral scruples but because the Casino's sternly enforced ban on patrons photographing what took place on stage meant that if I was caught I could expect not only to be physically tossed out by the lumbering louts employed as bouncers but also risked losing my precious Graflex.

Nevertheless I eventually gave in to temptation: Dave bought the tickets and I slunk in behind him trying not to look too dewy-faced. We slumped into seats near the front, where we tried to be as inconspicuous as possible. When Peekaboo came on stage in a blaze of crimson light and a skirl of seductive music, she so engrossed my attention that Dave had to shake my arm to bring me back to earth.

"She's goin' to take it *all* off!" he whispered hoarsely. "You ready to shoot?"

I eased my big machine out of the schoolbag in which I had concealed it; cocked the mechanism; raised it high; aimed; and, just as Peekaboo revealed her all, pressed the trigger.

There was no flash (I had not dared use one and could only hope the stage lights would suffice) but the racket made by the Graflex's focal-plane shutter and clattering mirrors sounded, at least in my ears, like the last trump. A hairy old man in the seat in front turned, shot me a furious look, and muttered:

"You get caught doin' that, kiddo – they'll kill ya!"

Fortunately the Casino's Wurlitzer organ was pealing out such a thunderous blast to herald the star's moment of truth that it masked the noise made by the Graflex, and I escaped detection.

I developed the precious negative that night and made an enlargement, watching nervously as the nude image of a woman swam into view beneath the rosy glow of the safety lamp. Fixed and dried, the glossy print revealed the statuesque Peekaboo in all her glory.

During the next few days I made three or four dozen eight-inch-by-ten-inch enlargements that I dutifully handed over to Dave. At his insistence I even loaned him the negative so he could have more enlargements made in a hurry if sales went well.

I never saw any of the prints or the negative again. Nor any of the money they were supposed to earn. Dave abruptly dropped out of my life, but years later I would learn he had become a successful entrepreneur with a mansion in Toronto's ritzy Forest Hill Village.

I like to think Peekaboo and I helped get him there.

· 3 ·

ESCAPE

Shortly before my arrival in Toronto, the TOFG had launched a little journal called *The Chat*. Consisting mostly of bird notes from club members, it was mimeographed and distributed when and if someone could be found to do the work. After I let it be known that I had founded and edited a somewhat similar publication in Saskatoon, I was catapulted into *The Chat*'s editorial chair.

My western publishing venture – ten mimeographed pages mostly written by me – had been encouraged by Canada's leading ornithologist, Percy Taverner. Hoping he might again be of help, I wrote to him at his Ottawa office.

November 15, 1937

Dear Mr. Taverner,

I have certainly been enjoying myself in Toronto going around with a bunch of young fellows who look out for birds.

I do not know if you have heard of the Toronto Ornithological Field Group or not. It is a club including all the younger bird enthusiasts in Toronto. The Club publishes The Chat *which is the only ornithological bulletin of its kind in Canada so I consider it of great importance. Its phenomenal growth in the last few months shows definite promise of a widely read organ if it is encouraged. I am the Editor and am endeavouring to push it to the full extent of my powers.*

What is most needed now is the attention of those who are most prominent in Canadian ornithology so at the risk of presuming too much I decided to ask you for an Article. . . .

My news seems to have stunned Mr. Taverner for there was no reply. A month later I tried again.

. . . Just to tell you The Chat *is becoming a nation-wide paper and our Subscription is rising in a very gratifying manner so we are very humbly expecting an article from you. . . .*

Eventually the grand old man of Canadian ornithology and author of our bible – *Birds of Canada* – did send a brief congratulatory message. Alas, it came too late to save my bacon.

During the winter of 1937–38 the TOFG had been instructed by its mentors at the museum to make an exhaustive inquiry into the feeding habits of *Asio flammeus*, commonly known as the short-eared owl. Members were ordered to collect and analyze the contents of "pellets" – compact little grey cylinders of bone, fur, and feathers – regurgitated by these owls at roosting sites.

Although we were told the project was of prime scientific importance, I had my doubts. It was well known that short-eared owls dined almost exclusively on small rodents such as meadow mice. Collecting, dissecting, and analyzing quantities of pellets was unlikely to enlarge upon that knowledge. I concluded the project was a waste of time and ignored it until the day Jim Baillie handed me a manuscript report on the investigation for publication in *The Chat*. It contained enough turgid scientific lingo, complicated graphs, diagrams, and drawings of mouse bones to fill the next several issues of our little journal. Appalled, I offered to publish a synopsis but Jim shook his head.

"Won't do, Mowat. Science is built on facts. *All* the facts. No short cuts. Print it *all*."

Reluctantly I obeyed, but was unable to resist adding my own editorial comment.

What We Have Learned About Asio flammeus

This owl has the revolting habit
(when dining on a mouse or rabbit)
Of glutching hair and bones and all,
Which, in its stomach, forms a ball.
So when the owl has had its sup
It turns its head and brings it up.
Could it be staying up so late
That makes this owl regurgitate?

Shortly thereafter I was replaced as editor of *The Chat*. This was not my first brush with duly constituted authority – nor would it be my last.

When Angus took over Ontario's public library system it encompassed more than a hundred libraries, some consisting of a couple of rooms in a village hall and some of grandiose monuments in the larger cities. He began his new labours by visiting all of them and was appalled by what he found. He reported to his superior, the provincial Minister of Education, that "most of Ontario's libraries seem to be little more than fossilized and badly housed collections of antiquated and worn out books cared for by underpaid and under-trained librarians who are expected to serve as custodians and guardians of relics rather than as purveyors of good reading to the public."

Angus Mowat set out to change all that. He began by ruthlessly ordering the discard of thousands of dusty and outdated volumes and their replacement (as fast as he could squeeze the money from a reluctant ministry) with books that had "a little life in them."

He was even more passionate in pursuing his second goal, which was to inculcate enthusiasm and a sense of purpose in the librarians, most of whom were single women underpaid and undervalued both by their employers and by their communities. Angus described this problem in a letter to a friend:

"I find I must invigorate a number of mainly moribund libraries and an even larger number of librarians who are pitifully unhappy with the way things are going in their public and private lives but can't do much about it. Quite a challenge for a little man with only one arm. [Angus had lost the use of his right arm to machine-gun fire during the Great War.] I don't quite know how I'll manage this, but I shall do my best for them."

As I was later to learn from certain of the librarians, he did very well. One woman recalled:

"Your father was like a banty rooster in charge of a flock of needy hens. The wonder is he lived as long as he did . . . or perhaps that is why he lived so long."

Although his contributions to Ontario's library service were many and sometimes momentous, the double (or multiple) life he led resulted in the cumulative erosion of my mother's sense of well-being. Having been brought up in relative innocence or, as it may be, ignorance, she did not know how to cope with the uncertainties that Angus's dedication inflicted upon her. She was unable, as she once told me, to set her mind at rest by "talking things out with your father" because Angus became furiously defensive if challenged on any issue, especially marital ones.

Helen had other problems too. On her return from western exile she had believed she was finally to have a home of her own instead of "always having to camp out like a gypsy in other people's houses."

She still nurtured this hope even after Angus rented 90 Lonsdale Avenue. But one early spring day in 1937, as a consequence of a trip my father made to Montreal, her hopes were shattered.

Nominally Angus's visit to Montreal had been about library affairs; in fact, he had gone to look at a sailboat being offered for sale there.

An avid sailor since childhood, he had ever since been seeking the ideal boat. The one he found in Montreal – a thirty-six-foot double-ended ketch of Norwegian design built for ocean cruising – turned out to be his "Dream Ship." Despite her hefty price, my father bought her on the spot.

For a month he delayed telling us what he had done, while taking every opportunity to extol the joys of life on the ocean wave. Helen may have smelled a rat but I never guessed what was coming until the late April day he made the momentous announcement that he had found the boat in which we three would one day embark upon a voyage round the world.

However, he added: in order to hasten that day we needed to economize, so we would have to move out of our present house, whose rental we could no longer afford.

"But where are we to go?" wailed my mother.

"We will live aboard our ship – she is to be called *Scotch Bonnet* – until I can buy us a house somewhere outside Toronto. It's not fair to keep Farley in the city when he wants to be close to nature."

Angus did not state the obvious: that a house in the hinterland would cost a lot less than one in the city. If indeed he ever did actually buy one.

It was all too much for Helen. Pleading a migraine headache she took to her bed, where she stayed incommunicado for a week. Many years later she would tell me:

"I really couldn't think what to do. I did think of leaving him but my own parents and family would have been bitterly opposed, and I would probably have lost you, my darling, for how could I have supported you on my own? So I decided I had to grin and bear it."

I had no idea of the tension *Scotch Bonnet* brought to my parents' marriage. For me her coming was an open sesame to a world of high adventure. I believed *Scotch Bonnet was* capable of carrying us to the ends of the earth. I listened enthralled to Angus's talk of voyaging across the Atlantic in the track of such bold venturers as Jacques Cartier and Martin Frobisher. My head filled with fantasies of sailing to golden islands "below the Line" (the equator), where the palm-fringed atolls were alive with exotic wildlife, including dusky maidens. It seemed to me that the adventures of *Robinson Crusoe*, *Swiss Family Robinson*, and *Treasure Island* were now all within my reach. It never occurred to me that *Scotch Bonnet's* acquisition sounded a death knell to my mother's hopes and dreams.

My closest human companion at this time was Andy Lawrie, a tall, curly-haired, blue-eyed youth who, like me, suffered from a name affliction. Even as I had been dubbed *Fartley* Mowat by schoolmates in Saskatoon until I changed my name to William, he had been mocked as *Annie* Lawrie. These shared indignities drew us closer together.

Andy was the only child of immigrant Scots parents who, having endured the economic purgatory of the Dirty Thirties, were determined their son should walk an easier path. When he showed a burgeoning interest in wild creatures, they set their sights on a university degree in zoology for him.

We young naturalists were all under pressure from our mentors at the museum to seek careers in biology. It was impressed upon us that this was as exalted a vocation as any to which we could aspire. Especially promising neophytes were taken on field expeditions and taught how to collect birds, mammals, insects, fishes, and any other non-human or non-domestic creatures they might encounter. The word "kill" was never used, "collect" being the preferred euphemism of those times for describing the slaughter of wild animals in what is now usually described as "harvesting."

The professional biologists who oversaw us on our field trips may or may not have known that the word *biology* translates as the study of *life*. *They* practised it as an exercise in death and taught us to do likewise, employing poisons such as arsenic, strychnine, and cyanide; snares and traps ranging from household mousetraps to steel leg-hold traps strong enough to hold a bear; and a fearsome array of firearms, including shotguns with which to bring down birds from hummingbirds to eagles, and rifles with which to collect mammals ranging in size from squirrels to elephants.

They also taught us acolytes how to preserve the creatures we "collected." Fishes, frogs, and most soft-bodied animals were immured in jars or vats of alcohol or formaldehyde. Insects were generally pinned in regimented rows to sheets of cardboard. Birds and small mammals were skinned then stuffed "in the round" with cotton wool before being laid to rest (birds on their backs and mammals on their bellies) in trays stacked from floor to ceiling in hermetically sealed steel sarcophagi built to keep their contents safe from the ravages of time. Such mausoleums are the inner sanctums of all zoological museums. So far back as 1938 the Royal Ontario Museum of Zoology possessed almost a million such "study skins."

Like all natural history museums, the ROMZ dispatched its collecting expeditions to the far corners of the globe, but relied heavily upon local collectors whose ranks Andy Lawrie and I and other members of the TOFG were being groomed to join. Then, as now, collectors were issued permits by the federal government, authorizing the killing of all manner of wild creatures in almost any place and at any season.

A chance to prove myself worthy of such a permit came early in December when somebody spotted a white-eyed vireo in the willow swales of Toronto's Ashbridges Bay. Since this southern species had previously been recorded only three times in Canada, the report of its arrival brought every birdwatcher in Toronto out to look for it. I was one of them, but in addition to my field glasses I carried a slingshot and a burning desire to prove myself worthy of the scientific mantle.

The odds against spotting this unobtrusive little bird were very high; yet I had barely parked my bike under a dripping willow when a flicker of movement in the branches overhead caught my eye. And there it was! A sparrow-sized little thing, its drab plumage fluffed against the chill, it seemed completely unremarkable except for chalk-white eyes that made its identity unmistakable.

It may have been too cold or too hungry to pay attention to me. I was not five feet from it when my third shot killed it. Hurriedly wrapping the tiny body in a handkerchief, I thrust it into an inner pocket, got on my bike, and hastened home.

That night in the privacy of my bedroom I skinned and prepared the specimen and a few days later proudly displayed it to Jim Baillie. Expecting a commendation, I was shaken when he launched into a tirade, accusing me of having deprived the museum of a rare specimen staff members had been searching for. He calmed down when I assured him it had always been my intention to donate the vireo to the museum. This was a lie but I made it true, and once the specimen was in official hands I was restored to favour.

A few months later federal authorities in Ottawa issued a permit authorizing me to collect up to six specimens a year of each and every species of bird I might encounter in Canada – a limit that would be increased as my scientific status grew.

In May of 1938, while Helen was sadly packing our belongings, I was suffering through the hours school demanded of me but spending my free time flitting around the city's parks and green spaces almost as actively as the birds I was watching. Angus, meanwhile, was devoting *his* weekends to sailing *Scotch Bonnet* west from Montreal. He had planned to bring her to Toronto but, unable to arrange a satisfactory (by which he meant free) mooring for her there, he instead chose Whitby, a small lakeshore town some thirty miles east of Toronto in whose uncrowded harbour *Scotch Bonnet* could lie at anchor while serving as our temporary home.

One May weekend he invited me to join him at Kingston for the last lap of the sail to Whitby. I was ecstatic, especially when he agreed to let Andy come along.

We took the train to Kingston where Andy and I got our first sight of my father's vessel. Her sombre black hull and ochre-coloured sails contrasted sharply with the gleaming white yachts among which she was moored. Heavily built and broad of beam, she seemed a bit like a water buffalo lording it over a herd of gazelles – tough, enduring, and unstoppable.

I was instantly in thrall to her. My memory of the next three days is a kaleidoscope of happy sounds and images: the rattle of the anchor chain coming up, the snap and crackle of canvas as she took the wind, spray whipping over her bluff bows as a hard gust laid her over, and the vibrancy of her passage through the water transmitted by rudder and tiller to my guiding hand.

Our course took us the full length of the Bay of Quinte where Angus had learned to sail and I, as a two-year-old, had made my first voyage happily splashing about in the wet bilges of a sailing dinghy. By the time we dropped anchor in Whitby harbour, *Scotch Bonnet* had established herself as a pivotal influence in my life, and I had contracted sailor's itch: a lively and incurable combination of exhilaration and apprehension.

That sail must have been just as memorable for my father. Not only had he brought his dream ship home but, on that same day, a Toronto firm had published his first book, *Then I'll Look Up*, a novel about nineteenth-century life on and around the Bay of Quinte. As one of the few truly Canadian books to appear that year in a field dominated as usual by British and American imports, it was seen by some as a bright omen of things to come.

Things were going well for Angus. And for me. By the end of June school was over. We had moved out of 90 Lonsdale and were living aboard *Scotch Bonnet*. Soon after dawn most days (sometimes before the dawn) I would climb into our little pram – a bathtub-sized dinghy – and ease my way into the dense reed beds that enclosed most of the harbour and were home to many swimming beasts and nesting birds. I did not yet have a collecting permit and went among them in peace. Carrying only field glasses, a notebook, and sometimes my camera, I entered a domain of the Others, not unlike some I had known in my Saskatchewan years.

Old friends were here: raucous red-winged blackbirds, reclusive marsh wrens, pompous bitterns, sprightly teal, moth-winged harriers, skulking rails. Engrossed in mating and nesting, some birds were so incautious as to alight on the gunwales of the pram and occasionally on my head or shoulders.

I even managed to establish something of a relationship with an enormous snapping turtle who liked to sun itself on a muskrat's floating lodge. About two feet in diameter, this hoary creature had a tail resembling that of an alligator. He (or she) may have been as much as a century old. Having survived so long it seemed to have no fear. When I approached it for the first time, it raised its gnarled old head, opened its eagle's beak, and hissed so fiercely that I hurriedly back-paddled. Nevertheless, I visited it again and again and in time it came to accept me. Or ignore me. One sunny morning I eased the pram so close alongside as to be able to tentatively touch its armoured back. Very slowly it turned its ancient head and looked full at me. Neither of us could have guessed that, with the passage of only a few more years, its sanctuary would be transformed into a dredged and regulated basin of polluted water inhabited chiefly by "stink pots," as Angus called powered pleasure boats.

I was content but Helen grew increasingly despondent as the days slipped by and Angus, who always seemed to be away in some far corner of the province on library business, did nothing about finding us a house ashore.

One day she revolted, announcing she was going to Montreal to stay with her spinster sister who had a spacious apartment there. Helen wanted me to go too but I begged off on the grounds that, if I did, there would be nobody to look out for Mutt. The truth was that I had not the slightest desire to leave my marshy world where eggs were hatching and abundant new life throbbed below and above the waterline. Moreover, having just turned seventeen, I felt quite capable of looking after myself, and was happy to have the chance to do so.

Next day I rowed my mother ashore. She took a taxi to the train station while I hastened back aboard to become, at least temporarily, master of my own destiny.

Andy came to join me and we had a splendid time in the ensuing week. We lived in an aquatic Eden through most of the daylight hours. When night fell we lit the gimballed brass lamps in *Scotch Bonnet*'s snug cabin, cooked our supper on the cast-iron Shipmate stove, drank cider (which our imaginations transmuted into rum), and fantasized that we were anchored in the lagoon of a tropical atoll where, next morning, we might encounter a Komodo dragon or some such semi-legendary creature.

My collector's permit arrived that week. The pleasure this gave me was marred by Andy's announcement that he had to return to Toronto and look for a summer job to help pay the expenses of his next year at school.

Then I had an inspiration. How would it be, I asked if, instead of his trying to find a job in a labour market swamped with the unemployed, he and I mounted an expedition to collect birds and small mammals for the ROMZ, which was then paying up to fifty cents apiece for specimens.

Deluded by the wilful optimism of youth, I predicted that such a venture would earn Andy at least double what he could expect to get from any summer job available to him in Toronto. He was intrigued but dubious. Where would we go and how would we finance an expedition of our own? I first suggested Saskatchewan, but the cost of travelling so far put it out of reach. Then I remembered Hawk Lake.

"We could go to my grandparents' place in Quebec. I heard Dr. Diamond [head of the ROMZ] tell Jim Baillie the museum needs stuff from Quebec. Hawk Lake's real wild. We could camp out and scrounge most of our grub off of the country. Wouldn't hardly cost us a thing. What d'you say?"

Andy said yes.

LOVE AND DEATH

I never knew what transpired between my parents after Helen's return from a prolonged visit to Montreal. The atmosphere between them was glacial, mostly I think because the question of where we were going to live when summer ended remained unresolved. I didn't really care where I lived because I was preoccupied with preparations for what I pompously described in a proposal given to Jim Baillie as *A Zoological Investigation of the Kazabazua Region in the Province of Quebec*.

Andy and I were soon in difficulties. By the time we had bought our collecting supplies (which consisted mostly of shotgun ammunition), we found we could not afford train tickets to Kazabazua. We had just enough cash left to purchase one-way bus tickets as far as Ottawa, well short of our destination. Worse still, dogs were not allowed on inter-city buses. To our great relief, Angus anted up the cash to ship Mutt from Whitby to Kazabazua by railway express.

Andy and I set off to hitchhike from Ottawa to our destination. We walked from the city centre to the northern outskirts burdened with a bell tent, bedrolls, and two enormous packsacks. One of these was stuffed with scientific equipment, including a hundred mousetraps, cartons of ammunition, skinning tools, and lethal chemicals. The other contained clothing and fishing, camping, and cooking gear. We also carried axes, two shotguns, and a .22 rifle.

Plodding along the verges of a gravel road north of Ottawa, begrimed with dust and sweat and bent under heavy loads from which the muzzles of our several guns protruded, it is little wonder the few cars and trucks we encountered gave us a wide berth. At dusk, well into the wilderness, we came upon a hulking group of rough-looking fellows milling about a dilapidated gas station in a roadside clearing. As we drew near we saw most were armed, and none looked friendly. We had blundered into a backwoods vendetta. The garage owner and some of his supporters were anticipating a raid and their guns (which they displayed prominently) were loaded. So were they.

Neither Andy nor I spoke French and the garage's defenders understood little or no English so attempts to explain who we were and what we were doing got us nowhere. When a black-bearded fellow pointed his .30-30 down the road we had just travelled and growled an imprecation, we hurriedly backtracked, stumbling under our loads while half-expecting to hear the whine of pursuing bullets. We retreated at least a mile before, too exhausted to go any farther, deciding to take to the woods and lie low until morning. Not bothering to erect the tent and not daring to make a fire, we burrowed into our bedrolls and gnawed on dry biscuits for supper as we tried to defend ourselves against a perfect passion of mosquitoes.

At dawn we headed north again. We had to, because Mutt was due to arrive at the Kazabazua station that afternoon and we needed to be on hand to claim him and free him from his shipping crate. We sneaked past the now ominously quiet garage to reach Kazabazua just minutes before the daily train arrived. Ecstatically relieved to see us, Mutt peed on everything in sight, including several bags of mail.

That night we pitched our tent beside a nameless little lake in a paradisiacal setting of old conifers and hardwoods that had somehow escaped "harvesting" by timber barons. This vestige of wilderness became the centre from which we set about denuding the region of as many of the Others as we could kill. We butchered birds, from woodland warblers to hawks and owls, and trapped and snared mammals ranging from tiny shrews to a lactating vixen who probably had suckling pups in a den not far away. We also collected a wide assortment of other animals, including fishes, reptiles, frogs, and invertebrates whom we preserved in jars and bottles recovered from the Kazabazua garbage dump and filled with formaldehyde.

This slaughter of the innocents resulted in no twinges of conscience because we were able to employ that supreme achievement of the human intellect – rationality – to suppress any feelings of guilt. We believed that what we were doing was fully justified, even laudatory.

At the start of our fourth week in the woods a letter arrived from Jim Baillie. Having expressed his hopes that we were amassing "a large and useful collection," he gave us the bad news that the ROMZ's budget had been cut. Consequently he would have no money this year to purchase specimens from "outside sources" such as ourselves.

"However," he added, "we will gratefully receive specimens as donations."

This news left Andy no choice but to return to Toronto where, for six dollars a week and his keep, he could get a job as a deckhand aboard a Lake Ontario cruise ship, scrubbing floors and cleaning up vomit, used condoms, and other debris left by holidaying passengers.

"It should be enough," he later wrote to me, "to buy my school books this fall, but I sure wish I was still up in the Gatineau with you and Mutt."

Shortly after Andy's departure, my mother arrived at Hawk Lake to stay with her parents until she had a home of her own to go to. Mutt and I remained with her there through the rest of the summer.

Since there was no money to be made continuing at the collector's game, I put aside guns, traps, and poisons and again began living the life that had been mine in Saskatchewan as an observer of rather than as nemesis of the Others.

One day I was canoeing on one of the larger lakes when I spotted a porcupine waddling purposefully along the shore of an offshore islet. Since porcupines do not normally swim, I guessed this one had crossed over on the ice the previous winter. It had outstayed its welcome. Having girdled the islet's few trees and eaten most of their bark, it was now in dire need of greener pastures.

I paddled up until only a few feet separated us. I thought its tuft of white whiskers and its yellowed, protruding teeth gave it some resemblance to my paternal grandfather and, since it seemed to be almost as amiable, I dared to gently touch it with my outstretched paddle. When it showed no resentment I grounded the bow of the canoe directly in its path. It paused, glanced at me, then reared back, and, before I could react, grasped the gunwale with its front feet, hoisted itself up and with a great rattling of quills flopped aboard.

For a startled moment I considered abandoning ship. However, this would have left *me* marooned on the islet. As the porky settled itself comfortably in the bow, I concluded I might be able to paddle both of us to the mainland.

I pushed off, carefully. My passenger remained motionless until the bow grated on a mainland beach, whereupon it thumped its tail, scrambled over the gunwale, and ambled off into the nearby forest. It did not give me even a backward glance but I had the feeling that if the time ever came when it could do *me* a favour, it would be glad to oblige.

Returning to the Thomson cottage I showed my mother and grandparents a six-inch-long quill retrieved from the bottom of the canoe and explained how it had got there.

Later I overheard Helen telling her parents:

"He takes after his father, of course. *Such* a vivid imagination. Perhaps he'll turn out to be a writer."

We saw little of Angus that summer. He had wrangled a free mooring for *Scotch Bonnet* at Toronto Island and was living aboard when not inspecting the far-flung bastions of his empire. He wrote occasionally to assure Helen he was diligently seeking a suitable home for us. The truth was that, having got his Dream Ship, he had no intention of taking on the financial burden of a house as well. He could hardly have afforded to do so. Buying and refitting *Scotch Bonnet* had left him barely enough money to rent a roof over our heads.

At the very end of August he finally appeared at Hawk Lake.

"Couldn't find quite the right kind of place to buy so I've rented one until we do. Bridge End House it's called. Twenty miles north of Toronto near a picturesque little village called Richmond Hill which has a small but excellent high school. The house is right out in the country with its own little stream running through it and birds and beasts galore. I'm sure it will suit all of us very well."

As with so many of my father's plans, there was a hitch: we would be unable to move into Bridge End House until mid-December when the current tenants were supposed to vacate. My mother, father, and Mutt could live aboard the boat, now moored at Toronto Island, until the house became available but I would have to start school in Richmond Hill on September 3. Angus solved the problem by finding me board and bed with an elderly couple near the school. They made a living selling "home bakes" and, though amiable, were not stimulating company. After the evening meal (which generally consisted of fried potatoes and fat sausages followed by stale pie), my hosts would crouch over a squawking table radio and listen entranced to *Amos 'n' Andy*.

In consequence I spent a lot of evenings in my room building model aeroplanes out of balsa wood, reading until my eyes ached, and fantasizing about accompanying a famous explorer named Frank "Bring-'em-back-alive" Buck on exploring expeditions deep into the heart of Africa.

The bright side of that long, dark autumn was that for the first time in my life I found myself in a school I really liked.

Richmond Hill High School was a red-brick 1920s-style structure, four-square and unpretentious. Its two storeys housed just eighty students in five grades. Grade 12 (which I had managed to scrape into) had only fourteen students, and Jimmy Stewart – our class teacher and also the school principal, a kindly, somewhat myopic middle-aged man – believed in allowing us lots of latitude.

Foremost among the teachers was our hawk-nosed, piercingly black-eyed English teacher, Miss Edna Izzard. Her "sidekick," Miss Jean Smith, was a mousy blonde who was supposed to teach us French and who did succeed in getting us to read a lot of French classics, if in English translation. These two shared a cat, a car, and a house, but nobody in that day and age would ever have admitted to the suspicion that they might also be sharing a bed. Their home was open to any of us who might be in need of advice or encouragement. Edna (I can call her by her first name now, though I would never have dared do so in life) gruffly assured me I could write, and her recognition of my efforts to do so gave me a status I had not known in any previous school.

Only a few of my fellow students were actually from Richmond Hill. Others came from adjacent farms or had been parachuted into our semi-rural school by parents from distant places chasing the few jobs to be found during the Depression. Whatever our origins, all

of us had been shaped to some degree by the adversity that charac-
terized those lean years. In consequence we had mostly put aside
competitive behaviour in exchange for the camaraderie, tolerance,
acceptance of singularity, and loyalty to the clan that I would later
encounter in the army and, later still, among the native peoples of
the Arctic and the fisherman of Newfoundland.

Late in December, Bridge End House finally became available. A
shoddy imitation of an English country cottage, it squatted forlornly
in what had once been a swamp but was now a muddy field drained
by a narrow ditch (the "stream" Angus had bragged about) running
through a rusty culvert (the "Bridge") under a rutted trail that dead-
ended at the house. Wind and rain blew through its scrofulous
planking and under its curling roof shingles. Its shallow and almost
certainly contaminated well (we never dared have it tested) ran dry
if the toilet was flushed more than three times a day. There was no
proper sewage system, not even a septic tank, just a cesspool with a
nasty tendency to back up and flood the bathroom.

The cellar was truly a nether region. Dark and airless, it grew
toadstools and harboured its own wildlife. It was also home to the
furnace, a coal-burning monster whose grates had long since melted
into slag. It was my duty to stoke this antiquity because Angus was
seldom home to do it and Helen wisely refused to descend the slimy
cellar stairs. I found it nearly impossible to keep the fire burning
properly so we endured the winter by piling on extra clothing and
by crowding around a kerosene heater in the frowsty kitchen.

Although my mother never summoned the courage to call it that
in my father's hearing, it was she who re-christened our new home
Dead End House. Life there must have been almost intolerable for
her. Being without a car (she never learned to drive nor did Angus
ever encourage her to learn) she was isolated from friends and
family in a rural ghetto.

While my mother suffered, I enjoyed a new life. On foot, bicycle, cross-country skis, or snowshoes, usually accompanied by Mutt, I ranged the back concessions where pockets of wilderness were still to be found. I did not carry a gun – only my field glasses and occasionally my Graflex. I was rewarded by encounters with flying squirrels, deer, a mink, pileated woodpeckers, a golden eagle, and many others.

School was an ongoing pleasure – not for what it could teach me but because the people I was with were willing to accept me on equal terms. For the first time I truly felt myself to be a social animal surrounded by my kind. My mentors and companions at RHHS were not inclined to view me as a wimp because of my lack of interest in competitive sports. Neither did they sneer at me as a "nature lover." Many actually seemed to admire my knowledge of wild creatures and several began developing their own interests in the Others.

Richmond Hill was the northern terminus of a rural streetcar line known as the Radial. Running on a track set close alongside Yonge Street, electric trolleys carried passengers between Richmond Hill and the outskirts of Toronto and so made it relatively easy for me to visit the ROMZ, and for Toronto friends to visit me. Sometimes on Friday evenings one or two of them would ride the Radial to Richmond Hill, walk the mile and a half to our house, and stay the night there so we could spend all day Saturday roaming the countryside together.

We also found time for some epic camping trips. Andy Lawrie, Al Helmsley, and I spent the 1938 Christmas holidays at the Helmsleys' summer cottage on Lake Simcoe. This flimsy board-and-batten structure was put to the test by the fiercest storm of the winter. A four-day blizzard piled drifts almost to the top of the rattling cottage windows and dusted the interior with so much snow not even the pot-bellied wood stove stoked to incandescence could melt it all.

Fuel was a problem. During the first night of the storm the stove consumed the scanty wood pile. With the return of what passed for daylight, we ventured into the blizzard to look for more. All we could find was a snake-rail fence almost buried in snow. Its cedar rails burned hot, but so swiftly that by evening most of it had also been fed into the insatiable stove.

Fortunately the cottage had for several generations served as a depository for cast-off family furniture. These oak, maple, walnut, and mahogany relics burned even hotter (and longer) than cedar rails. And were far handier.

There was, however, one antiquity of such commanding presence that nobody felt like putting an axe to it. A wind-up Edison gramophone housed in a towering and ornate teak cabinet, it played music through an immense cherry-wood horn. Or had done so once upon a time.

When, on the third day of the storm, I began to look speculatively at the massive teak cabinet, Al forestalled me.

"We have to leave that one, Farl. Aunt Jane'd kill me if anything happened to it. Was a present from her husband back about 1900, and it still works . . . kind of."

To prove the point he carefully cranked up the machine's coil-spring, placed one of only three surviving record cylinders in position, and engaged the playing head.

I could distinguish nothing above the tumult of the storm until I pushed *my* head deep into the flaring mouth of the horn, where I heard a distant, glassy tinkling sounding vaguely like an insect mating song. The effect was as odd as if I had tuned in to the voice of some unimaginably distant planet . . . or, as Andy suggested, to a spaceship from a Buck Rogers comic.

He and I were fascinated. Breathing frostily into the cavernous horn while the heat from the stove toasted our backsides, we listened intently. The garbled snatches of music and words that came through to us made little sense . . . except for a single verse of a single song.

> *When you're trapped on the second floor*
> *And someone bangs upon the door:*
> *"Any old bones or rags to sell?"*
> *Ain't that a grand and glorious feeling? . . .*

Early in the new year, principal Jimmy Stewart called me into his office. He spent some time deploring the rising tide of fascism in Europe before coming to the point.

"I believe, Mowat, you wish to become a zoologist and hope to take a degree from Queen's University." He paused to look me in the eye in fatherly fashion. "Are you not aware that something more than passing grades are wanted for entrance into Queen's? Your Christmas examination results were appalling. You failed chemistry . . . physics . . . algebra . . . and geometry. And Latin and French both seem to be truly dead languages insofar as you are concerned. Would you care to explain where the difficulty lies?"

I usually had no trouble producing excuses. Not for nothing did Angus sometimes call me Alibi Ike. This time, however, I could not find my tongue.

Jimmy gave me a knowing glance. "So," he said gently, "perhaps your inability to concentrate has something to do with a certain young lady in your class? Yes?" He sighed a little. "Well, I can recall the feeling. . . ."

Marie Heydon was a slim, supple, dark-haired, and dark-eyed seventeen-year-old. Although no pin-up, she had a vivacity that made her irresistibly attractive, to me at any rate. The only child of the railway station agent in Richmond Hill, Marie liked birds, photography, and poetry. *My* poetry especially. We were simpatico . . . and brimming with hormones. We had begun eyeing one another early in November and by the end of January had become a couple.

Although we were in love, love-*making* was almost impossible. None of us owned a car or had ready access to one. Our parental homes were small, crowded, and the domain of mothers who did not go off to work and so could (and did) keep sharp eyes open for "goings on." We occasionally attended parties at the girls' homes, where we sat around listening to the Big Bands on radio while eating gooey cake and drinking Coke. The best we could hope for would be a little feel or a quick smooch if no adult member of the hosting family happened to be looking.

If the indoor scene was pretty hopeless, the outdoor one in winter was little better. Walking a girl home on a sub-zero night; accompanying her on a sleighing party; snowshoeing through a frozen forest – all these served to inflame the mood but seldom resulted in satisfaction. One could only expect so much from a girl who was being embraced in a snowbank, or under an old buffalo rug shared by several other couples. There was little chance of making out until spring finally transformed the great out-of-doors into something more accommodating.

This was the way it was for Marie and me until Aphrodite took pity on us.

After badgering my parents for two months, I finally persuaded them to let *me* have a party at Bridge End House. I planned to invite a dozen close friends on a Saturday night to eat hot dogs and listen to records, to dance, and to breathe steamily over one another. However, on the Thursday before the chosen date Angus announced that he and my mother were going to Winnipeg for a three-day library conference and so, without the presence of a supervisory adult, my party could not be held.

I protested so vigorously that my parents relented.

"Very well then," said Angus, "perhaps you *are* old enough to act like a responsible human being. You can have your party if you behave yourself!" Then, assuming his most military bearing, he laid down the rules.

"There's to be no more than eight guests, none of whom will enter the bedrooms or go upstairs for any reason other than to use the bathroom. Singly. No alcohol will be allowed on the premises. Guests will depart by 9:30 p.m. leaving the house in immaculate condition and, I trust, remaining in that same state themselves. Is this fully understood?"

I whittled the guest list down to seven: Marie, and three couples who had been suffering the same restraints that had been making life a torment for me. There was insufficient room for more. If one excluded the cellar (and one would) and the bedrooms (which were strictly *verboten*), the only rooms suitable for what I had in mind were the living room, my father's office (he refused to call it a "den"), which had a daybed, and my mother's sewing room, which had a couch.

There was *also*, however, our caravan, parked a few hundred feet away. Once my parents had departed I cleansed the battered caravan of its accumulation of mouse droppings and dead flies, aired the mattresses and pillows, and set an array of tumblers and glasses on the dinette table.

Determined to make this a truly memorable affair, I spent most of Saturday preparing dinner. The *pièce de resistance* was a silver serving dish filled with curried veal on a bed of rice and garnished with apple rings dusted with cinnamon. For dessert there was chocolate trifle and brandied pears. Apart from the pears I cooked all of this myself, following recipes in my mother's well-worn copy of the *Fannie Farmer Boston Cookbook*. The pears were a present to Angus and Helen from a gourmet friend in England and had been set aside for some special event.

I served the meal on a mahogany dining table that had belonged to one of the founding Fathers of Confederation, my great-great-uncle, Sir Oliver Mowat. The silver, which I had polished to a silken gleam, bore the Mowat monogram. The dining room was lit by tall wax tapers.

The wine was Four Aces Sherry, brought by one of my male guests who got it from the local bootlegger. The wine bottles and two dozen beer bottles stayed in the caravan, sequestered but frequently visited. No alcohol was available *in* Bridge End House that night.

After dinner we played some records on Helen's phonograph and did a little torrid dancing. Then the couples began drifting away. Where the others went and what they did I cannot say. I whispered in Marie's neat little ear:

"Ever wonder what it'd be like living the gypsy life in a caravan?"

The early days of 1939 were cold and leaden until April brought the benison of spring. When I opened the kitchen door one morning I inhaled the sensual smell of warming earth. Mutt could smell it too. He was old now but still game.

"Spring's here, old-timer. Ducks'll soon be back. How's about a walk?"

Wagging his tail, he pushed stiffly past me, nostrils wrinkling as he tested the fleeting breeze. I returned to the kitchen to pull on my rubber boots and when I went outside again he was not in sight.

His tracks were there – meandering to and fro across our field toward the county road. I followed them to a snake-rail boundary fence with flocks of juncos bounding over it. He had taken his time here untangling the identities of the many foxes, farm dogs, and hunters' hounds who had come this way during the long winter months.

After a bit his tracks left the road for fallow fields where he had paused now and again to sniff at old cow flaps or at collapsing field mice burrows revealed by the melting snow.

His tracks led me to the beech woods, taking me under the red tracery of budding twigs wherein a squirrel jabbered its defiance at the unheeding back of a horned owl brooding her round eggs.

A small pond lay near at hand. I scanned its only recently ice-free surface with my field glasses and, although I could see no ducks, I knew that somewhere in the yellowed cattails a mallard drake and his mate were waiting for me to go away so they could resume their courtship.

The first bee flew by. Then, suddenly, I heard a familiar voice raised in wild yelping somewhere among the dead cattails. There followed a frantic surge of wings as the drake lifted out of the reeds with his mate close behind. They circled heavily while Mutt reared below, plunging recklessly through the tangle, revelling in a surge of the lithesome energy that had been his when guns had spoken over other ponds in years long gone.

I ambled after him as his tracks led me through a cedar tangle into the tamarack swamp and on into a small clearing where the soft leaf mould had been churned as if by the hooves of a herd of deer. But these tracks were all Mutt's. I was baffled by them until a butterfly fluttered through the clearing on unsteady wings. Then I remembered the many times I had watched him leap and hop and circle, mocked by just such a one as this.

Now the tracks led me beyond the swamp into another field, where they hesitated before a groundhog's den. I could envisage Mutt's bulbous nose wrinkling with interest as he wondered if it might be worth his while to do a little excavating with his blunt old claws.

Then a rabbit passed close by and the rising breeze must have brought Mutt its scent. His tracks veered off abruptly, careening recklessly over the soft and yielding furrows of October's plowing. I followed more sedately to where his progress had been interrupted by a bramble thicket. He had not stopped in time. The thorns still held several tufts of his long, silken hair.

A new scent must have reached him on the wind for now his tracks moved purposefully toward the county road again, and toward the farms that lay beyond. A new mood was on him. I knew it, for it was in my blood too. I even knew the name of the little collie bitch who lived on the nearest farm. I wished him luck.

My boots were sucking in the mud of the road when a truck came howling up behind and showered me in dirty water. I glared angrily after it as it swerved abruptly to avoid a bend in the road. It vanished from my view and I heard the sudden shrilling of brakes, followed by the roar of an accelerating engine. . . .

That evening I drove along the county road in company with the silent farmer who had come to fetch me. We stopped beyond the bend. The tracks I had followed ended here. Nor would they ever lead my heart again.

It rained that night and when dawn broke even the tracks were gone.

The pact of timelessness between the two of us was ended, and I went from him down the narrowing tunnel of the years.

ᛡ 5 ᛡ

THE GREAT ADVENTURE

Andy's resolute pursuit of a scholarship tied him to Toronto through most of that winter. I did not miss his company as much as I might have, because of a new friend, Harris Hord, a dreamy-eyed, six-foot beanpole who was in my class. Harris was the only child of yet another family driven to the wall by the Depression. He had planned to quit school at the end of this year and indenture himself as a bank clerk in order to help his family but, through his association with me, became enamoured of the world of the Others and concluded that what he really wanted to do was become a scientist. Although there seemed little prospect of this ambition being realized, I felt he at least deserved a fling and, since I was then nurturing a fantasy of my own, made room in it for him.

Ever since leaving the west I had dreamed of returning to it and of eventually becoming Saskatchewan's premier ornithologist. Early in 1938, after learning that the ROMZ's budget for the purchase of specimens had been restored, I asked Jim Baillie if the museum would be interested in financing a freelance collecting expedition to Saskatchewan that coming summer.

"If you're able to put it together we'd consider buying the bird and mammal skins you might collect" was his reply.

This wasn't much, but it was enough to set me off. What I needed next was a partner. I first tried selling the idea to Andy who, perhaps disillusioned by the outcome of our Gatineau trip, turned me down. I tried Harris next.

Harris was a tough sell but eventually I was able to persuade him to take part in what I grandiloquently termed a *Faunal Survey of Saskatchewan*, by assuring him the experience would open doors for him into the sacred halls of science. Or words to that effect.

The next problem was how to finance the plan. When the ROMZ refused to make a cash advance, I emptied my own bank account of the $26.47 it contained; borrowed forty dollars from my father, twenty from my mother; and wheedled a cash advance of thirty more from a rich Chicago surgeon who claimed to own the largest private collection of bird skins in America, but wanted more.

This was the sum total of our capital. We still needed to get to Saskatchewan and find a means to get around once we were there.

The solution turned out to be Frank Banfield, a rather oleaginous Toronto youth about to enter university as a zoology student. Frank was the only child of a pair of Methodist missionaries who had done well for themselves during three decades in China. Now retired, they wanted for nothing. Nor did Frank, to whom they had just given a brand-new Dodge sedan as a reward for having passed the Fifth Form examinations he had yet to write.

Frank's interest was in mammals. An avid collector, he had already amassed several hundred skins in his own personal collection.

When, one March weekend, he unexpectedly showed up at Bridge End House behind the wheel of his fabulous new car, I seized this God-given opportunity to tell him about my Saskatchewan plans and to paint a glowing verbal picture of the mammalian wealth of the Great Plains.

"Frank," I enthused, "you could *triple* your own collection in a summer out west as well as make a pile of money. Oh boy, just think of the rarities! There's probably a dozen brand-new subspecies of desert mice alone, just waiting out there to be discovered by somebody. Could be you. . . ."

Before the afternoon was over Frank was hooked.

Little more than a month later his waxed and polished Dodge drew up in front of Donnelly's Café in Richmond Hill, where a group of friends waited to speed Frank, Harris, and me on our way to the Golden West. Somebody took our photo grouped beside the car. In it Marie stands beside me holding my hand and wearing the Scotch bonnet that was my trademark. The Dodge is crouched like a racing car, heavily laden with two tents, camping gear, five rifles and shotguns, enough ammunition to start a minor war, scores of traps, skinning and preservation equipment, and personal belongings. The load flattens her springs almost to the ground.

Nevertheless, she bravely set off down Yonge Street with Frank at the wheel and Harris and I waving last farewells out the windows.

Ten miles down the road, Frank swerved violently at a stop sign and mashed a fender against a lamppost. It seemed an inauspicious omen, but our prospects improved when halfway between Toronto and Hamilton we came upon an enormous Heinz Company truck overturned and smouldering in the roadside ditch. The wreck was surrounded by people, many pushing baby carriages or towing children's wagons into which they were urgently loading canned goods that had scattered from the crash. During these hard times, people had learned to seize upon every opportunity.

To us, setting out on an expedition of at least two months' duration, with practically no money and almost no food (a dozen cookies, a few chocolate bars, and a bag of apples), this was a gift from the gods.

When we drove on again the car was, as Harris happily put it, "really dragging her ass." Dozens of tins, many with their labels burned off or scorched beyond legibility, filled every nook and cranny. The unidentified contents, including fruits, vegetables, spaghetti, beans, and soups, became the surprise mainstays of our menus for many days to come.

Crossing into Saskatchewan, we found that a storm had turned the gravel-surfaced highway into a quagmire of greasy muck known locally as gumbo, in which the car was sometimes mired to its axles. A back wheel fell off, then we cracked the pan and the engine lost its oil. A farmer towed us to his farmyard, where he welded the cracked pan. He would not accept so much as a nickel for his help and his emaciated-looking wife insisted on giving us a loaf of soda bread to help us on our way.

Even with all three of us taking turns at the steering wheel, it required almost a week to drive through the province to the town of Prince Albert where we paused long enough to pick up Murray Robb, my friend from Saskatoon days, whom I had inveigled into joining us on what he mistakenly thought was to be a holiday venture.

Our immediate objective was Emma Lake, four hundred miles north of the Canada–U.S. border, at the edge of the coniferous forest that blankets central and northern Saskatchewan. I had chosen Emma Lake as our first "station" because I had previously camped there with my parents and knew the region to abound with animal life.

Having pitched our tents in the "bush," we set about scouring the country for miles about by canoe and on foot, collecting material for our faunal survey – which meant killing everything within range that was not too big for us to handle.

The then director of the Department of Mammals of the American Museum of Natural History eloquently described the rationale underlying what we were doing.

"The building up and serious study of a collection of study skins is well worth the time devoted to it. The sentimental reluctance one naturally feels at killing these wild creatures may be set at rest by the realization that the forces of the wild environment and the tremendous sacrifice of life extracted every twenty-four hours by Dame Nature herself make the activities of the collector a very trivial consideration; and it is better to devote a few specimens to such a serious and lasting purpose than to forego the capture and surrender the victim to a Snake, Hawk, Weasel or predatory House-cat. The collector is usually the least of many enemies an animal may have."

So we busied ourselves far into mosquito-ridden nights, working under nets by the flaring light of a gasoline pressure lantern, skinning birds and mammals, cleansing their skins of fat with carbon tetrachloride, and preserving them with powdered arsenic. We stuffed them with cotton batting and pinned the mammals' carefully cleansed little skulls beside them. To one leg of each specimen of bird or mammal we tied a neatly inked label on which was recorded such invaluable scientific data as the body length, tail length, sex, condition of the gonads, presumed age, location where the kill was made, and the name of the killer (whichever one of us had set the trap or pulled the trigger).

Our lives were not entirely dedicated to science. The shores of Emma Lake and nearby Prince Albert National Park had a sprinkling of human occupants – Metis, Indians, wardens, trappers, and on occasion a Royal Canadian Mounted Policeman on patrol.

Frank became enamoured of the girlfriend of a large, heavily bearded trapper who was not amused by Frank's interest. One morning while Frank was checking his mouse trapline, bullets began whistling through the trees around him. When Frank appealed to the police for protection, an RCMP patrol canoed across the lake to our camp to recommend that Frank "desist from bothering the locals." After this Frank and Murray were ready for a change of venue but Harris and I were not. Harris had found favour with the wife of a trader at Okema, while I had fallen under the spell of a legend.

Anahareo was an Iroquois, the recent widow of a man calling himself Grey Owl who claimed to be half-Scot and half-Apache and who, greatly influenced by Anahareo's convictions and example, had become an impassioned defender of the Others. Before his death in 1938 Grey Owl had become hugely famous in Canada, Britain, even in the United States. During the mid-thirties he and Anahareo had lived beside a remote lake in northern Saskatchewan, sharing a semi-aqueous log cabin with a family of beavers. Grey Owl wrote several books about the mingled lives of the two species, all of which I had avidly read.[*]

When a local friend of Anahareo's invited me to meet this young woman who had been the imperative in Grey Owl's life, I eagerly accepted – perhaps partly because I had recently received my first "Dear John" letter. It was from Marie Heydon, telling me her parents were so opposed to our romance that it would have to end, though we could remain "good friends."

When I first saw her, Anahareo was standing in the doorway of a log cabin wearing high leather boots, jodhpurs, an open-necked white shirt, and a fringed deerskin jacket. Although a decade older than I, she was slim, vivid, and beguiling. I have no idea why, but she treated me kindly. Suddenly and utterly smitten, I was soon dreaming of a time when she and I would travel together by canoe to some unsullied northern lake where we could continue living the kind of life she and Grey Owl had made their own.

---

[*] *Pilgrims of the Wild* (1934), *The Adventures of Sajo and Her Beaver People* (1935), and *Tales of an Empty Cabin* (1936).

It was not to be. Just two weeks after we first met, she gave me a pair of beautifully beaded moose-hide gauntlets and told me she would soon be marrying a wealthy Swedish businessman who was prepared to underwrite her continuation of Grey Owl's work.

I did not sleep at all that night. Next morning I told my surprised companions to break camp – that we were moving to a new location and the sooner the better.

We drove south out of forested country onto a rolling prairie dotted with bluffs and laced with mostly dry stream beds. The heat was intense, and dust was always with us as we jounced along dirt roads toward Fort Carlton, a long-abandoned trading post on the bank of the North Saskatchewan River. This river's headwaters rise among Rocky Mountain glaciers that maintain a flow even when drought desiccates the broad plains through which the river runs.

At the turn of the eighteenth century the North Saskatchewan was a major artery of the northwestern fur trade. In 1810, the Hudson's Bay Company built Fort Carlton on its banks roughly halfway between Winnipeg and Edmonton. Grandiosely named after King George III's London Palace, Carlton became a mid-way depot for canoes and York boats transiting the Great Plains. It also served as a meat post, where huge quantities of buffalo pemmican were collected from native hunters to fuel the web of traders and transporters pursuing the fur trade across half a million square miles of wilderness.

In 1885, Fort Carlton found itself at the centre of a war that we, the victors, call the Riel Rebellion. It was fought between government soldiers and police armed with machine guns and artillery, and prairie Indians and Metis with rifles and smoothbore guns desperately trying to retain ownership of their homelands. Fort Carlton was where one of the greatest freedom fighters in Canadian history, the Cree chief Big Bear, eventually surrendered to the paramilitary

Northwest Mounted Police. Before another decade had passed, the buffalo upon which the plains people had depended for their existence had been destroyed and the People of the Buffalo were being submerged beneath the first waves of European immigrants come to occupy their lands.

Abandoned Fort Carlton burned to the ground. Berry bushes and cottonwoods took over the ruins until, by the time we arrived, nothing of it remained visible.

We descended into the river valley along a narrow dirt road that ended at the water's edge but began again on the far side of the river a quarter of a mile away. The river could be crossed on a wooden scow capable of carrying a car or two, or up to six cows. This ferry was on the far side when we arrived. We were awaiting its return when a rangy little man, burned and wrinkled by fierce prairie suns and sporting a tattered straw hat and ancient overalls, came striding down the road. He introduced himself as Servais Rahier, and when we asked where Fort Carlton was he led us through a tangle of berry bushes to an overgrown clearing where we found a few bones exposed by the upturned roots of a fallen tree and some crumbled rocks and mortar that may once have been part of a chimney. This was what remained of Fort Carlton. When we asked permission to camp, Servais invited us to set up our tents wherever we pleased.

"You will be my guests, *n'est-ce pas*? This is our land, but what we have is yours. Then please come to my house and meet my family."

Servais's weatherworn, rough-planked home standing just below the protective lip of the river valley housed him and his wife, Isabella, and several children ranging from eight to eighteen. He had emigrated to Canada in 1919 from a farming village in Belgium that had been all but obliterated during the First World War. Barely eighteen years old and on his own, he had jumped down from a railway colonist car one spring morning at the Metis village of Duck Lake.

Within a month he had staked a claim to a homestead embracing a quarter section (160 acres) of virgin prairie overlooking the valley of the North Saskatchewan. Then he dug a windowless dugout in the valley wall, where he lived for two years while clearing fifty acres with an ox and a single-furrow sod-breaker plow in order to plant his first crop.

When he had harvested it, he sent for the girl he had left behind and, while she was en route from Belgium, built her a one-room, sod-and-log cabin.

Servais, Isabella, and their children had only just begun to make ends meet by 1929 when the world of finance collapsed and the Great Depression swept over them. This disaster was close followed by a prolonged and consuming drought. At the time we met them, the Rahiers were effectively penniless (as indeed they had been during most of the previous two decades), yet were as ebullient and seemingly as contented as if they were on top of the world.

Frank and Harris had never met their like before. I had, and I knew them as avatars of mankind's ancient stock, survivors winnowed by rigorous adversity that had given them a willingness – indeed a compulsion – to help one another and others no matter what the cost.

The Rahiers took us under their wing. We were ordered to present ourselves at their table for at least one meal a day and if we failed to show up the children would bring us hot dishes from the family table. We ate bread baked from grain they grew and milled themselves; potatoes and other vegetables they somehow managed to grow in their dusty garden; pies and puddings stuffed with cranberries, wild raspberries, or strawberries picked by the children; delectable fishes called goldeyes caught in the nearby river; prairie chickens, jackrabbits, and wild ducks, all gifts of the prairie, its sloughs, and marshes. They also fed us sauerkraut, salt pork, and bottled meat from the steer they butchered every fall or from white-tailed deer shot among the tangled woods in the river valley. Eggs, milk, butter, cream, and even handmade ice cream were pressed upon us. On special occasions they gave us heady saskatoon berry wine or barley beer they had brewed themselves.

They were a musical lot. Led by Servais playing a shiny old fiddle, the children constituted an orchestra. Playing banjos, Jew's harps, mouth organs, and a rebuilt accordion, they achieved something akin to harmony. They liked to perform at our campfire, sometimes joined by youngsters from Cree families who lived seasonally in tents at the river's edge while netting and drying goldeye for winter use.

As we sat at their family table, the Rahier children sometimes entertained us with operatic records played on an old Victrola. Although the mainspring was broken, they made the machine work by spinning the turntable with their fingers while coaxing music from worn old records with thorn needles harvested from Isabella's one precious rose bush.

Katherine, the eldest daughter, would sometimes sing along with the scratchy voice coming from the Victrola's horn. Her extraordinarily inventive renditions of arias from *Aida* remain with me long after the best efforts of the Metropolitan Opera Company have faded from memory.

Frank, whose boast was that he never missed an opportunity to collect a new mammal, quickly became interested in Katherine, who one day responded by inviting him to accompany her to the village of Carlton, fifteen miles away across an ocean of shimmering prairie. She volunteered to drive Frank there in the Rahiers' automobile, a 1919 McLaughlin-Buick touring car whose superstructure (including windshield and doors) had long since vanished. So had the seats, to be replaced by wooden slats. When all six cylinders were firing, this massive vehicle could attain a speed of twenty-five miles an hour. This was quite fast enough because the car had only one functional brake – a handbrake – on just one of its wooden-spoked wheels.

Frank offered to drive but Katherine would have none of that. The pair set off in a cloud of yellow dust and we saw nothing more of them until late next morning when Frank appeared at camp subdued and chastened and reluctant to talk about his experience. We eventually learned that he and Katherine had surprised a coyote on the track that passed for a road. Frank did not yet have a coyote in his collection and desperately wanted this one so, eager to oblige, Katherine had wheeled the car out of the ruts and headed it off across the prairie in pursuit.

Wildly bouncing into and out of gopher and badger holes, flinging dirt and tumbleweed in all directions, they were gaining on the coyote when it reversed its course and disappeared. Katherine hauled on the brake handle, which made the big car slew sideways so abruptly that a wheel broke and Frank was flung out of the car and into a patch of Russian thistle – nature's version of barbed wire.

Frank and Katherine walked the ten miles back to the farm, where, without a word of censure or complaint, Servais hitched up the ox and went off to haul the car back home. Then he and the boys carved new spokes for the broken wheel. Two days later the old vehicle was back in service.

During the remainder of our stay, Frank concentrated on four-legged mammals, which were in great abundance at Fort Carlton. But then there are few places in the world where small mammals are not abundant, though humans are generally unaware of this because most four-legged creatures are too small or of too little monetary worth to merit our attention.

As a case in point, the places we visited in Saskatchewan were home to some sixty different mammalian species. Rodents alone included meadow jumping mice, woodland jumping mice, pocket mice, house mice, deer mice, white-footed mice, grasshopper mice, harvest mice, red-backed voles, meadow voles, sage voles, prairie voles, blond-faced voles, heather voles, bog lemmings, kangaroo rats,

wood rats, Norway rats, pocket gophers, flying squirrels, red squirrels, grey squirrels, fox squirrels, prairie dogs, pocket gophers, wood
gophers, common gophers, striped gophers, chipmunks, muskrats,
beaver, cottontail rabbits, snowshoe rabbits, and jackrabbits.

Then there were the members of the shrew family: short-eared
shrews, arctic shrews, masked shrews, prairie shrews, dusky shrews,
the truly diminutive pygmy shrews (half a dozen of which weigh
less than an ounce), and water shrews (creatures smaller than one's
little finger living, as the name implies, in and under the water).

All are preyed upon by martens, ermines, minks, otters, long-
tailed weasels, least weasels, black-footed ferrets, red foxes, kit foxes,
black (silver) foxes, badgers, and coyotes.

To be added to the list are the mammalian aeronauts. Those
living in Saskatchewan include the big brown bat, little brown bat,
silver-haired bat, red bat, hoary bat, long-eared bat, and small-
footed bat.

The little people of the mammalian world were almost unbelievably abundant a century ago when a single acre of virgin prairie
could harbour thousands of shrews, mice, voles, ground squirrels,
and their ilk. However, their once-thriving communities have since
been decimated by the destruction of their habitat, by deliberate
poisoning and trapping campaigns, and "incidentally" by herbicides
and insecticides.

During the summer of 1939 we four budding scientists did our
bit to hasten the decline. Fort Carlton's primary attraction for us was
that it was the "type locality" for two species of ground squirrels.

In 1825, John Richardson, second-in-command of a Royal Naval
expedition charged with making a land-based exploration of the
coast of the central Arctic, was delayed at Fort Carlton for a few days
while en route north. Typical of his kind and of his times, Richardson
amused himself by wandering around shooting whatever creatures
came within range. Among his trophies were two small mammals

which, when sent to London, turned out to be unknown to science. British zoologists christened them Richardson's Ground Squirrel and Franklin's Ground Squirrel.

Europeans who later settled the prairies called them wood gophers and common gophers and, because those fed on grasses (including grains), stigmatized them as worthless vermin and spent enormous amounts of time and money trying to eradicate them.

For us, however, they had real commercial potential. Scientific collectors paid handsomely (and still do) for type specimens – *topotypes* they are called – and since nobody had collected topotypes at Fort Carlton since Richardson's visit we hoped, as my journal attests, to make a killing there.

July 27: Our job is to get as many topotypes as we can. We go after them every day with guns and traps and snares. Frank even used most of the arsenic from our skinning kits in bait but the gophers that ate it probably died in their burrows. Anyhow we are getting so many that gopher carcasses are in everything from the stew pot to bedrolls. And if anything stinks worse than a three-day dead gopher in hot weather I don't want to know about it. We sometimes skin all night because it's too hot in daytime with the temperature going as high as 107 degrees by noon. The worst was when Harris was trying to skin a big fat wood gopher that got so hot its intestines burst all over the skinning tent. Murray says he'll never go fer a gopher again. I'm with him, even though that really is a lousy pun.

‹ 6 ›

BEFORE THE STORM

Our next station was near Dundurn, some eighty miles south, where I had spent my bittersweet sixteenth birthday. Now, in early August of 1939, Murray Robb and I, accompanied this time by two new companions, again pitched our tent in the same magical place.

Although the Big Slough had become little more than a vast alkaline puddle it still nurtured abundant life. Around and beyond it the shortgrass prairie, including a military preserve and an Indian reservation, had escaped the settlers' plows and so still provided a home to many of its original inhabitants, except buffalo, wolves, and prong-horned antelope, all of whom had been exterminated by modern man.

The survival of this oasis seemed something of a miracle. Not far from our camp stood a monumental example of the forces that had been deployed against it – an abandoned steam tractor almost as big as a turn-of-the-century locomotive, whose iron-cleated drive wheels ten feet in diameter and five feet wide had once provided traction to haul a gang plow capable of scalping fifty acres of native grassland every day.

Thirty years earlier this clanking invader had been mysteriously halted at the border of the Indian Reserve and had never moved again. Summer storms and winter blizzards had conspired to rust its mighty shafts and wheels into permanent immobility. It stood (and for all I know may still stand) as a monstrous testimonial to mankind's relentless efforts to reshape the natural world.

Grain fields stretched to the horizon south and west of the dead monster. Seed planted in them that spring had sprouted, but the young stalks had grown only a few inches before drought withered them. To the north and east, however, the native prairie grasses had survived. Although a hot wind rippled through them, they bent before it and rose again when it had passed.

The south and west was now an incipient desert – a man-made one – while to the north and east lay a parched but living world in which Harris, Murray, and I assumed the role of the Grim Reaper.

With August drawing on, our time was running short so we decided to spend what remained to us "investigating" a rolling plateau not far from the U.S. border. Straddling the boundary between Saskatchewan and Alberta, the Cypress Hills rise some two thousand feet above the surrounding prairies, achieving the highest elevation in mainland Canada between British Columbia's Rocky Mountains and the Torngat peaks of Labrador. A fertile island in the prairie sea, the Cypress Hills once supported a verdant sprawl of pine, spruce, birch, and poplar copses that were home to an enormous assemblage of plants and animals.

Their survival and variety was due largely to the fact that all through the last great continental glaciation (which ended about twelve thousand years ago) the Cypress Hills miraculously remained ice-free, a haven for all living things. During the short time we had to prowl its high plateau, we found the bones of bison, the horns of big-horned sheep, a puma's jaw, and part of the skull of what must have been one of the last of the Great Plains grizzly bears – now fabulous creatures who had still been at home here when the first Europeans arrived.

The Cypress Hills had also been a haven for aboriginal people. As late as the nineteenth century, when the Indians of what would become the western United States were being harried toward extinction, many came here seeking sanctuary. They did not always find it. In 1873, thirty-six Indians fleeing the U.S. Army's genocide were massacred here by marauding American bounty hunters. But, in 1875 the Canadian government sent the newly formed Northwest Mounted Police to the Cypress Hills to build wooden-walled Fort Walsh as a bastion against American incursions. To the surprise of all concerned, Fort Walsh and its handful of defenders managed to do the job.

My journal has this description of *our* meeting with the successors of the NWMP upon *our* arrival at the Cypress Hills.

> We set off from Dundurn in mid-morning and on through the night to Swift Current, before heading to Maple Creek, just north of Cypress Hills. What a weird country! Arid semi-desert for miles and miles of mostly abandoned farms doomed by the drought, then the land starts to roll as if a big sea was building under it, except the surface is covered with sage brush. Hardly any sign of living people. The hills got bigger and higher until suddenly we were in a pine forest. It smacks of the miraculous. Pine trees, and a cool breeze and even some green grass!
>
> We didn't think they would let us into Cypress Hills Provincial Park since we were collectors, but the park warden winked an eye. We set up camp then drove to a sparkling little clear-water lake we'd passed on the way in.

We were stripping off in the car for a skinny dip and were mostly naked as frogs when another car pulled up and four big guys hopped out. They were Mounties. A corporal came loping over, peered through the back window, saw some of our guns and let out a shout.

"They're armed!"

At that they all pulled out revolvers and scurried for safety behind their car before ordering us to come out with our hands up.

We were kind of slow, being nude and not too amiable after driving all day and night. We lined up, looking like a bunch of skinned rabbits. There was nothing on us to search so they searched the car and hauled out guns and ammo. They told us we were under arrest because we were a bunch of bank robbers from Ontario trying to make a getaway to B.C.! They'd been looking for us, they said.

Frank and I dug out our collecting permits and all the other papers we could find and we tried to explain who we were. They just kept their revolvers pointed at us. Finally I told them Inspector Mundy of the R.C.M.P. in Saskatoon was a friend of my family and they should phone him. They let us get dressed but took the keys to the car and our guns and told us to stay in our camp till they came back. Which they did in about two hours. Inspector Mundy had vouched for me, but they were still suspicious and hung around asking more questions until I got out a mickey of Scotch whisky we were saving for a special occasion.

Soon thereafter Frank and I made an expedition of our own to the U.S. border, looking for a prairie dog town we had heard about.

Drove south over the Frenchman River Flats, the most desolate country I've ever seen. From its few hills we could look pretty near as far as the border across a rolling yellow desert dotted with clumps of sage bush and not much else. Suddenly came upon a flock of birds as big as turkeys crossing the road. They were our first Sage Grouse. We brought down four and stowed them away to skin that night then we followed a cart track across the desert till it petered out. We set a course by the sun and bumped along until we reached the edge of a dry valley. Down below we could hear whistles and yelping as if a thousand puppies were on the loose. It took us an hour to find our way down to the "dog town." It consisted of some three hundred burrows, each marked by a cone of dirt two or three feet high, with a prairie dog (they look like small groundhogs) sitting perched on top of each, keeping an eye on us. Frank was desperate to collect some but every time he hit one it would drop down into its burrow and we'd lose it.

It was dusk before we gave up and coming upon another dirt track followed it although we had no idea where it went. Burrowing owls flitted ahead of us like giant bats. Then a coyote trotted across the track with a prairie dog in its mouth.

I jammed on the brakes and Frank grabbed his rifle as the car slewed to a stop. The coyote vanished into the sage brush, but dropped the prairie dog. Frank was delighted to get the specimen and I was happy the coyote escaped.

We eventually came to the small village of Val Marie, a "one-elevator dump," Frank called it, where we found an emaciated young coyote chained to a post in front of a gas station. Frank was desperate to get it for his collection, but I was determined to save its life – which I did with one of my last remaining dollars.

In deference to the array of sharp white teeth with which the pup warned all comers to keep their distance, I named him Fang. Although not aggressively hostile, within minutes of our arrival back at camp in the Cypress Hills he had validated the name by putting his mark on Murray for attempting to give him a patronizing pat on the head.

During our absence, Harris and Murray had collected the two rarest birds of the trip: a Bullock's oriole and an Audubon's warbler. They had also had a visit from the park warden, who warned them that the troubles in Europe were threatening to lead to war. We were not much disturbed by this news. Whatever might be happening overseas, we did not expect it to impinge upon our lives. Such was the extent of our innocence.

The summer of 1939 was now nearly at an end. We were almost broke, were a little homesick, and were very tired of our own cooking. So, on September 1, we set out for Ontario by a circuitous route that would take us into northern Wyoming to see the wonders of Yellowstone National Park.

On September 3 we stopped at a gas station near the Grand Canyon of the Yellowstone, and the fellow manning the pump saw from our licence plates that we were Canadians.

"You Canucks going off to war again, eh?" It was more of a statement than a question. "I guess them English bastards given you your orders. Expect you'll get your asses in a sling and it'll serve you goddamn right! That'll be two bucks thirty for the gas – and don't give me none of your funny money."

We abandoned our sightseeing shortly thereafter, not because we had seen enough but because our remaining money was all Canadian currency. In anticipation of Canada's imminent destruction at the hands of the Nazis, most American stores and gas stations were refusing to accept our cash.

Driving by night and by day and living mostly on crackers and stolen fruit, we headed east through a miasma of hostility. Some Americans were actively sympathetic to the German cause and many were isolationists, as their refusal to join the Allies in the war until two years later would demonstrate. We became edgy, Fang edgiest of all, perhaps because he was being subjected to a meatless diet. He rode on the ledge under the rear window and I have a vivid memory of Harris's expression as Fang leaned over his shoulder one day and snatched a banana out his hand – perhaps hoping to get the hand as well.

It was with considerable relief that, on September 6, we crossed the border at Windsor and regained our own country again.

Three days later, Canada declared war on Hitler's New Order.

I returned to school determined to get good enough grades to let me become a professional biologist, but what I really wanted was to regain the limitless horizons of Saskatchewan after graduation.

I had much to do that winter, but still found time for the Others. Andy occasionally came out for a weekend of birdwatching, and Harris and I spent a lot of time tramping over fields and through woodlots, making countless small discoveries about the lives of the "lesser beasts." I tried to train Fang to come along for I was certain he would be able to show us many hidden things. It was not to be. Fang belonged to the wild. He hated being on a leash and one morning when I went to get him I found a gaping hole in the mesh of his enclosure.

Though I never saw him again, I did hear from him – as did many others. He took up residence in the Honey Pot, a swatch of unfarmable wooded ridges a few miles west of Richmond Hill. From there, when the moon and the mood were right, his laments sounded across the countryside. Reports of an invasion of wolves, "the first to be reported since a wolf was killed here in the 1890s," appeared in the local paper. Only Harris and I and a few fellow con- spirators knew who the singer *really* was.

Late in 1940, a duet was heard from the Honey Pot hills. The sex of the newcomer was established the following summer when the singing from the Honey Pot swelled to a chorus of half a dozen voices, some of them quaveringly juvenile. It delights me now to realize that, even if only by accident, I helped bring the coyote to Ontario, where his kind are now firmly established and where I hope they will continue to prosper, despite all that human beings can do to put them under.

The end of 1939 was fast approaching and Andy, Frank, and Harris had all agreed to come along on a new expedition to Saskatchewan if I could organize it. However, I had not yet found financial support and, sensing that their commitments were weakening, I suggested a Christmas get-together in a semi-abandoned cabin a hundred miles north of Richmond Hill. I kept no journal of this but later wrote an account for a never completed book.

A cracked iron range billowed acrid smoke into the cabin, further dimming the flickering light from an oil lamp. The wind snoring across the burnished ice of the big lake had no trouble finding its way through the log walls.

It might seem a peculiar way for four town-bred eighteen-year-olds to be spending New Year's Eve. Some of our more dashing contemporaries were at this very hour disporting themselves at Bill Beasley's Esquire Club on Toronto's waterfront. Others, more sedate or better heeled, were squiring their dates to a glittering prom at Casa Loma. Those who were neither rich nor dashing were partying at home or, if they lived in little towns like mine, swinging their partners around high school gym floors, sweating in the heat of adolescent sexual miasma.

"Time for a drink!" I cried.

Someone hauled a gallon jug of cider out from under the table and tilted it to fill our mugs. Alas, the cider had turned to frozen mush that had to be tickled out of the jug with a fork.

"Music, maestro!" shouted Andy.

I fiddled with the knobs of a battered Stromberg-Carlson radio whose battery was almost dead, or almost frozen. Through a blur of static I could only get a thread of band music, barely recognizable as Tommy Dorsey playing "Smoke Gets in Your Eyes." We began to sing along – with feeling – as the wind bellowed across the lake blowing smoke down the tin chimney until we could hardly see each other.

When the music lost itself in static I spun the dial, and suddenly a clear, calm, male voice broke through:

. . . report several German aircraft shot down over Alsace-Lorraine . . . At sea, German activity has increased but the Royal Navy is countering . . . On the ground in France only patrol activity has been reported on this, the last day of 1939 . . . We return you now to the ballroom of the Royal York Hotel here in Toronto where, in just five minutes, we will welcome the New Year. . . .

Five minutes later we four linked arms around a rickety old table, raised our mugs of icy cider, drained them to the bottom, and joined the distant revellers in singing "Auld Lang Syne."

And never realized that not only were we bidding adieu to the year just passed, but that this was a final farewell to the last hours of our unfettered youth.

· 7 ·

WAR DRUMS

Despite the fact that there was a war on, the outlook for 1940 seemed reasonably bright to me. The initial gloom cast by the outbreak of hostilities had largely dissipated as the situation overseas stagnated into what came to be known as the Phony War. Except for bombings by the Luftwaffe, the Germans appeared to be content to sit tight behind their borders. Nor were the Allies inclined to provoke them. Many people actually thought Hitler would make peace with France and Great Britain, or at least arrange an armistice with them in order to free the fascist forces for a massive assault upon the Soviet Union. Many resolutely neutral Americans would have been happy to have seen this happen and might even have supported the Nazis in a crusade against Godless Communism.

The jobs and money so suddenly produced by a war economy fostered a feeling of optimism in Canada that my father did not share. The Hastings and Prince Edward Regiment (a rural south-central Ontario peacetime militia unit in which he held a captaincy) had mobilized for active service in mid-September of 1939, and Angus had ever since been trying to find an active role for himself in this new struggle for world dominion. Despite having lost the use of his right arm, Angus yearned to be a warrior again. To prepare the way, he had finally given my mother what she most desired. In November 1939, he had actually bought a comfortably aged house in Richmond Hill, where he could leave her when he went off to battle.

Two days before my nineteenth birthday, the Phony War ended as the *blitzkrieg* shattered the defences of the Maginot line, overwhelmed Holland and Belgium and thunderd westward toward the English Channel.

A devastation which would snuff out at least fifty million human lives along with the lives of thousands of millions of the Others had begun. Though we could not even begin to comprehend its ultimate horror, we knew our world had shifted and a terrible darkness was descending.

It is hard now to remember, let alone describe, the conflicted state of mind into which we so suddenly and tumultuously found ourselves thrust. Personal hopes and plans were swept aside as we sensed, if dimly still, that everything we had believed secure was now in jeopardy. There was a rush to take up arms.

By the end of May many of my closest male friends had enlisted in the army, the navy, or the air force. On May 28, I headed for the Royal Canadian Air Force's manning pool in Toronto's Exhibition buildings to become part of a long line of (mostly) youths trying to enlist. After a cursory preliminary interview, I was passed along for a medical examination by a harassed doctor. He pronounced me underweight.

A few minutes later a tired recruiting sergeant glanced at my medical report and confirmed my lack of suitability.

"Shove off," he said. "The air force don't need no peach-faced kids."

Although I knew I looked younger and more fragile than I really was, I was still furious. Once back home I unburdened myself to my father, who was now under orders to report for duty with the Hastings and Prince Edward Regiment.

Angus attempted to soothe me with some derogatory comments about the air force being "the junior service" before casually mentioning that there were still openings for junior officers in the "Hasty P's" as the regiment was familiarly known.

I had no interest in becoming an infantryman or in joining my father's old outfit, but I was not going to be left behind while all my peers got into uniform so I agreed to try the army.

On June 18, Angus and I set sail in *Scotch Bonnet* from Toronto, bound for the regimental depot at Picton on the Bay of Quinte. When we arrived there, it was to learn that my father had been made a major and given command of Headquarters Company of the 2nd Battalion, based in Trenton. I was told to proceed to the headquarters of Military District No. 3 in Kingston for a medical examination.

I feared I would fail this examination too but the staff of HQ MD 3 included a number of my father's aging cronies from the Great War. One of them ordered me to drink six large glasses of water – seven if I could get the last one down – before presenting myself to the medical team.

Bollocks naked, I went before the three doctors, one of whom eyed my rotund stomach with interest and made as if to poke it with his finger. He was restrained by the one who had told me to drink up.

"For God's sake, Harry, don't *do* that! You'll drown us all!"

Then they put me on the scales and to nobody's surprise found I weighed enough to pass medical muster.

Having been declared fit to die for my country, I was returned to Picton. There, after taking the oath and being duly attested, I was enrolled in the ranks of the 2nd Battalion as Private Mowat, F.M., was issued a moth-eaten First World War uniform meant for a much larger person, and provided with two threadbare blankets of equal antiquity. I was not issued a weapon because at this stage of the war there were not even enough military rifles in Canada to arm the *active* battalions, let alone the militia.

I had no need of a weapon anyway. My first assignment was as a batman (officer's servant) to the elderly lieutenant who was the depot's assistant adjutant. I spent the first month of my service life shining his boots, polishing his brass, burnishing his Sam Browne belt, and helping him get over his hangovers, for he seldom went to bed sober.

Determined to become a good soldier I worked to such effect that I was promoted to lance corporal (acting) and put in charge of the bar in the officers' mess.

This happy state of affairs ended as soon as my father got wind of it.

Angus had my career firmly charted. He was determined that I follow in his footsteps by becoming a platoon commander, even though he of all people must have realized this was likely to get me killed or maimed.

After he discovered that, instead of slamming my feet up and down on a parade ground, I was "slinjing" (his word) in the officers' mess, I received orders to report to HQ Company in Trenton.

Headquarters Company of the 2nd Battalion was run by a handful of mostly over-age soldiers commanded by my father. It consisted of three rifle platoons, composed of men who were either too young, too old, or too disabled for active service, or those who could not be spared from war-related civilian jobs but could "soldier" two nights a week and on weekends.

Most of our training was of First World War vintage. A farmer's field became our training ground and here we laboriously dug a full-scale 1918-style trench system. On those rare occasions when we could scrounge a little ammunition from District Headquarters, we practised marksmanship at targets illuminated by the headlamps of parked cars. On weekends we engaged in war games, during which we were sometimes attacked by antiquated RCAF biplanes whose pilots dropped paper bags filled with flour on us as we pointed wooden machine "guns" at them and shouted "*Bang!*"

Because I had spent much of my young life in the wilderness, I got the job of field-craft instructor. With the coming of winter I wangled thirty pairs of ski boots from a Bata shoe factory, miscellaneous skis and poles from Trenton and Belleville merchants, dressed my platoon in white cotton smocks, and so created the Canadian army's first ski unit. This improvisation may have had something to do with my finally being commissioned an *acting* second lieutenant.

To avoid any possibility of finding himself accused of favouritism, Angus treated me with rigorous severity. "You may be my son," he told me one day after chewing me out publicly for being sloppy on parade, "in fact, I'm fairly confident you are, but in this regiment you're just another snotty-nose who has to be taught to change his diapers and respect his betters."

Off duty Angus was more of a comrade. Helen had remained in Richmond Hill with her new house while Angus and I lived aboard *Scotch Bonnet*, moored in Trenton harbour. We took turns doing the cooking, drank together, read together, and talked more than we had ever done before. But from the moment we stepped ashore in the morning, uniforms pressed and boots polished, he became an alien martinet who seemed determined to grind me into the ground. I hated him, yet I had never loved him more.

Determined to dispel any vestiges of peacetime torpor in the local population, Angus displayed a Churchillian inventiveness. To bring the reality of war home to Trenton, he staged a raid by a German U-boat — or what *could* have been a U-boat but was, in fact, *Scotch Bonnet*. With her black hull and a very dark night, she was practically invisible as she eased slowly and silently into Trenton's inner harbour. Once there she discharged several "torpedoes" at the dim outlines of three coal barges and a small freighter moored to the docks.

The torpedoes were army-issue "thunder flashes" — powerful fireworks — lashed to small cedar rafts which, using *Bonnet's* dinghy, I towed close to the targets and released after igniting the fuses.

No damage resulted but the tumult and confusion following the explosions was spectacular. Sirens rent the air. HQ Company was called out to defend the town. Not until next day did the absurdity of the supposition that German submarines were active in Lake Ontario strike home. By then my father's purpose had been achieved.

The 2nd Battalion was a way station from which I impatiently waited to be transferred to active service overseas with the 1st Battalion. But the 1st Battalion was not in action and was enduring no casualties, so there were few openings in its ranks. As autumn drew on, I became increasingly frustrated with soldiering in Trenton. When Sergeant-Major Bill McCoy, a leathery backwoodsman from north Hastings County, suggested he and I spend a few days at his hunting cabin, I jumped at the opportunity.

I asked for leave and, for once, my CO proved accommodating.

"Just make sure you bring back some venison. And maybe a brace or two of partridges."

Bill and I shed our uniforms and drove north through the mining town of Bancroft to a great granite dyke with a break in it called Hole in the Wall. Here we pulled on packsacks and snowshoes and tramped off into the winter woods. Three hours later we reached Bill's cabin, chased out a porcupine who had taken up winter quarters in the woodshed, built a fire, fried up some bannocks, and had a belt of rum.

During the next few days we mostly went our separate ways, Bill following deer trails while I wandered along a frozen river that snaked a convoluted course through hard-rock country. I carried my shotgun but though I saw rabbits, a bobcat, a belligerent ermine weasel, and many birds including ruffed grouse, I did not fire a shot. My rationale for this restraint was that I did not want to alarm the deer and so spoil Bill's chances. The truth was that I was far too happy at once again finding myself in the company of the Others to even consider using my guns against them.

A blizzard kept us stormbound in the cabin for a day and Bill grew fretful. A legendary deer hunter, he believed it was imperative that he return to Trenton with at least one carcass tied to the fender of his car. Deer were remarkably scarce, however, and by our next-to-final day he was still "skunked" and getting desperate about it. On the last day he persuaded me to lend him a helping hand.

I was to take station at the head of a gulley while he made a wide sweep through the surrounding country and circled back toward me, occasionally baying like one of the hounds with which he hunted in peacetime. Although I could hear him coming a mile away, no deer appeared. Bill was almost upon me and I was about to come out of hiding when, soundless as a ghost, a big buck materialized out of the dusk not fifty feet away.

For a moment the buck and I looked straight into each other's eyes, then he whiffled lightly in the friendly way deer do with one another, walked unhurriedly into the gulley, and disappeared.

A minute later Bill appeared, sweating heavily and looking angry.

"Didn't you *see* that goddamn deer?"

I nodded my head.

"You *saw* him? And never took a shot?"

Again I nodded apologetically. There was a long, pregnant pause before Bill spoke again, bitterly emphasizing the "mister" which was my due as an officer.

"Well, *Mister* Mowat . . . you just went and spoiled a damn good hound!"

Christmas came and went and I was still stuck in Trenton. Applications by militia officers to be given active status and sent overseas were a dime a dozen. One needed powerful influence to gain acceptance. Angus used all he had, but to no avail.

I still have the official reply to one of his attempts:

> *To: O.C. HQ Coy, 2nd Bn. H.P.ER. Trenton.*
>
> Re: F.M. Mowat, 2/Lieut, Non-Permanent Active Militia.
>
> *1. The further request of the m/n officer to transfer to Active status is herewith noted.*
>
> *2. It is not considered that the services of this officer with the Non-Permanent Active Militia should be dispensed with at this time.*
>
> *[signed] L.E. Grant, Col.,*
>
> *H.Q. Military District No. 3.*

Scrawled in ink at the bottom of the page is this addition:

> *Sorry Angus, we just can't do it. He looks so damn young there'd be bound to be questions asked in Parliament about the Army baby-snatching.*

Finally, on February 17, 1941, I was TOS (Taken On Strength) of the Canadian Army (Active) and posted to Fort Frontenac in Kingston. My stay in Kingston was a happy time. There really wasn't very much for me to do while I awaited posting to an officer-training centre. I was given nominal command of a few troops in transit, and when one soldier came down with measles the lot of us were quarantined together in an old stone warehouse on the lakeshore. We were not allowed out but abundant quantities of beer came in. And, in the dark of night, sundry local girls who, I assume, must have had an immunity to measles, came in too.

Ten days before my twentieth birthday, I was dispatched to an officer candidates training unit in Brockville. Enclosed behind a ten-foot barbed-wire fence, almost as formidable as that of a concentration camp, it was commanded by a very tough colonel (Whitehead was his name, so of course we called him Blackhead) whom we concluded must have been the peacetime warden of a penitentiary. He ran a classic U.S.-style boot camp where sadistic permanent-force corporals and sergeants did their level best to reduce us officer cadets to the emotional level of snivelling worms, while at the same time trying to imbue us with the physical attributes of pit bulls and the bloodthirstiness of demons.

I am happy to remember the day of our departure from "Brockville Military Academy." Colonel Whitehead owned an Irish wolfhound bitch of which he was inordinately fond, seeming to prefer her to any other being. She happened to be in heat on the weekend my class graduated, so some of us scoured Brockville for its most disreputable mongrel dog. Having fortified him with a huge steak we then, in the dark of night, hoisted him over the wall into the garden surrounding the colonel's private quarters and let nature take its course.

There was bloody hell to pay next day, but we already had our marching orders.

Although I was now a fully qualified first lieutenant, I did not get the immediate overseas posting I had anticipated. Instead I was seconded as an instructor to an infantry training centre at Camp Borden in central Ontario.

Outraged, I had myself paraded before the camp commandant there (another has-been resurrected from the last war) and demanded to be put on draft for England.

He was adamant in his refusal and I found myself fated to spend a rotten fall and winter in Camp "Boredom," doubtful that I would ever be released to join my regiment in England.

Eventually the fates relented, but it was not until July 18, 1942, that I found myself on a troop train entering the seaport of St. John where, along with a thousand others, I boarded the *Letitia*, a former luxury liner converted to serve as one of His Majesty's Transports.

Short hours later we were under way "across the Pond."

Part Two

INTERLUDE

· 8 ·

A GREEN AND
PLEASANT LAND

The transatlantic passage turned out to be something of a holiday cruise, with pay. The weather was calm, clear, and warm. The sea was gentle. Although we had to eat kippers, oatmeal gruel, boiled meat, and Brussels sprouts, liquor was abundant and, at sixpence a shot, well within our reach.

Five of us reinforcement lieutenants shared what had been a first-class cabin for two, and we behaved somewhat like youths at a summer camp, filled with the boisterous exuberance of those who, for the first time in their lives, truly feel free of the restraints imposed by family and society. The prospect of soon being set ashore in "England's green and pleasant land" before marching bravely off to war was overwhelmingly romantic.

I spent a lot of time on the upper decks observing the escorting corvettes and destroyers, half hoping and half fearing to glimpse the deadly dorsal spike of a periscope or the rushing white track of a torpedo, but the war seemed intent on avoiding us . . . until one evening a three-inch gun mounted aft on the poop deck opened fire.

I was in our cabin when the cannon roared. Almost simultaneously the ship's warning siren signalled an attack while the loud-hailer ordered us to action stations. My station was with the troops below decks so I missed seeing "the show" that followed.

One of *Letitia's* lookouts had reported seeing the wash of a barely surfaced submarine almost directly astern of us, and our naval gunners had reacted with commendable speed, sending half a dozen fifty-pound shells screaming toward the target, which disappeared. Two escort destroyers came foaming toward it at flank speed. Penned below decks, we *felt* the sickening thuds as depth charges began exploding and desperately hoped they would find their mark.

They did. Some hours later we learned via the ship's scuttlebutt that the target had been rammed and cut in half by a destroyer travelling at a speed of twenty knots.

This would have been a notable victory had the target been a U-boat instead of a whale.

One of my cabin mates expressed the general disappointment:

"Goddamn whales sure screw things up!" he lamented. "Teach them a fucking lesson! Keep out of our way."

In due course we raised the lush, green hills of northern Ireland, and a day later *Letitia* and her convoy sisters steamed slowly up the Clyde to dock at Greenoch.

The roadstead was packed with shipping ranging from camouflaged luxury liners and brooding battleships to dirty little tugs and sinister submarines. Both banks of the Clyde appeared to be sinking under a proliferation of shipyards whose stocks were filled with the skeletons of new vessels being hastily riveted together to help fill the voids created by U-boats.

The summer sky was everywhere streaked and soiled by gouts of coal smoke rising from the roaring maze of industries associated with the yards. Over our heads barrage balloons tugged at their tethers like blind, bloated beasts striving to escape a sea of suffocating fumes. Riverside streets and quays were encrusted with masses of trucks, horse-drawn wagons, and human beings. There was a continuous heavy-bellied rumble punctuated by strident metallic shrieks. Though I did not comprehend its significance at the time, what I beheld on Clydeside that day was a classic battle in the never-ending war between Man and Nature.

There was little time to dwell upon this monstrous spectacle before we were hustled off *Letitia,* herded over incredibly cluttered wharves, and wedged into the tiny carriages of British trains whose engines hooted like demonic owls.

Jammed into claustrophobic compartments, my companions and I peered eagerly out at a land that seemed grotesquely out of scale. Small as I am, I felt large and loutish in a landscape where everything was as if seen through the wrong end of a telescope. The illusion was heightened by the onset of darkness as the engine of our train snuffled southward into night. Tiny towns, Lilliputian cattle, handkerchief-sized fields, toy trucks and autos grew vague and disappeared. The blackout blinds in the carriage were pulled down, leaving one small bulb to illuminate two rows of white and astonishingly childlike faces staring palely at one another in the coal-reek gloom. All that long night we slept or dozed as best we might.

Dawn brought us into an immense industrial sprawl somewhere in the Midlands, through which our troop train crawled in fits and starts. Early as it was, the chimneys of Blake's dark satanic mills were already smearing the pallid sky with dust and smoke. The train jolted at a walking pace past endless rows of tenements backing so closely on the right-of-way that we could stare directly into the wan faces of men, women, and children crowding at their open windows to see us pass. They did more than stare. They leaned out toward us over blackened walls and waved and grinned and shouted raucously: "Good show, Canada!" "Up the Can-eye-dee-ans!" "Give the Heinies hell!"

Munching bully beef sandwiches and taking the occasional swig from a bottle of gin someone had thoughtfully brought along from *Letitia*, we waved and shouted back. We were moved by this reception, yet perplexed. Nothing like it had ever happened to us in Canada, where for the most part the civilian populace tended to treat the armed forces as some sort of necessary but essentially unpalatable aberration.

The train inched across a mighty bridge and as we reached the far side we saw why we had been delayed. Work crews were swarming over one of the spans, some of whose massive iron girders were strangely twisted and distorted. Below us lay a waste of tenements and factories reduced to unroofed and still-smouldering ruins by a Luftwaffe bombing raid the previous night.

Passing beyond the city, the train gathered speed and trundled into another world – the Ancient Island, at peace in the shimmer of a summer's morn. We caught glimpses of hoary villages and stately homes shrouded from vulgar view by moss-grown walls. Massive copses of oak and elm stood upon a land that curved and rose and fell away again in sensuous somnolence. Everything was unbelievably green, even, it seemed to me, the translucent sky itself. Our toy train, its little whistle keening at the many crossings, was an invisible time machine. Neither men nor animals in the fields and byways so much as raised their eyes as we went past. It was as if the train and we ourselves were from some future time.

War did not belong here, yet every now and again we glimpsed a distant aerodrome with tiny fighters lazing high above, or dingy rows of what looked like huge metal culverts cut in half lengthwise. We would become all too familiar with these unlovely objects –

corrugated iron Nissen huts, the standard shelter provided for the armed forces throughout Britain.

On the last day of July we halted at a little station whose identifying sign had been removed "for the duration" so as not to afford aid to German columns if they should invade. This was Witley, well south of London on the edge of the Salisbury Plain. A herd of double-decker London buses repainted a bilious khaki waited to trundle us the final few miles to 1-CDRU – First Canadian Division Reinforcement Unit – a gloomy collection of Nissen huts and ancient brick barrack buildings where each unit in the division maintained its own reinforcement company. Ours was commanded by Major Stanley Ketcheson, a raffish, slightly balding young man with a refreshingly unmilitary manner.

"Glad to see you horny young bastards . . . though you might better have stayed home. The regiment don't need you. It's up to its ass in officers right now and the only casualties we get are from syph or the clap. You'll stay here until you're wanted. We'll teach you something about real soldiering." His sharp-eyed glances flicked from face to face and stopped on mine. "You there, Mowat! How in hell did *you* lie your way into the army? Can't be a day over sixteen and still a virgin by the look of you. We'll fix that, by God!"

Ketcheson was as good as his word. He gave us into the charge of Captain Williams, a suave and cynical "older" man of thirty. Williams began our education by taking us in a battered fifteen-hundredweight lorry to Windsor where we spent the day learning about right-hand drive, charabancs, pillar boxes, tea shoppes, queues, bobbies, Hore-Belisha stripes, and sundry other local mysteries.

Williams explained that this expedition was intended "to acquaint you with some of the more superficial aspects of life in this loony bin. Tonight I'll show you the *real* thing!"

The real thing consisted of a pub crawl through Guildford, the nearest large town to Witley. Here in short order we learned the vital distinctions between saloon, public, and private bars; 'arf-and-'arf and gin-and-it; and members of the Wrens (Women's Royal Naval Service), WAFS (Women's Air Force Service), ATS (Auxiliary Territorial Service, also female), and Land Army girls. The differences between these groups consisted mainly of variations in the uniforms, all of singularly hideous design, clothing a breed of young woman the likes of whom most of us had never encountered before.

In the last of the several pubs we visited that night, Williams conferred earnestly with a Land Army girl named Philipa, whereupon this rather lumpy lady wearing a sweater and manure-stained green jodhpurs invited me to take a walk along the adjacent riverbank. Woozily I wondered if Philipa might be interested in birds – owls perhaps – for the night was very dark.

Her interest *was* biological, but not ornithological. In what must have been one of the most undignified and most uncomfortable seductions of modern times, she got me under some dripping bushes and deflowered me upon the soggy sod.

"There you are, luv," she said brightly as I fumbled to get my fly buttoned up again. "Captain Willy told me the Major said you needed doing and there's nothing I wouldn't do for a Canuck."

Having accomplished our introduction to the basic facts of civilian life in England, Ketcheson sent us off on an assault training course. The sadist in charge of it chillingly explained: "We're going to teach you to kill or be killed. If you live through it, you'll think taking on the Jerry army single-handed is a piece of cake!"

We did our stuff on a waste of blasted heath – a dusty semi-desert filled with thorny gorse. Our day began at 0500 and never really seemed to end. Everywhere we went, and everything we did (with the sole exception of defecating *if* and *when* one had time for this), was done at the double, running full-out while wearing full battle kit, including rifle, bandoliers of .303 ammunition, small pack, and sundry other impediments that weighed about sixty pounds at the beginning of the day and something like two tons by the end of it.

The training syllabus for Battle Drill (as it was called) demanded that we march (read: *run*) a minimum of ten miles a day (twenty on Sundays); that we crawl, squirm, and wriggle for endless terrifying hours over gorse-covered heath while homicidal maniacs masquerading as training staff fired live ammunition over, under, and all around us; threw percussion grenades between our out-flung legs or heaved gas canisters (which made us puke) under our noses as we tried to dig slit trenches in the flinty soil. For variety, we played unarmed combat games with bronzed killers who hit us in the windpipe, kicked us in the testicles, cart-wheeled us over their shoulders into gorse bushes, and belted us with rifle butts.

Although the bayonet was as outmoded in modern warfare as the horse, training in its use was still encouraged in order to instil in us a proper degree of "bloody-mindedness." So we lined up in squads in front of rows of straw-filled dummy Germans swinging from rough wooden gibbets. On command we lowered our rifles and thrust our bayonets into the dummies to an accompanying litany screamed by a hoarse-voiced instructor.

"IN . . . OUT . . . SHOVE IT IN HIS FUCKING GUT . . . IN . . . OUT . . . SLIT HIS BLOODY THROAT . . . IN . . . OUT . . . STICK HIM IN THE BALLS . . . IN . . . OUT . . ."

The instructor of one squad (thank God it wasn't ours) collected a load of offal from a local abattoir and stuffed some of the dummies with rotten tripe and with balloons filled with pig's blood.

The actual assault course, mostly constructed of barbed wire, was half a mile long and had to be surmounted or crawled through or under in a maximum of four minutes. If you were one second over, you repeated the torture and kept on doing so until you either beat the stopwatch or fainted dead away.

On the fourth day of this torment, our demon of an instructor added a particularly diabolical wrinkle. As we staggered over the last barbed wire obstacle, he screamed at us to *"double to the right, over the hill, down the slope, and swim the pond at the bottom!"*

We managed the hill and fell rather than ran down the far slope to the pond, which was what in England is discreetly referred to as a sewage farm. In this case, it was a gigantic open septic tank containing the sewage from most of the military camps in the Witley area.

The leaders of our panting mob drew up in horror on the verge of this stinking pit, but the demon was right behind us tossing percussion grenades under our tails, so in we plunged. There is no need to dwell upon the details.

Two weeks passed and the assault course was nearing its end. We had lost eight or nine of our number, three of them wounded (one fatally) during live firing exercises. The others had simply collapsed and been returned to their units as "unsatisfactory combat material." I was barely a hair's breadth from this fate myself. Nevertheless, I hung on until one morning I woke to find myself with what looked like the symptoms of a dose of gonorrhoea.

I was revolted, horrified, and frightened. I was a product of a time and society where the stigma attached to venereal diseases was the equivalent of what might attach itself to the hatchet murderer of a crippled old lady.

Overwhelmed with guilt, shame, and dread, I actually contemplated getting myself accidentally shot on the assault range, but somehow screwed up my courage and reported sick.

The camp M.O. was a young and recent graduate, humourless or perhaps just uncertain. He made a quick examination, muttered something unkind about people getting what they deserved, and ordered me to collect my kit and report to the transport lines en route to hospital. I sneaked into the officers' quarters for my gear and sneaked out again like the invisible man.

Three ghastly hours later I was admitted to No. 5 Canadian General Hospital to be examined by a doctor who told me the diagnosis would have to wait until the following morning. The nursing sister who saw me to my bed was an attractive woman whom I was too shamed to look in the face. I put in one hell of a night. But next morning the sister flung into my room, threw wide the curtains, and brought joy back to a blighted life.

"Well, Lieutenant, lab report is in. Nothing to fret about. Only a little non-specific urethritis. Bit like a sinus infection . . . except not in your nose. Clean it up in a day or three. Meantime, kippers for breakfast, or would you like some nice scrambled egg powder?"

God, how I loved that woman! I hope she reads this and remembers the frightened little subaltern to whom she restored the desire to go on living.

Later that day the M.O. came by and asked some questions about what I had been doing with myself. When I told him about the sewage farm, he grimaced and guessed that this was where I had picked up the infection. Freed of my incubus of dread, I began to take notice of my surroundings. They were quite extraordinary. No. 5 CGH was a brand-new, handsomely designed, and luxuriously fitted hospital built on the Cliveden estate of Lord and Lady Astor on the banks of the Thames in dreamily peaceful countryside near Maidenhead.

The luck of the gods had sent me here but it was entirely thanks to the sadists of the assault course that I remained, not just for the three or four days it took to cure my drip, but for three glorious summer weeks.

During my final days on the course, I had become agonizingly aware of swellings in both knees resulting from the interminable pounding across the heath loaded like a mule. Severe bruising of the knee cartilages was the diagnosis, and when it was also discovered that my weight was down to 116 pounds the doctors ruled I should remain in hospital until my bones had more upholstery.

I wrote home to my parents:

"I have a room to myself complete with radio and big bay windows looking out on a park of giant oaks. A luxurious bed, easy chair, semi-private bathroom, and three edible meals a day in a panelled dining room. I'll have walking-out privileges when I can walk again. This is the army? I don't believe it!"

An extraordinary bonus for me was that Cliveden then harboured one of Britain's leading ornithologists who, with his father and grandfather before him, had amassed an enormous collection of rare bird skins and eggs from all over the world. These included *three* great auks, together with the last known egg laid by that ill-omened species before mankind exterminated it; an egg (the size of an ostrich egg) of the legendary dodo of Mauritius; and two mounted passenger pigeons, relics of North America's most infamous extirpation.

Learning during a visit to the hospital of my interest in birds, the current guardian of these glories, a retired brigadier of First World War vintage, kindly invited me to view the collection and later gave me sherry in a magnificent library that boasted a portfolio of Audubon's paintings of American birds.

The brigadier led the good life as custodian of several thousand dead birds and many more of their eggs. His one complaint was that the current war had put a halt to the acquisition of additional specimens.

"Frightful loss to science, you know. But I trust young chaps like yourself will soon be able to take up the good work again. We'll drink to that, shall we?"

Cliveden also possessed an ornate boathouse containing several sculling punts and, wonder of wonders, a Canadian-made cedar-strip canoe. These were available for the use of patients so, being unable to walk any distance, I appropriated the canoe and used it to explore the back reaches of the Thames, stopping often to sample the wares of the many pubs along its banks. My favourite was the Compleat Angler, a pub frequented by an international collection of civilian pilots belonging to Ferry Command, in the dicey business of ferrying warplanes from Canada and the United States to and around the British Isles. They included bush pilots, stunt pilots, test pilots, and commercial pilots too old (one or two were in their fifties), too ruggedly individualistic, or of the wrong sex (there were several women among them) to fly in the air forces of their respective countries.

A hell-for-leather, hard-drinking but kindly lot, they responded to my admiration by tolerating me in their circle as a sort of mascot. They called me their Pongo Penguin – Pongo being a derisive name for an infantryman, and Penguin because I was flightless.

It was through them that I met Penelope. She was sitting at a table on the Angler's river terrace one evening when I arrived in my canoe. Petite, blond, and amber-eyed, she was suffused in that diaphanous glow which is the hallmark of an English beauty.

I was instantly enthralled, but the ferry pilots surrounding her presented such formidable opposition I was afraid to intrude. When it grew dark and everyone moved inside to drink and dance, a pilot jokingly introduced me as Ferry Command's pet penguin. To my delight she allowed me to buy her a drink and I was emboldened to, in the language of the times, pitch her a line.

Penelope listened with gratifying interest until a handsome Yank (who *claimed* to have flown in the Antarctic with Admiral Peary) sauntered over and shot me down in flames.

"Enough of your crap, Penguin," he said sternly. "You wanna fly with pretty birds like this you gotta have wings! C'mon, Penny baby, let's cut a rug."

She smiled kindly at me as she took the Yank's extended hand. Somehow I managed to smile back, the sardonic grin of One Who Does Not Care, before slipping miserably off to my canoe.

It was an awfully dark night and just below the Angler I found myself paddling into a side channel that turned out to be blocked by an ancient weir over which even the sluggish Thames poured with unexpected vigour.

The canoe tipped forward, burying her bow and spilling me out. I floundered ashore on a muddy little islet, where I was immediately attacked by two spectral beings clad in white who beat me savagely about the kidneys with what felt like flails. By the time I had leapt back into the river and splashed my way to the mainland, most of the Angler's customers, including Penelope, had assembled on the bank to see what all the fuss was about.

Although it was not one of life's great moment (I had come ashore in a sorry state), my misadventure awakened Penelope's protective instincts. She demanded towels and hot whisky for me and as she drove me back to the hospital in her little red MG sports car proceeded to make amends.

"Someone really *ought* to have told you about the swans. They're royal birds, you know, and they do get frightfully huffy when someone trespasses on their breeding grounds. But not to worry, dahling, I'll make it up to you."

We were barrelling along in almost total darkness (the little car's normally ineffectual lights had been further dimmed with blackout tape) when she jammed on the brakes and brought us to a squealing stop beside a roadside callbox erected by the Royal Automobile Club for the benefit of members who might experience a breakdown.

Penelope slid smoothly out of her bucket seat and with her member's key unlocked the door of the callbox. Then she beckoned me to join her in the glass-enclosed little cubicle. Puzzled but willing, I did as bid. When we were jammed inside, she scrunched the door shut and began making passionate and acrobatic love to me.

Nothing had prepared me for the likes of Penelope.

A day or two later she drove me to her home – a mansion surrounded by impressive lawns and guarded by a grim-visaged Scots nanny who met us at the door holding a year-old infant in her arms.

Penelope fondly took the child and in reply to my mute inquiry explained that "Baby Dumpling" was hers.

"Daddykins," she would later tell me, was a senior staff officer "doing something frightfully important in Cairo for dear Alex – *General* Alexander, you know" – but who expected her to "live a normal life" in his absence. This she was doing to the best of her ability.

Life in Penelope's England was heavy going for a callow youth from the Colonies. The doctors at the hospital were puzzled to find I was no longer gaining weight and, in fact, had actually lost a pound or two. God only knows where it would all have ended had not the black tragedy of Dieppe intervened.

On August 19 most of the Second Canadian Infantry Division made a foredoomed raid on the German-defended French Channel coast. The Channel and the beaches of Dieppe ran red with blood and the crimson welt soon extended back into England as far as sylvan Maidenhead.

At 2:00 a.m. on August 20 the ambient patients in No. 5 General Hospital, myself among them, were rousted out of bed and dispatched to their holding units to make way for some of the flood of shattered men returning from the shambles of Dieppe.

By the time dawn broke, I was back at 1-CDRU in Witley – never to encounter Penelope in the flesh again.

⟩ 9 ⟩

SETTLING IN

Having missed my turn in the queue to join the regiment, I was fated to spend the next month in limbo at Witley, where the colonel commanding 1-CDRU concluded I was unlikely ever to become a useful infantry officer and decided to make me permanent camp adjutant. Although this would eventually have brought me the rank of captain and ensured a safe and easy life, the prospect filled me with dismay. I ran to Major Ketcheson for help.

His solution was to tell the camp commandant he simply could not have me. Why not? Well, Ketch lied, because I was a nephew of Canada's Minister of Defence, who would be *most* upset if I was prevented from joining my regiment.

The commandant decided to dispense with both of us. Next morning Ketch and I were on a train to, as our orders read, "join the Hastings and Prince Edward Regiment in the Field."

In this case "in the Field" meant the lovely, rolling Sussex countryside in the valley of the River Wal. Here we found the regiment billeted on farms, in little villages, and on a few large estates scattered around the district. Battalion headquarters was in a rambling old vicarage in the hamlet of Waldron and when we arrived was in a state of some confusion as a result of a shake-up of its officers, a number of whom were being shifted to rear area jobs or sent back to Canada.

The new commanding officer, Lieutenant Colonel Bruce Sutcliffe, welcomed Ketch with open arms and immediately made him second-in-command. Ketch's first act was to appoint *me* as battalion intelligence officer. I had expected to be posted to a rifle platoon and had only the vaguest idea what an I.O. was supposed to be, or do, but I liked the sound of the title and the prospect of living at headquarters, where I would be in the heart of things.

Waldron consisted of half a dozen thatched cottages; a tiny pub that looked and felt as if it belonged to the days of Robin Hood; the vicarage, a sixteenth-century brick-and-timber warren with leaded windows; and the parish church which, the old verger told me, had been built by the Saxons about A.D. 600, refurbished by the Normans around 1100, and hadn't had much of anything done to it since.

This crumbling, square-towered little church, plastered with bright green moss, stood half buried in a grove of ancient linden trees and was surrounded by stone walls and yew hedges pierced by a canopied lych-gate (literally, a corpse gate). The lushly overgrown churchyard, richly manured by more than a thousand years of human burials, was bursting with birds, rabbits, and other creatures but rarely visited by living human beings since even the verger had given up the struggle to keep nature under control. It was my kind of place and I felt instantly at home there.

Headquarters was small, cozy, and friendly. Since almost all of its half dozen officers were new to their respective jobs, nobody put undue pressure on me and I had time to find my feet. My "command" consisted of a ten-man Scout and Sniper Section and an eight-man Intelligence Section. Fortunately they were a kindly and forbearing lot – old hands who knew their jobs inside out – and they carried me until I began to learn the form. They also taught me the joys of swanning.

Swanning was not, as the name might imply, a specialized form of birdwatching. It was the art of escaping from the clutches of one's superiors in order to do what we now refer to as one's own thing. Thus, on the pretext of looking for possible spies, organizing intelligence exercises, or undertaking reconnaissances of various kinds, I was able to absent myself and explore the surrounding countryside, and meet many of the English Others.

I had bought a pocket bird guide with whose aid I was able to tally many new species. I particularly recall the day I spotted my first bearded tit. Eventually my British list included such notables as the chough, hoopoe, capercaillie, twite, chiffchaff, whinchat, wryneck, knot, dotterel, dabchick, and corncrake. English ornithological nomenclature was anything but dull.

By now I had spent nearly two years preparing myself to be a fighting soldier; but life that autumn with the Hastings and Prince Edward Regiment was a far cry from what I had anticipated. Most of the troops were living in distinctly unmilitary ways, preoccupied by unmilitary tasks. Widely dispersed across the countryside, companies and even platoons were spending much of their time helping their farmer-hosts with farm chores. This was a happy time for most of us. I was able to spend long hours in company with foxes, badgers, hedgehogs, rooks, pheasants, magpies, barn owls, and the like who were also living in happy times because the war had effectively brought an end to sport hunting in Britain.

Such a happy state as we were in could not last. In mid-November the regiment was ordered to exchange its comfortable civilian billets for a bleak collection of newly erected Nissen huts slowly sinking into a quagmire of sticky mud on a large estate called Possingworth Park.

Nobody was happy with the change. As the autumnal rainy season melded into the winter rainy season we again became just another part of a great khaki gob that was overwhelming England.

Our new quarters (lightless metal tunnels from whose cold corrugations condensation was forever dripping) were dismal, frigid, and dispiriting. Opportunities for supplementing army rations with fresh vegetables and fruits were much reduced. To make things worse our lordly masters at First Canadian Corps Headquarters concluded we had become too relaxed in our habits, so it was time for a turn of the disciplinary screw. As Allan Richmond, my intelligence sergeant, put it:

"The silly fuckers up above have to justify their useless existence somehow so every now and again they shove a rocket under the tails of the poor bloody infantry."

Worst of all, Canadian Military HQ in London now afflicted us with a new 2 i/c – a hard-mouthed, spear-tongued major with the double-barrelled Anglo-Irish name of O'Brian-Bennett. He wasted no time letting us know we had a tiger in our midst. Mud or no mud, rain or no rain, the whole regiment went back to parade-ground bashing, arms drill, and close-order drill in the mindless ritual that is supposed to turn men into soldiers, but that tends to turn them into automatons instead.

Keeping out of O'Brian-Bennett's way became synonymous with survival. Evasive tactics were possible for some junior officers in the rifle companies but were generally impossible for me. The 2 i/c's cold glance seemed always to be on me and clearly he did not approve of what he saw.

"Smarten up, Mowat!" and "You'd bloody well better get with it!" were his two favourite salutations.

I was not even able to escape his hostility in the presumed sanctity of the officers' mess. As we were eating dinner one evening a mess orderly brought me a small, beautifully wrapped parcel which had just arrived by registered mail. There was no return address or name on the outside so I rather casually ripped it open. It contained an ornate silver automatic pencil in an alligator leather sheath. While I turned this expensive trinket over in my hands wondering rather stupidly who could have sent it, Lieutenant Jerry Austin, fumbling through the wrapping paper, uncovered a gilt-edged card. He read what was written on one side in copper-plate script then loudly demanded, "Jeez, Farl, who's this Penny bint? And what's she mean, '*May you always have lots of lead in your pencil*'?"

The gilt-edged card was passed from hand to hand down the long table, accompanied by laughter and wisecracks – until it reached O'Brian-Bennett. He glanced at it, turned it over, and saw what none of the others had noticed: the neatly engraved name and rank of Penelope's husband.

O'Brian-Bennett's raised voice cut like a machete.

"It is despicable for a man to accept valuable gifts from *any* woman except his wife and especially so from a woman married to another serving officer!" He paused for effect. "Lord Jesus Christ, what could be *more* despicable?"

I should have held my tongue, but foolishly tried to defend myself.

"She's not his wife . . . she's his daughter . . . sir."

A smile touched his lips but there was no smile in his eyes.

"*Wrong*, Mowat! As you so often are! I have met this officer . . . *and* his charming wife. Are *you* calling *me* a liar?"

This was my first trial-at-arms with O'Brian-Bennett. Another soon followed. Having had enough of being referred to as Junior, or the Babe, by superiors, inferiors, and peers alike, I had begun to grow a moustache. It was not much – a few pale yellow hairs – but the best I could manage.

One rainy afternoon O'Brian-Bennett decided to hold a ceremonial parade. The entire regiment had to turn out and stand in the drizzle for his inspection. When he got to the Intelligence Section, he halted in front of me and in a voice that could be heard all over the parade square shouted, "MISTER MOWAT!"

"Sir?"

"WHAT IN HELL'S THAT ON YOUR UPPER LIP?"

"Moustache . . . sir."

"LORD JESUS CHRIST, THAT'S NOT A MOUSTACHE . . . IT'S A DISGRACE! SHAVE IT OFF!"

Although quaking inwardly, I was not to be cowed into silence. Too much was at stake. The whole regiment was listening and I knew that if I did not make a stand I would never live it down.

"Can't do that . . . sir. King's Regulations and Orders, Section 56, paragraph 8 states that a moustache, once begun, may not be removed without permission of the commanding officer . . . sir!"

I had him there. Lieutenant Colonel Sutcliffe was a gentleman and also a gentle man. He never did give the requisite permission. In fact, he was overheard to take my side to the extent of remonstrating with the 2 i/c for "riding me too hard." O'Brian-Bennett's attempted explanation – also overheard – did not endear him to me.

"The little piss-pot *needs* riding. Toughen him up! Make a man of him!"

Perhaps this really was his motive. On the other hand, he may have guessed who had tagged him with the sobriquet by which he became known both within and beyond the regiment: Lord Jesus Hyphen Christ.

His antipathy seemed to embrace the whole of the I Section, both as to its functions and its personnel. In our hearing he would fulminate about us. "Lazy as cut bitches . . . useless as tits on a bloody bull!" were typical assessments.

We were neither lazy nor completely useless but there may have been a grain of truth in his criticisms. None of my men was what might be considered an average soldier. In truth, most had gravitated to or had been banished to the section because they did not fit the army pattern. One of my best men had been a commercial artist in civilian life and was an accomplished and vitriolic cartoonist whose savage caricatures of certain senior officers (printed on jelly pads and anonymously distributed) delighted the troops as much as they infuriated their subjects. Another of my men was a self-confessed anarchist who would rather talk than eat, and much rather fight than talk. His concept of an ideal society was one in which the officers dug and maintained the latrine pits, peeled the potatoes, and in general acted as servants for private soldiers. A third was a sometime lecturer in classics reputed to have been a Rhodes scholar, something he vehemently denied except when drunk, as he often was. My chief sniper was a homicidal maniac with a passion for the poetry of Robert Service and the reputation of being able to put a .303 bullet through the eye of a squirrel at two hundred yards.

My batman (who had been assigned to me at Witley by someone who probably thought he was playing a practical joke) fitted into the I section perfectly. Doc Macdonald appeared to be bashful, awkward, and ineffectual, someone forever destined to be a victim of the system, military or civilian. This was protective camouflage. Inside his bumbling, innocuous outer self lived a shrewd and talented manipulator. What Doc set out to get, sooner or later Doc got.

He and I had been together at Witley less than a week when one evening I missed the bus to Godalming and began fulminating about how much I wished I had a car. Some hours later Doc came to my room and, ducking his head humbly, reported that "my car" was ready.

I didn't know what he was talking about but I followed him outside, where he proudly led me to a regal-looking Bentley parked in front of our Nissen hut, its engine purring invitingly.

Doc accepted my vehement order to return the bloody thing to wherever he had "liberated" it, but I had disappointed him.

· 10 ·

BOMBS AND BIMBOS

As winter lengthened and the mud at Possingworth deepened, a surly mood afflicted officers and other ranks alike. The troops of First Canadian Division were fed up with waiting, so we were greatly excited when in early December we were suddenly ordered to proceed to the very secret Allied Forces Combined Operations Centre on Scotland's Loch Fyne, for sea-borne invasion training.

December was hardly the best month to visit Scotland's western coast. Fierce Atlantic gales blew up and down the lochs; bitter rain and sleet storms lashed the training areas and sprawling encampments (consisting mostly of the ubiquitous Nissen huts); snow fell on the slopes and crests of the surrounding hills, turned to slush in daytime, and froze again at night.

Nevertheless, for two exhausting weeks we enthusiastically practised the techniques of landing troops and weapons on a defended coast. By day we scurried up and down scramble nets dizzyingly suspended from the sides of troopships, loading ourselves into and out of heaving little cockleshells called LCAs (Landing Craft Assault). By night, under the lash of the winter rain, we pitched through the darkness and heaving seas in LCAs to stumble ashore through freezing surf onto beaches that crackled with simulated machine-gun fire and glared palely under the light of flares.

There were lighter moments. In the middle of one particularly miserable landing exercise, an unidentified voice came on the regimental radio net to announce that "Blue Beach has been taken and we have captured six polar bears, three walrus, and four Eskimos." This was followed by another voice complaining plaintively that his LCA was sinking "after collision with an iceberg."

There were even some pleasant interludes. Our camp stood on the edge of the Duke of Argyll's estate, and the duke's jealously guarded herds of red deer proved an irresistible temptation to my scouts and snipers who several times invited me to dine on fresh venison steaks and marvellous stews unsmilingly identified as beef. Some, who were trout fishermen but possessed no rods, substituted percussion grenades.

Did we feel any sense of guilt at despoiling the aristocratic duke? As my section anarchist put it, "If that fat-assed old son of a bitch gets himself into a private's uniform and slogs along with me on the next exercise, I just *might* leave his fucking deer alone."

On arrival at Inveraray, I had been issued an ancient and asthmatic Norton motorcycle on which I spent a good deal of time trying to locate far-flung fragments of the regiment that had become lost during landing exercises. One afternoon in a sleet storm, I was cautiously descending a steep side road leading to the camp when I saw a cluster of uniformed Wrens waiting for a bus. I opened the throttle and my poor old machine managed to work herself up to forty miles an hour, at which speed I attempted a flashy skid turn onto the main road. And found myself on my belly in a deep ditch with the Norton sprawled on top of me. The sweet cooings of concern from the Wrens as they pulled me free was little solace for having made such a fool of myself.

Worse still, my rescue was observed by our signals officer – a loathsome type who was notorious for sucking up to his seniors. He made such a yarn out of it that night in the mess that Lord Jesus Hyphen Christ was moved to strike again.

"So, Mowat . . . you can't handle four wheels, and you can't handle two. A tricycle ought to be about your style. We'll order one from Harrods toy department for your exclusive use!"

A bone-weary regiment arrived back at Possingworth early in the first week of 1943. We were not, however, discontented. Indeed, we felt sure our moment of glory must now be close upon us and guessed it would be an invasion of Norway. Our good spirits were reinforced when our miracle-working quartermaster, Captain Hepburn, having finagled several quarters of prime beef and vast quantities of whisky and beer, gave the whole regiment a stupendous Christmas blowout. It was held on January 6, the Old Christmas Day of the Russian Orthodox Faith. The choice of that date made Sergeant Richmond unusually thoughtful.

"Don't figure it's going to be Norway at all," he told me confidentially. "You mark my words . . . Churchill's sending us off to Russia to restore the Czar."

When time passed and nothing further happened, we began to think the Inveraray experience had been just one more false alarm. Winter dragged on, wet, cold, and dreary. Training languished and even O'Brian-Bennett seemed to have lost some of his blood-and-guts attitude. Instead of going off to battle, we found ourselves sending squads of men to the south coast to demolish defences that had been feverishly erected against invasion in 1941. We took this as an evil omen, perhaps presaging the regiment's demotion from a front-line fighting unit to some kind of work battalion.

Then, war came to us. Early in February the Luftwaffe tried to seize the initiative in English skies by mounting hit-and-run bombing raids by day and night on London and on industrial targets in the Midlands. But the RAF defence intercepted most German planes en route forcing them to jettison their bombs and streak for home.

Since Possingworth lay under one of the Luftwaffe's major flight paths, we got our share of unexpected presents. This kept me busy for I was now also the Bomb Reporting Officer for the district. Whenever an "incident" occurred, it was my job to rush to the scene, identify the type and weight of bomb, and assess the damages if any. If the bomb was a dud or I suspected it to be of the delayed-action variety, I arranged for a bomb disposal squad to deal with it.

I welcomed this new role for it provided me with my own Jeep. It also gave me the opportunity to meet civilians at many social levels.

I particularly remember an elderly lady who lived alone in a small cottage, supporting herself on a minuscule pension and by the sale of eggs from her dozen or so hens. One afternoon a two-hundred-kilo bomb from a fleeing Messerschmitt fell close to her cottage, broke all her windows, blew most of the tiles off her roof, killed her hens, and turned her garden into a muddy pool fed by a broken water main. By the time I arrived, she had just finished tacking brown paper over the broken windows and was calmly making a pot of tea, which she warmly invited me to share. After examining the still-smoking crater, I took a cup from her and, in what was probably a rather patronizing manner, tried to soothe and sympathize. She would have none of it.

"Tish and tush, my dear young man! What's this little bit of non-sense amount to when you think of what our brave chaps at sea and in the air and in North Africa are putting up with? Now this is the way *I* see it . . . if those nasty Germans drop their bombs on the likes of me, well then they won't have so many to drop on our Armed Forces, will they now?"

It was logic of a peculiarly English kind.

One night in February hundreds of one-kilo (two-pound) incendiary bombs intended for the London docks were dumped over our district. Falling into soft and sodden fields, many failed to detonate. I brought several of the "duds" back to camp, where out of simple curiosity Sergeant Richmond and I proceeded to take the sinister metallic tubes apart on the floor of the Nissen hut the Intelligence Section shared with the Catholic chaplain. This padre, a kindly older man, was accustomed to our odd ways but when we accidentally triggered an incendiary and it spouted a white-hot geyser of molten thermite through the flimsy partition separating his part of the room from ours, he lost his cool.

"Damn your eyes!" he cried as he stumbled through the thick white smoke toward the door. "It isn't *me* that's supposed to roast in the fires of hell! It's heathen dolts *like you!*"

A few nights later I was having a drink with the padre in the mess when the tin building shuddered under a tremendous concussion. After a stunned moment, the padre raised his gaze to mine and spoke in the tone of one who is sorely tried:

"Well, I suppose I must forgive you again. God would expect me to."

This time, however, it was not my fault. Earlier on this foggy evening we had heard German bombers overhead and one of them had jettisoned a one-ton delayed-action land mine. It had swayed to earth under its enormous parachute unseen by anyone. When its timing mechanism detonated this monster, it blew a crater more than fifty feet broad in a plowed field just outside the camp perimeter. It was a close call.

I was examining the crater by flashlight when Sergeant Richmond hailed me from the far side of the field. I made my way over and found him standing as if hypnotized in front of a large grey cylinder draped by a grass-green parachute.

My somewhat frenzied call to Divisional HQ brought two polite young Englishmen in civilian clothes who quietly suggested we evacuate the western portion of the camp. The young men then set to work "debollocksing" this second land mine, using nothing much more sophisticated than a crescent wrench and a set of screwdrivers.

A tense twenty minutes later, they rather shyly reported that all was well. When we took them into the mess and plied them with Canadian whisky, they admitted that the time fuse on the bomb had had only a few minutes left to run and, moreover, that the fuse had been booby-trapped to explode if handled the wrong way.

Several days later we learned that both men were already recipients of the George Cross – the highest award for valour that can be bestowed on a British civilian. The incident was a salutary way for us to learn that there are many unsung ways to fight a war.

Leaves of absence were being granted very sparingly during this time, but I was lucky enough to wrangle one to London in company with a close buddy, Lieutenant Frank Hammond. Franky was small like me but sported a bushy RAF-type moustache and a dashing manner, both of which I greatly envied.

Franky used his swagger to get us a hotel suite normally reserved for generals, then he acquired tickets to some of the most popular London shows, including a box at the Windmill Theatre, famous for nude strippers so thickly coated with metallic bronze or silver dust that they resembled statues in a fountain.

On our third night Franky met a "smasher" in a Kensington bar and vanished from my ken. I mooched moodily about at the Overseas League Club until I met a friendly girl named Hughie – a corporal in the ATS. Alas, Hughie was happily married and made it clear from the outset that though her husband was safely distant driving a tank in Libya there would be no hanky-panky between us. During the next few days Hughie and I chastely visited bars, restaurants, and shows.

By the final day of my leave, my mood was singularly gloomy. I took the tube to Waterloo to catch the midnight train back to Possingworth to discover that the previous night's bombing had disrupted the schedule and there would be no train to my destination until sometime next day.

I was staring morosely at the departure board when a young, handsome, if rather rakish-looking RAF flying officer appeared beside me.

"Missed your train, old chap?" he asked sympathetically in a cultivated public school accent.

Mournfully I admitted that I had.

"Well, not to worry! I've a little key flat a few streets away. Come along for a drink and I'll give you a kip for the night."

The invitation seemed so marvellously fortuitous that I accepted without second thought. The flat consisted of a bed-sitting room and a tiny kitchen. We had two or three drinks of very good scotch as we chatted in desultory fashion. My host was wearing the ribbon of the Distinguished Service Order. He was a fighter pilot – one of the Battle of Britain boys – but did not seem inclined to talk about his exploits. Instead, he yawned largely and suggested we turn in.

"There's just one bed, old boy. I'll take the inside. I'll set the alarm for six. Give you lots of time to catch your train." At this he rapidly stripped to his underwear and slid between the sheets. A worm of suspicion must have stirred in my subconscious because I retained my trousers, shirt, and socks. And when I lay down it was at the very edge of the bed, leaving as much space as possible between me and my host. I dropped off to sleep almost instantly and swam back to consciousness some time later to realize that I was being groped.

In those days I was as unversed about homosexuality as I was about space travel. Consequently the shock was every bit as severe as if I had awakened to find I was in bed with a cobra. Driven by an uncontrollable reflex, I shot out of bed and across the room with such alacrity that I all but brained myself against the far wall.

The blackout curtains were tightly drawn and the only illumination was from a tiny, glowing bed light. It was just sufficient to help my shaking hands find my web belt with its holstered .38 service revolver, which I had left hanging on a chair. I fumbled out the heavy gun, cocked and pointed it, and quavered:

"D-d-d-don't you c-c-c-come a step c-c-c-closer or I'll sh-sh-shoot."

The only reply was a heavy snore. But what else was that poor Battle of Britain ace to do? He may have felt he was in greater danger at that moment than when he had had a Messerschmitt on the tail of his Spitfire.

· 11 ·

THE BALLOON GOES UP

I was away from the regiment on an Air Liason course when I got an urgent summons to report myself to the Canadian reinforcement depot at Witley. There I learned that the entire First Canadian Division had been moved, with the greatest secrecy, to Scotland.

Witley depot was itself in ferment. It was clear to all that at long last the balloon was going up.

I was given charge of a draft of reinforcements just arrived from Canada and ordered to rejoin the regiment.

I hardly recognized my old outfit, now billeted in the town of Darvel in Lowland Scotland. Many of the officers I had known were gone – culled out as medically or otherwise unfit. There were many other changes. The unit had been lavishly re-equipped with brand-new Jeeps, trucks, and armoured carriers, and issued new types of weapons, some of which I had only heard about before.

A feistiness infected everyone from the C.O. down. The ambience was so powerful I hardly cared when I was told I had been replaced as I.O. by an English captain seconded to us from the British Intelligence Corps. I was not even greatly perturbed to find Lord Hyphen back in his old ringmaster's role, wielding his whip with renewed enthusiasm. He had me into his office an hour after my arrival "home."

"So-o-o Mowat. Back again. And bloody time you stopped farting about. Report to Captain Campbell, commanding Able Company. Tell him you're to have Seven Platoon and" – he paused for a significant moment to give me his mirthless grin – "I wish you joy of it!"

Alex Campbell was an elephantine lump of a man and a gung-ho warrior. I doubt that he gave much of a damn about Making the World Safe for Democracy; he simply had a ferocious compulsion to kill Germans – as they had killed his father in the Great War and his elder and only brother in this one. However, apart from this obsession he was one of the most kindly men I have ever known. Self-taught, well read, and a bit of a poet, he must have been nearly unique in the regiment for he never cursed or swore. I liked him at first meeting.

"Seven Platoon, eh?" Alex mused after he had welcomed me into his company. "You surely must have stepped on the 2 i/c's toes good and proper. I'll give it to you straight, Farley." (He never called me by my last name, or by any of my nicknames either.) "Seven's the unit's penal colony. It's where the regiment's been dumping its hard-case lots, troublemakers, misfits, odds and bods, for years. My predecessors used to send the toughest subalterns they could find to try and tame that lot. Never worked . . . they'd just chew each other into a ruddy stalemate."

He paused and stared searchingly at me for a moment out of his pale blue eyes, and a ghost of a smile creased his massive face.

"Fancy the 2 i/c sending *you* down there . . . a lamb among the lions . . . and yet, you never know, he might get hoisted with his own petard. Anyway, here's my advice: don't try to face them down. Kind of throw yourself on their mercy, if you take my meaning." He chuckled. "They're a bunch of carnivores but they just might make a pet out of you . . . instead of eating you for lunch."

I was buckling at the knees the first time I walked out on the parade ground to take over my new command. With a shaking hand I returned the sergeant's punctilious, if clearly sardonic salute, and gave the platoon its first order.

"Seven Plato-o-o-o-n! . . . ST'NDAT . . . EASE!"

It was not badly done, except that my voice shot *up* on the emphasis, instead of down, startling everyone within hearing distance.

I trotted alongside as Sergeant Bates marched the platoon off to a corner of the field, where he told them to break ranks and gather round to hear my introductory spiel.

"Listen, fellows," I said meekly, "the fact is I don't really know too much about a platoon commander's job, but I'm sure as hell willing to learn. I hope you'll bear with me until I do . . . and give me a hand when I need it, which may be pretty damn often. Uh, well, uh, I guess that's about all I have to say."

It stunned them. They were so used to being challenged by tough new officers that at first they did not know what to make of this twenty-two-year-old-who-looked-seventeen, with his frail wisp of a moustache, his falsetto tones, and his plea for mercy. Probably I seemed contemptible but their attitude toward me in the days that followed was one of amused condescension rather than bare-fanged hostility.

I actually saw rather little of my platoon during the remainder of our stay at Darvel. While the NCOs kept the men busy on training exercises, we platoon officers spent most of our time on refresher courses in weaponry, field tactics, and, not least, combined operations. When we weren't attending lectures and courses we were wrestling with administrative problems of infinite variety and complexity. I spent two whole days arranging to draw thirty-one folding bicycles from a Glasgow ordnance depot – and two more days trying to find the tires that should have come with them.

Folding bicycles? The very idea of pedalling gaily ashore on an enemy-defended beach, or even wading ashore with these ridiculous machines hung around our necks boggled the mind!

From the emphasis on combined ops training, we knew we would be making an opposed assault landing but the burning question was where would it be. For a few days a new clothing issue that included tropical bush shirts and cotton shorts and slacks convinced everyone we were bound for Burma or the Pacific. Then we were ordered to repaint all our vehicles the colour of desert sand and replace the RAF rondels on their roofs with large white U.S. stars. *That* had to mean we were going to the Middle East. There was no end to the number and variety of rumours about our ultimate destination.

It was a time when one made bosom friends almost overnight. One of my fellow platoon commanders in Able Company was Al Park, a tall, loose-limbed youth of my own age. Park and I were billeted in the same private house and before a week was out we were as close as brothers. For a time we shared the services of Doc Macdonald, who during my absence had been serving as a batman-driver in the HQ Company but was now returned to me. He seemed glad to be back.

"Jeez, boss, I couldn't stand that goddamn Headquarters Company one more day. They got no sense of humour there!"

This was in reference to an occasion when Doc had generously donated a turkey – an almost priceless luxury – to the HQ Company officers' mess. Only the rankest of bad luck led to the discovery that the turkey was a prize peacock belonging to a wealthy local landlord, and only the rankest ingratitude on the part of the HQ Company officers had led to Doc's detention for "ten days without pay."

Being reunited with Doc was a great stroke of luck. An even greater one was to follow. One glorious day the Lord Jesus Hyphen

Christ came a cropper while riding a motorcycle too fast on a curving road. At least that was the *official* story of what happened. Some of us had reason to suspect the bike's brakes had been adroitly sabotaged. We even had a shrewd idea who the saboteur was, and there was a move to take up a collection to buy him a gold wristwatch as a token of our appreciation.

So O'Brian-Bennett was carted off to hospital, badly enough injured to be out of circulation for some time. His replacement was surely the last man an Ontario county regiment could have anticipated: Major Lord John Tweedsmuir – a bona fide Lord of the Realm – whose father, the onetime Governor General of Canada, was the famed adventure novelist John Buchan. Unlike Lord Jesus Hyphen, Lord John was an amiable, sympathetic soul whom we came to cherish and admire.

During the first week of June the unit was granted four days' leave. It was not called embarkation leave, and we were told it was nothing special – which fooled nobody. Men streamed out from Darvel to all points of the British Isles knowing full well that this was their last opportunity to drink in English pubs, make love to English girls, and "live, laugh, and be merry – for tomorrow we go battle fighting."

My friends mostly headed south to London but I had no desire to renew my acquaintance with that city. Furthermore, I thought it foolish to waste half of a too-brief leave riding around on crowded trains. It was springtime and the Others were calling me, so I settled on the Trossachs, only a couple of hours' rail distance from Darvel.

I packed my haversack, binoculars, and bird book and departed on a meandering local train that deposited me at what seemed to be an abandoned station in a valley of misted, glimmering lochs fed by shining tarns that plunged down the slopes of green-mossed mountains.

Things all seemed slightly out of focus behind a shimmer of rain as I stood on the empty platform wondering what to do next. There was not even a station master from whom to inquire about accommodations, but as I belted my trench coat and prepared to go in search of people, a rattletrap taxi came snorting toward me. The driver seemed amazed that someone had actually descended from the train. When I asked if he could find me a place to stay, he drove me up an ever-narrowing valley on a gravel road that ended in the driveway of a nineteenth-century castle towering under the shoulder of a massive sweep of barren hills.

Once the summer seat of a rich marquis, this rococo pile had been closed since the beginning of the war but was now attempting a new lease on life as a hotel. It was sadly bereft of guests. Besides me there were two New Zealand nursing sisters, a Free French naval captain, and a young American armoured corps lieutenant – surely a strangely assorted little gaggle of *wandervoegel* to have come together in this remote cul-de-sac.

The staff, which outnumbered the guests, consisted of old servitors of the marquis. The aged butler, now acting as maître d', pressed on us the finest foods the estate could provide: venison, salmon, grouse, fresh goose eggs, butter, Jersey milk, and clotted cream – and pleaded with us to avail ourselves of what remained of the marquis's wine cellar. We slept in regal, if slightly musty, splendour in vast echoing apartments and dined, the handful of us, in a glittering hall beneath chandeliers and candelabra. In the evenings we danced to 1920s music from a wind-up gramophone in the richly panelled trophy room before a mighty fireplace.

By day, in the soft veil of warm June rain or under the watery warmth of a shrouded sun, I climbed among the hills; saw herds of red deer on high, windy ridges; flushed black grouse and even a capercaillie from the redolent heather; picnicked on venison patties; and drank the bitingly cold tarn water mixed with malt whisky.

One brilliant morning I boarded an old fisherman's little boat and was taken to an island uninhabited by man, far out in the salt waters of the loch. The fisherman left me there for most of the day while he hauled his crab pots along adjacent shores. That night in my castle room I wrote this verse:

Holy Isle

There's a sweetness in the greening,
and the rich tang of decay
in the pungent sharpness of seaweed
and the salt tingle of spray.

There's the free song of the plover,
and the deep roar of the surf,
and the thunder of shaggy cattle
on the sounding board of the turf.

The high flight of the whitewings
curves to a curving sky,
and a recognition of Oneness
gleams in the dog-seal's eye.

There's a kiss from the soft sea breezes,
a caress from the sun-soaked sod,
a peace beyond all knowing . . .
for here is the living god.

A different world lay waiting.

Early in the afternoon of June 13 Able Company of the Hastings and Prince Edward Regiment embarked on His Majesty's Transport *Derbyshire* where she lay at anchor in Greenoch Roads. Two weeks later, in a blood-red dawn, *Derbyshire* steamed out to sea.

Part Three

SEEKING

· 12 ·

MOWAT'S PRIVATE ARMY

In the thunderous dawn of July 10, my platoon and I waded ashore to face our baptism of fire on the saffron sands of Sicily. The assault upon Hitler's and Mussolini's Fortress Europe had begun.

I remained in nominal command of Seven Platoon until our capture of the mountain fastness of Assoro in central Sicily. During this campaign the man who had replaced me as regimental Intelligence Officer was killed and I found myself back in my old role.

I held the job of I.O. until the end of 1943 when I was seconded ("kicked upstairs") to HQ First Canadian Infantry Brigade, of which the Hasty P was an integral part. Eventually I was promoted to the rank of captain and became Brigade I.O.

On March 9, 1945, after twenty months' service in Italy, I found myself aboard an LSI (Landing Ship Infantry) bound from Leghorn for Marseilles. The vessel's engine kept breaking down so we made a slow passage, which gave me time to bring my journal up to date.

. . . This morning we could still see the grey loom of the Ligurian alps astern. Watching them slowly diminish, many things came to mind. I thought of the burning beaches of Sicily we stormed in July of 1943, and of the high mood of exaltation that was on us during our first action. We thought we would live for ever. I did, anyway, until I saw Sergeant-Major Nuttley lying in the foaming wavelets, unable to speak because he had been shot through the throat and was already as good as dead.

. . . Our first winter in Italy, and the darkening mood as casualties increased. The bloodbaths at the Moro River and Ortona, our rifle companies reduced to platoon strength, and Alex Campbell sprawled in a shell-shredded vineyard, weltering in his own heart's gore.

. . . The spring of '44, when even the war-torn Italian fields seemed to sprout new life, while our forgotten little army grew thin and tattered and shrank into itself. Reinforcements did not come and we railed against the Judas politicians who had sent us here, then abandoned us.

. . . The May day shortly after my twenty-third birthday when we broke through the "impregnable" Hitler Line to liberate Rome. Followed all too soon by the bleak winter wallowing in the mud and blood of the Lamone and the Montone River holocausts.

. . . The Tri-wound scheme: if you'd been wounded in action three times you could apply for home leave, but probably would not get it. You could not be spared because the conscripts in Canada were rioting against being sent to Italy, where we were fighting our all-but-forgotten war.

. . . Well, arrivederci to all that. It's spring again and we are bound for the Low Countries, where schnapps flows, the sun shines, and the war correspondents smell victory in the wind.

Landing at Marseilles, we put our vehicles ashore, climbed into them, and set off to join the rest of the Canadian Army in Holland, where I was given a new job, evaluating and assessing German weaponry. Then, in mid-April I was assigned to liaison duties with the NBS (the Dutch underground) in German-occupied Amsterdam. Working and living behind the German lines provided some exciting moments until May 7 when, just five days before I turned twenty-four, the German army in Holland surrendered.

For us Canadians the shooting war was over and we were at loose ends. I did not remain so for long, as these excerpts from letters home attest.

June 2 Ouderkerk [near Amsterdam]

I've gone back to work. In effect I've made myself a new job because the army had absolutely nothing interesting to offer, but I owe the idea to Colonel Michels, chief of staff of the Dutch underground. He and I have had some interesting discussions about the future, and we agree there is no way Uncle Joe and Uncle Sam are going to stay pals. Michels believes the big boys will be toe-to-toe in short order and he's afraid all us little countries will get squeezed to death between them. I talked to a senior US officer in Antwerp not long ago who told me: "We are going to pulverize Ivan and anything and everything that gets in our way."

So what we've got now isn't peace. It's a delusion of peace – a standoff. The big boys are getting ready for the next act. Yankee and Limey boffins are already crawling like lice over the wreckage of the Jerry war machine and presumably the Russkies are just as busy.

Churchill and Truman have decided the rest of the western Allies – all the little brothers – are to be denied access to advanced German military science. I've seen the orders. We are "forthwith" to turn over all innovative German weapons and tech gear to our Limey and Yankee colleagues; and all enemy experimental facil-

ities, especially rocket or V-1 sites, are now strictly off limits to us.

On top of this, Supreme Allied HQ is now implementing something called Operation Eclipse. On the face of it this seems to be a program for collecting run-of-the-mill Jerry weapons and putting them out of reach of baddies. In fact, it is intended to ensure that all German war materials not in Russkie hands be collected and concentrated in secure dumps solely controlled by the U.S. and the Brits.

Michels believes this is all part of a concerted plan to keep the Yanks and the Brits dominant during the build-up to a showdown with the Russkies, which he believes (passionately) is what we face.

What's to be done? Michels says he won't stand by and see his nation turned into a patsy for either of the warring giants. He wants the smaller nations to band together as a sort of buffer block between the two Goliaths.

The upshot of all this is that I have revived my job as a Tech I.O. and am again busy as a little beaver collecting Jerry stuff, especially his newest and bestest. Only (and here's the twist), instead of sending it all back through "channels" to end up in an Eclipse dump, I bring it to an old Dutch army barracks at Ouderkerk recently abandoned by the Jerries and now in the hands of the Dutch Underground boyos. This is my (very) unofficial base. The NBS supplies me with accommodations and guards my collection. In exchange I collect two of every piece of Jerry weaponry and equipment I can lay hands on, and Michels gets the second one.

Officially I'm on detached duty from First Corps HQ at Hilversum, but they only see me when I need something I can't get from the NBS, such as a twelve-ton Mack breakdown truck with a crane on it, and 60-hundredweight lorries to transport my "finds." Three young lieutenants just arrived from Canada have attached themselves to me since nobody at Corps wants them, so I'm putting them to useful work.

Whether what I'm doing is good for anybody else, I know it's good for me. My eye shineth again, and I am full of piss and vinegar as I *organize and lead my crew on scrounging expeditions all over north-ern Europe.*

June 15.

In future you will kindly address me with all due deference as Officer Commanding, First Canadian War Museum Collection Team. A sonorous title, ain't it? Ought to be – I concocted it myself.

How it came about is quite a story. Last week I got back to our base with a truckload of purloined German radar equipment and found Lieut. Mike Donovan (an Irish boyo who has become my right-hand man) growling over an order instructing him and Lieuts. Jimmy Hood and Butch Schoone to report to Hilversum for duty with the Army of Occupation in Germany; and an order for me to return to the Intelligence Pool (unofficially called the cesspool) for reassignment.

Panic!

Doc, my trusty batman, suggested we all go AWOL and head for Italy, but wiser heads prevailed. I drove up to the lions' den – Army HQ – where I had some quiet conversations with and delivered some magnums of vintage champagne to sympathizers who feel, as I do, that all staff officers and staff decisions should be consigned to hell. I told my friends as much as I felt they ought to know about my activities. They were sympathetic to my problem and supportive of my proposed solution.

My plan is to convince the Powers-that-be of a need to assemble a collection of the most fearsome German weapons and ship it to Canada's national war museum as a way of honouring the memory of our dead and to help keep the reputation of the peacetime army in good repute. I did not tell anyone that our real intention was to feed the latest Jerry military technology into the hands of our own research boffins.

Well, the Big Brass bought it. Donovan, Hood, Schoone, and I have been placed under the (purely) nominal command of Col. Harrison, boss of the army Historical Section. He is a good guy and au fait with our real purpose. He has made it clear that the less he hears from us, or about us, the better. "I'm sure you know your job better than I do," he told me pleasantly, and didn't even wink.

We have taken over the house once occupied by the Jerry commandant of the Ouderkerk barracks and are making ourselves comfortable for the duration. Equipped with letters of authorization from Col. Harrison bearing the Army HQ stamp, I requisition whatever I need from both army and civilian sources. I am also authorized to travel anywhere, to enter any German installations, and to remove whatever I may in my wisdom consider essential to the War Museum Collection.

We have been busy, busy, busy. Already we have about 200 tons of loot (pardon me, exhibits), including a 30 cm (12") calibre siege gun, several panzer tanks and self-propelled guns, masses of radio equipment, and no inconsiderable collection of shells, bombs, flares, rockets and pyrotechnics with which we sometimes entertain ourselves and scare the bejesus out of our Dutch neighbours.

So here I sit, captain of my own ship, eating and drinking of the best with bon (occasionally bonne) companions. Tonight I go to a soirée at Tyce Michels's house in Amsterdam to celebrate the rebirth of the Dutch Armed Forces. I think I'll drive there in the Opal sedan that used to belong to the Jerry commandant of Amsterdam before Tyce took it away from him and gave it to me as a token of his appreciation.

But my life is not all beer and skittles.

I'm getting scared.

It is now the second month since the war ended, taking with it my excuse for carting around an empty skull. I should snap out of it, but I can't seem to snap. I can't seem to "rehabilitate."

I sit down to write, for I believe I can write. A para or two of reasonably good descriptive stuff comes out and I stare at it. But no more comes. No story comes. So what do I do? I rip the paper up and spend the rest of the afternoon or evening stripping down some piece of Germany military wizardry to see what makes it tick. It seems I'd rather dice with a deadly device that might blow up in my face than seek a sensible future. I seem to be trying to escape reality by an infatuation with mechanical toys – like a grown-up with an electric train set. There's no real satisfaction in it – just a way of passing the time away. It may be better than passing the bottle, but it leads nowhere. I even have to flog my interest to keep this war museum caper going and persuade myself I'm doing something worthwhile.

Where, for Christ's sake, is a real purpose? Could it be learning how to properly become part and parcel of the animal kingdom – trying to learn the secrets of how they manage to make things tick without blowing the world to hell and gone. The devil of it is I've pretty well lost touch with them in the past four or five years, and I don't seem to know how to get back in touch again.

I wrote a poem after the Ortona show called The Fascination of Destruction. It was about the way we've turned ourselves into slaves of the Machine. How the Machine made slaves of us and maybe planted the seeds of our own destruction in us. Yet here I am, up to my ass in killer machines, trying to preserve them for posterity! What a laugh. Trying to preserve them so they can continue to blow us off the face of the planet is more like it. I must be nuts! But I'll be goddamned if I can get hold of anything else that really seems worthwhile, so I guess I'll just have to stick with what I've got until something else turns up. If it ever does. Meanwhile, as Mehitabel the cat used to say to Archie the cockroach:

"Wotthehell . . . wotthehell . . . wotthehell . . ."

To which, in his next letter to me, Angus replied:

"Purpose, my son, is everything. Should a man find himself without a useful enterprise and a clear objective he had better contrive them pronto, even if they are only temporary stopgaps.

Inaction will cause him to sink into the slough of despond and vanish without a trace."

This was good advice and I took it.

July 15 Ouderkerk

Col. Harrison just came over from London to see us. He was stunned when he saw the size of our collection and told me we would probably only be allowed to ship about a tenth of our stuff home and would have to dump the rest. He suggested we take a holiday.

The hell we will! I decided to raise the ante. When in doubt, go on the offensive! So we all fanned out on super-swanning expeditions.

I did one into the Russian zone. Doc and I drove there in my Jeep, Lulu Belle, hot on the trail of a top-secret, heat-seeking, experimental rocket the Jerries codenamed Rhineland.

The bridge over the River Elbe we had to use was a pontoon affair built by the Yanks who manned the checkpoint on our side. They were hesitant about letting us cross but the fistful of authorizations (some of them actually authentic) I produced finally cleared the way.

We were stopped on the other side by a clutch of businesslike-looking Red Army types and escorted to a guard post, then to a regimental HQ, where a young chap who spoke a sort of English listened to my attempts to bluff our way on through and burst out laughing. When Doc whispered tensely, "What's up, boss?" I could only reply, "I don't think they buy it."

They didn't. But whatever they may have thought we were up to, they didn't hold it against us. Instead of being shot or sent to Siberia, we became the centrepieces of a party the like of which I cannot remember. The truth is I don't remember a damn thing after the first few rounds of toasts to Churchill, Stalin, mothers, wives, and girl-friends, until late next morning, when I was wakened by a kindly U.S. sergeant proffering a cup of coffee as I lay in a bunk in the Yankee guardhouse.

"*Goddamn!*" *he said respectfully when I came to.* "*Musta been quite a party you guys had with Ivan. Dead to the world when they drove you back in your Jeep. They left a message for you.*"

It said, You good fellow come again.

Well, I don't know about that. . . .

My other lads had better luck, or different luck. Butch Schoone, who is German-speaking, and Jimmy Hood tracked down a factory in an old salt mine near Würzburg where V-1 "buzz bombs" had been manufactured. They are a bit vague about what followed, but they showed up in Ouderkerk a couple of days later with two V-1s on tractor-trailers. And – hear this – the second one was a piloted prototype for a new version of the flying bomb to be used in suicide missions against Allied shipping in the Channel. So far as we know it's the only one in existence. Hood and Schoone have become quite insufferable about it and Donovan was darkly swearing to cap their exploit.

Which he did.

Mike went off on a recce and was gone three days. Somewhere near Hamburg he happened on a railroad spur filled with flatcars laden with V-2s: forty-foot rockets with one-ton warheads whose like bombarded London during the closing weeks of the war. These were virgins, closely guarded by a company of Limeys who were not letting anybody come within shouting distance of the big, black monsters.

What followed would make a pretty thick book, but I'll cut it short. With the help of the Mack breakdown, a Jerry midget submarine trailer, thirty litres of DeKuyper's gin, and his Irish gift-of-the-gab, Mike sprung a V-2 and brought it home to us.

We hauled the ugly beast into one of our big storage hangars then put all hands to work on it. When I inspected the result I found a rather peculiar-looking one-man Jerry "submarine." A wooden conning tower had been fitted amidships. The great rocket fins had been masked and a wooden propeller added. And the lads had painted the whole contraption a nice nautical shade of blue.

We are now waiting for the shit to hit the fan. Colonel Michels is very mad at me because I didn't get him a V-2 too. But it is obvious that this is the ultimate weapon of the future, and it is an offensive, not defensive weapon. In a sense the Brits and Yanks may have it right: the fewer powers to get their hands on these things, the better for the world.

I think it's time we moved out of Canadian Army territory, and I know which way to go. If you really have to hide, get as close to the hunter as you can. When I phoned Harrison's London office to tell them what was afoot, the staff captain there just gulped and said, "Tell us about it. When it's done."

I've certainly got myself a purpose now, if only to bring our collection home intact. With Harrison's help, we'll do it somehow. If we can arrange shipping. But if you've got enough nerve you can arrange just about anything in the current situation where the whole vast military organization is breaking down. B.B.B. – Bullshit Baffles Brains – is our modus operandi, and it works. Bamboozling the cement heads in authority is such a satisfaction.

There are other things that are making life worth living. Not least is the powerful affection I've developed for my lads. Not just Schoone, Hood, and Donovan, but all twenty of the best bloody rascals in the army, who now call themselves, with pride would you believe, Mowat's Private Army, and will tackle anything I think needs doing or getting. If I asked them for a German battleship, they'd try to get it. We may be the only unit left in the army that still has esprit de corps, even if (and maybe because) our "corps" is one we invented for ourselves.

Aug. 2 Oostmalle

The Cdn War Mus Col Tm has now established itself in Belgium in the quiet little village of Oostmalle, fifteen miles northwest of the port of Antwerp, from which we hope someday to sail for home.

Col. Harrison came over from London again a couple of days after we arrived here. He seemed nervous and a little grim. Did we or did we not have a V-2? All hell had broken loose at Cdn Army HQ as a result of a blast from Supreme Allied HQ. The search was on for some unidentified Canadians who, presumably as a lark, had snatched a V-2 from the Brits.

Harrison surely guessed the worse, but what a guy! When I took him to view the collection, never letting on what was what, he stared at the "one-man sub" for quite a time, then smiled a little crookedly. "Fine specimen," he says. "Looks a bit odd, but I suppose it's an experimental job."

So nobody told any lies, but we will keep a low profile for a while. Meantime, the V-sub and the rest of our 700-ton collection (yup, 700 now) skulks in the wooded grounds of a big chateau behind a high stone wall guarded by my lads, who aren't about to let any strangers in.

As for me, I'm not unhappy. I feel like the captain of an independent tramp steamer with a sterling band of deck officers and an unbeatable if disreputable crew, the lot of them loyal to a fault. Tramp steamers mooch around the world picking up cargo wherever they can find it and taking it where it needs to go. They have purpose. And so, thank God, have we. At least for now.

Aug. 20

Live, laugh and be merry now that the age of the atomic bomb has come upon us! After hearing the news of the big blast in Japan my new plan for the future is simplicity itself. I shall skedaddle to a point in the middle of the Barren Grounds somewhere west of Churchill and start digging a hole. Meanwhile, I am in Belgium with enough war material to outfit an entire Wehrmacht division, while the search for the missing V-2 goes on. Little wonder the powers want it under wraps. Clearly it was designed to deliver the atomic bomb, and the Jerries had a new generation of rockets on the drawing boards capable of delivering the bomb a distance of four thousand miles. Little wonder that Donovan's peccadillo has raised such a ruckus in high places. A friend at Army tells me our V-2 is now thought to have been stolen by French operatives disguised in Canadian uniforms. Of course it was! I could have told them that!

Sept. 23 Oostmalle

This letter may be premature but I'll take the chance. If the Gods of War are willing, and the fates smile, I ought to be on the high seas headed for Canada with my collection in a few weeks' time. And after five months of floundering around inside myself, the currents may have at last carried me close enough to shore so I can touch bottom and still keep my head above water. How's that for a contribution to the Department of Mixed-Up Metaphors?

As an indication of my current state of being I've finished the draft of a five-thousand-word story I've been thinking about for a couple of years and simply couldn't write. It isn't much good yet, but that's not the point. The point being that at long last I seem able to focus on something beside fun and games. So this is "ver goot!" as our Belgian town major likes to say.

Oct. 25 Antwerp

After more ball-ups and shenanigans than you could believe, the First Can War Mus Col Tm is about to haul anchor and go to sea. I am writing this aboard the SS Blommersdiik, moored to a dock in Antwerp with orders to sail on October 28. With luck I should see Montreal two weeks from then.

Our departure from Oostmalle for the twenty-mile trip to the docks must have been one of the strangest convoys of all time.

It was led by Lulu Belle flying an enormous Canadian flag just in case the Belgians might think the Germans were returning. Sure looked that way! Swastikas were very much in evidence on most of the vehicles, which included seven Jerry tanks, one of them a Mark V Panther, and six self-propelled guns on tank chassis.

Lulu was followed by a fifteen-ton Jerry half-track mounting a four-barrelled Flakvierling (anti-aircraft gun) and towing a heavy artillery piece, which in turn was towing a huge trailer carrying our real one-man U-boat. The rest of the mile-long column included a rich mix of heavily loaded Canadian Army transport trucks and Germany Army vehicles, most of them towing trailers, and all of them groaning under guns, torpedoes, searchlights, buzz bombs, our V-2 sub, a Kreigsmarine torpedo boat, a couple of Luftwaffe fighters, an ME-103 jet engine, and miscellaneous items "too numerous to mention" as the auction posters say.

This, my friends, was Mowat's Private Army putting on a final show.

It almost seemed as if the Jerry vehicles knew it was the last-time trip for them. Jimmy Hood and Mike Donovan rode herd in an amphibious Wehrmacht Volkswagen, along with a couple of ex-Wehrmacht mechanics we sprung from a POW camp to keep the machinery running. The column clanked and clattered along at about five miles an hour, tying up all traffic in the northern part of Antwerp for three hours. The folk we encountered en route, whether military or civilian, must have had trouble believing their eyes. The Limey military police patrolling the city went quite insane. Nobody had told them what was coming and they were fairly gibbering with outrage.

The column wobbled on until it reached dockside. Then Mike gave the signal to halt and from every vehicle came a last salute of horns hooting, gas warning sirens wailing, guys drumming on empty jerry cans, signal flares and crackers being fired, and a ragged cheer from all hands.

It took two days to load and stow everything aboard ship. And no, I did not take the horse the pretty American nurse in Brussels wanted me to carry back to Montana for her. But I am taking Cpl. Roy Weatherdon and his dog, Spike, a hairy mongrel from Germany who has attached himself to us for rations. Spike plans to become an illegal immigrant to Canada.

We hope all goes well. Crossing the North Atlantic at the beginning of winter with a V-2 and a midget sub lashed on deck ought to be interesting. And, ah yes . . . the Limey embarkation officer wouldn't permit our collection of experimental artillery shells, rockets, naval mines, and aircraft bombs to be stowed in the holds. Claimed it might be dangerous. So the big wooden crates containing them are lashed onto the afterdeck all around the little cabin I now call home. Nobody aboard but me and Roy knows that some of the crates contain Jerry shells filled with the latest Nazi horrors in the way of nerve gas. I do hope they aren't going to leak. . . .

· 13 ·

HOMEWARD BOUND

SS *Blommersdiik*, the vessel chartered to carry me and my collection to Canada, was one of the so-called Liberty ships mass produced in the United States for wartime service. "Built by the mile, and cut off by the yard," the Liberties were four hundred feet long, twin-decked, and propelled by a triple expansion steam engine. They were slowpokes, barely capable of maintaining a speed of ten knots.

In addition to the 930 tons of "freight" put aboard by my crowd, *Blommersdiik* loaded a number of locomotives belonging to the U.S. Army. By then she was, as the bosun, a black-bearded seaman from Bristol put it, well down to her marks.

"Maybe it'll keep the bitch from rolling her guts out when we strikes dirty weather. Or rolling right over, like a fucking filly. No, sir, don't you laugh. Her kind's got a wicked way of disappearing without no survivors to tell the tale. The Disappearing Liberties, some calls them."

If such gloomy talk was intended to put a pongo into a cold sweat, it had little effect on me. My life during the past several years had not been devoid of risks and since I was at last going home I would probably have been willing to set sail in a sieve.

The voyage turned out to be one of relative luxury. Although *Blommersdiik* had no passenger accommodations as such, she did have a spacious cabin on her afterdeck built to house the crew of a three-inch gun, her only defence against German submarines and planes. The gun and its crew were long gone and the cabin provided more than enough room for me and Roy and Spike. Although the rest of my private army would be returning to Canada packed into troop ships, we three would sail home in what amounted to our own private yacht, low-powered and ill-omened as she might be.

Roy and I were in goodly company. The crew consisted mostly of men who had survived a long and bitter war at sea. They treated us (and Spike) as their own kind. The ship's master, sixty-seven-year-old Hans van Zwol, was an omnivorous reader who spoke three languages fluently. He had spent fifty years at sea and could have stepped out of a novel by Joseph Conrad. He was one of the larger-than-life ship's masters who sailed and steamed across the oceans in the early twentieth century, men of whom it was said salt water instead of blood ran in their veins, and they came ashore only to die.

I was wakened at dawn on November 1 by the hoarse blast of a tug's whistle and the scurrying of feet outside my porthole as *Blommersdiik's* lines were let go. As the engine throbbed and the great propeller shaft revolved I climbed to the bridge to stare at the frieze of bombed and sunken ships and skeletal remains of smashed loading cranes bordering our passage through the Schelde estuary.

A pilot came aboard to guide us through the narrow and tortuous channel leading to the North Sea, thirty miles to the westward.

As we came abeam one of the many buoys marking a sunken ship, a lone RAF Spitfire came skimming low up the channel toward us. As it roared close overhead, the pilot dipped a wing in salute. Punctiliously, Captain van Zwol responded with a pull on the whistle lanyard, then turned to me.

"So now we will leave the wartime behind. Come to my cabin and we will drink a little schnapps to celebrate the end of all that bloody nonsense."

As I turned to follow him off the bridge I saw a black-backed gull hovering over our stern and trained my binoculars on it. The captain paused.

"You like to watch the birds?" he asked with a smile. "Since first I go to sea I watch them very much. In the tropics, in the Antarctic ice. Masters of air and water! Typhoons cannot stop them. They go their ways and no man can say what course they steer or why, or how they hold to it."

Listening to him was like hearing a familiar voice calling me awake after a long and deeply troubled sleep.

As night fell we entered the English Channel. The lights came on in Calais to the south and Dover to the north, and the many ships crowding the passage were bedecked as if for Christmas with red, green, and amber lights. Before turning in we celebrated the end of the obliterating darkness that had shrouded Europe for almost five years. And the chief engineer, an English veteran of two wars, proposed a toast.

"Lights is back on at last! Any son of a bitch tries to turn them off ever again may he rot in bloody hell!"

Spike wasted no time turning himself into a seadog. This nondescript street mongrel so ingratiated himself to officers and crew alike that he soon had free run of the ship. He was careful not to alienate his new companions. Right from the first he used a scupper hole to discharge his cargo into the sea. He was equally careful where he pissed, and it was some time before I discovered his private urinal.

I kept a sharp eye on the crates of shells and bombs lashed to the deck outside our cabin. If any of those containing liquid chemicals should spring a leak, I wanted to be the first to know about it.

On the morning of our third day at sea, I was horrified (and terrified) to find a rivulet of orange-hued liquid apparently seeping out from under a crate of shells. Frantic, I dashed into our cabin to alert Roy and to fetch a knife with which to cut the cargo lashings so we could heave the suspect crate overboard. Ever interested in what was afoot, Spike followed us out on deck and while we fumbled with the ropes took the opportunity to empty his bladder on an adjacent case. His relief could hardly have been a match for what Roy and I felt as we realized who was responsible for the liquid that had sent me into a panic.

By noon on the second of November we were abeam of Eastbourne. The chart indicated that Dieppe lay hidden in the haze forty miles to the southward. I had spent many quite pleasant months in Eastbourne when my regiment, together with the rest of the First Canadian Division, had been standing guard to repel the threatened German invasion of Britain.

Dieppe, on the other hand, was a name to instil horror in those who knew the grim story of the attempt made in August 1942, mostly by the Second Canadian Division, to force a landing on the Channel coast of Hitler's Fortress Europe. The ensuing disaster had cost Second Division more than a thousand men killed, wounded, or taken prisoner.

But as *Blommersdiik* plodded past Dieppe the air about us came alive with birds. I climbed up to the open upper bridge called "monkey island" to welcome this manifestation of life in a place that had seen the slaughter of so many Canadians, and of so very many mariners who, over the hellish years, had sailed this ditch of death under the assaults of U-boats, E-boats, mines, coastal guns, fighters, and bombers.

Now common, herring, and lesser black-backed gulls were eddying above freighters, tankers, coasters, lighters, and ferries peacefully making their way up, down, and across the Channel. The gulls were happily gleaning garbage, something that had been in short supply during the war but was now becoming plentiful again.

Keeping their distance from the ships, occasional fairy-winged kittiwakes, skimming shearwaters, and a few mighty gannets ignored the passing parade and went about the business of fishing for a living.

For years I had not had the opportunity, nor the heart, to watch so many and such varied kinds of birds, and my exhilaration was such that when I returned to the wheelhouse I brashly addressed the captain as "Skipper."

This might have been regarded as presumptuous aboard any other ship I had ever sailed in. Van Zwol just smiled. Later I would learn that the term skipper, so lightly used by yachtsmen, is a Dutch title of great antiquity reserved by Hollanders for respected masters of real working or fighting vessels. As it turned out, every man aboard our ship called van Zwol Skipper. *Blommersdiik's* bosun gave me one reason.

"I shipped with him in 1943 on a tanker bound from Aruba to New York carrying ten thousand tons of bunker-C. We was in company with another tanker full of petrol, with an old Yankee four-stacker destroyer for escort.

"Just west of Bermuda the other tanker stopped a torpedo and went up like a bloody torch. The destroyer signalled us to run for it while she went haring off to look for the sub; but instead of running, van Zwol rang for full ahead and steamed straight for the burning ship to see could he save any of her people afore they was fried or boiled.

"The destroyer seen what we was about and flashed a lamp signal: YOU ARE STEAMING INTO DANGER REVERSE YOUR COURSE.

"Skipper van Zwol never paid no heed. He held on until we see one of the other fellow's boats drifting out of the smoke. They was ten men aboard of her – six still alive – though by the time we snatched them out of the boat flames was licking all around it. Seemed like the whole bleeding ocean was aflame!

"The skipper hauled her off then and we run south at full revolutions until we dropped that devil's tower of smoke below the horizon. When night fell we come about and headed north again.

"After that we never saw the destroyer nor nobody else either until we raised Cape Hatteras and a guard boat led us into Norfolk, where those poor burned bastards was put into hospital.

"That's the sort of man van Zwol is. *You* can call him captain if you wants, but he's our *Skipper*. The finest kind."

For his part, van Zwol was punctilious about using my military title. This resulted in the peculiar paradox that I, the rankest amateur sailor, was the only person aboard to be called captain, though most of the crew used the title with more than a hint of mockery. The first mate, a lanky Friesian with a perverse sense of humour, always made a point of greeting my appearance on the bridge with an impeccable salute and a resounding "Goot day, mein Kapitan!"

Because the bridge was the heart of the ship as well as the best vantage point, I spent much of my time in the wheelhouse, in the adjourning chartroom, out on the port or starboard wing, or up on monkey island. Sometimes I would have the entire structure to myself except for the mate on watch and a helmsman gently handling the big mahogany wheel.

Those were times for dreaming dreams, especially one I had nurtured all through the war of someday sailing *Scotch Bonnet* among palm-fringed Pacific atolls inhabited by languorous, brown-skinned *wahines*. When I rather diffidently confessed to the skipper that I harboured such a fantasy, he was sympathetic. He told me that in his own youth he had sailed as mate on an island schooner trading for copra in Samoa.

Encouraged, I described *Scotch Bonnet* in detail and told him about a promise my father had made that, after the war, *Scotch Bonnet* would be mine to sail wherever I wished.

Van Zwol responded favourably to *Scotch Bonnet*.

"I know her kind. Go anywhere in any kind of weather. Slow, yes, but very strong and" – he paused to give me a sideways look – "forgiving of a green hand at her helm."

"I'm green, all right," I confessed. "I've only sailed in fresh water and never far from shore but I believe I could learn to handle a boat in salt water. The thing is, I don't really know how to navigate. Once out of sight of land, I'd be like a dog chasing its tail."

He laughed. "Ah then, Captain, perhaps I can show you what little I know of navigation."

So during the homeward voyage I had two things to help me distance myself from my bleak and bloody memories. I was re-entering a world shared with the Others, and I was being inducted into the mysteries of how seafaring men found their way across trackless waters.

On November 4 the skipper rolled out a chart of the entire North Atlantic. Touching the points of his dividers to Bishop's Rock in the Scilly Isles, which were then abeam of us, he explained:

"Here we will take our departure from European waters. North latitude 49 degrees and 50 minutes, west longitude 6 degrees and 27 minutes. We will steer now a great circle course for Belle Isle, 1,823 nautical miles – that is 2,096 landsmen's miles – to the westward. If the weather behaves and the Chief keeps his machinery working, we should raise Newfoundland in seven days."

He paused to ask: "What do you know of the sextant?"

When I admitted I had never even handled this fabled instrument, he set out to teach me how to use it. Every day thereafter, weather permitting, I reported to him or to the first mate on a wing of the bridge to be shown how to "shoot the sun" or, at night, to take a sight on Polaris, the North Star.

I was not an apt pupil. When plotted on the chart, my results often put our vessel so much as a hundred miles off course. Once I put her a hundred and sixty miles inland – on the Greenland icecap.

The skipper did not give up, although the mate did. After the Greenland fiasco, the mate told me with painful honesty:

"Better you stay on land, Kapitan. I wash my hands."

There would be times later in life when I wished I had listened to him, but by then I was following a different drummer.

The first day out of sight of land broke warm and clear with a brisk nor'wester making *Blommersdiik* kick up her heels. The bosun set his deckhands to checking the hatches and making everything secure in case "it come on to blow up dirty." As I watched the oilskin-clad seamen putting extra lashings on the miniature submarine and the massive bulk of the V-2, I wondered what the bosun might be thinking about them. Later on I asked him.

"Tell you the truth, Cap'n, if 'twas me, I'd-a cut them fuckers adrift and pitched them overboard. Subs and rockets! Maybe not the worst things we ever invented but, by Jesus, pretty fucking near!"

I spent most of that day watching birds: fulmars, Manx shearwaters, kittiwakes, jaegers, and even a great skua. To see them was exciting, but I was surprised at how few of each kind there were. The vast sweep of sky and water surrounding us seemed relatively empty. I mentioned this to van Zwol at supper. He was a while replying.

"I wondered if you'd notice the lack of birds. There's only a drift of them now. Handful of chaff in a gale, you might say. Six years ago starting an Atlantic crossing you'd have seen rafts of them on the water or flying around the ship thick as snow.

"Not long after the war started their numbers began falling. I didn't give it much heed until one day in 1942 we were steaming over the Grand Banks after a U-boat pack had caught a convoy there.

"The water looked as smooth as cream though there was a good sea running. But it wasn't cream – it was bunker oil. All the way to the horizon. And it was lumpy with dead and dying birds coated with oil.

"There was every kind, though most seemed to be eiders and murres. The few still alive were starving or choking to death.

"I knew, of course – what seaman didn't? – that tankers laden to their marks with crude and refined oil were going down every day all over the world. Men were being lost by the hundreds, but until then I'd never given a thought to what else was being lost. Millions of birds. Tens of millions maybe, killed by oil.

"That wasn't the whole of it. Pretty well everything in and under the sea was getting hammered. Whales and porpoises used to be common on the Western Ocean but by '43 they were mostly gone. Whales give off an echo the asdic and sonar operators on naval vessels can't tell from a submarine, so every time they got a contact, over would go the depth charges. Planes spotting the wakes of big whales at the surface would drop bombs on them in case they might be subs. I've even seen a cruiser with eight-inch guns *shelling* what any fool could tell was a whale. And coastal command planes regularly used them for target practice.

"Dead whales bloated up like blimps and stinking rotten were a common sight. Live whales were something we hardly ever saw, and don't see now.

"Even that wasn't the worst of it. When something big blew up, like a ship laden with munitions, the shock would kill everything in the water for miles around and, I don't doubt, for miles below.

After a depth-charge attack by the navy on a sub, I've seen the surface white as winter fields with dead fish floating belly-up.

"Men, too, of course. One fine summer day in the North Sea we picked thirty-seven men from a big freighter out of the water. They were all wearing life jackets and from our deck looked unharmed. All were dead save two. Those two lasted a few hours in our sick bay. Our third mate – he was our 'doctor' – called me down to see them.

"When their ship was torpedoed the escorts had dropped depth charges all around her hoping to get the sub. Those poor chaps hadn't had time to launch their boats so they'd just jumped overboard and were all in the water when the charges started going off. . . .

"The bottom half of their bodies looked like they had been run over by a steam roller."

During the war at sea more than twenty-two hundred merchant ships were sunk in the North Atlantic alone. Many thousands of human beings lost their lives. The destruction wrought upon oceanic life defies comprehension. No merely human nightmare could begin to encompass its catastrophic magnitude.

November 8 found us being bludgeoned by a full nor'west gale some 390 nautical miles from Kap Farvel, the southernmost tip of Greenland, and 432 miles east of the Strait of Belle Isle. By noon *Blommersdiik* was making very heavy weather of it. Towering grey-beards were bursting clean over her bluff bows and water was running so deep and fierce over her open decks that Roy, Spike, and I were effectively marooned in our cabin all that day and most of the succeeding night.

I was convinced the V-2 and the submarine would be swept overboard, but no, when dawn came again they were still with us though they had a different look. White-streaked with salt, they seemed to have been shriven of their aura of death and destruction. Perhaps they were undergoing a sea-change, even as I was.

The following day we entered the Labrador Current and the temperature dropped ten degrees, bringing a change in our avian escort. Jaegers vanished to be replaced by a scattering of sooty shearwaters, a greater black-backed gull, common murres, and dovekies – sparrow-sized seabirds that flew like bullets so close to the surface they seemed to be running on the water as storm petrels do.

As I tried to plot our position on the chart by dead reckoning (it was too foggy to get a sight with the sextant), the skipper came and looked over my shoulder.

"If you are not sure where we are, Captain, you must ask the birds. The black-back out there, and the murres will tell you we are closing with the land. Yes, just as they told old-time sailors who came to fish on this side hundreds of years ago with no sextants, charts, and, more often than not, not even compasses. Often all they had was the lead to find the depth; a chip of wood, a piece of knotted string, and a sand glass to estimate their speed; and the fetch of the seas so they could steer a course. But always they had the birds. *Those old fellows kept their eyes peeled.* Ja, they had to, or never would they have got home again."

I took special mental note of the emphasis on keeping one's eyes peeled if one was to find the way home. For that, of course, is what I was trying to do.

· 14 ·

WINTER OF MY DISCONTENT

I came on deck on November 10 to find *Blommersdiik* almost abeam of Belle Isle, that massive granite plug in the strait of the same name. I was almost home. The black hills of Labrador rose distantly off the starboard bow, and off to port snaggle-toothed Cape Bauld, the northeastern tip of Newfoundland, thrust out of the sea.

As the bleak indentations of Château, Red, and Forteau bays along the Labrador coast slowly fell astern, the Strait of Belle Isle funnelled us into the mediterranean sea that fifteenth-century whalers knew as *la Grande Baie* and we now call the Gulf of St. Lawrence. We continued unhurriedly into the estuary of the great river which would take us another thousand miles westward, deep into the vitals of the continent. *Blommersdiik* was bringing me home, not with the ferocious abruptness and soul-shattering immediacy of a jet airplane but gently, gently, giving me time to become aware of just how far I had gone astray. .

Our voyage ended on November 15, when a tug nudged *Blommersdiik* into a berth in Montreal harbour. Canada was indifferent to our arrival. Although I had not expected a hero's welcome I was a bit chagrined that *nobody* was on the dock to welcome us. However, when the ship's agent boarded, he gave me a wire from my father.

DESOLATED UNABLE MEET YOU STOP APPARENTLY NEITHER DEFENCE HEADQUARTERS NOR GOD KNOWS WHEN YOUR SHIP DUE STOP WE AWAIT YOUR CALL.

There was also a telegram from Major General Howard Graham, deputy chief of the General Staff at National Defence Headquarters in Ottawa. Graham had been the lieutenant colonel in command of my regiment when I first joined it in England in 1942, and he had been one of my father's friends in Trenton between the wars. His telegram, however, did not sound a welcoming note. Marked URGENT, it ordered me in no uncertain terms to notify the general's office IMMEDIATELY REPEAT IMMEDIATELY UPON ARRIVAL CANADA.

With some trepidation I called National Defence HQ from a dockside phone and after considerable telephonic shuffling was connected to the general.

"Damn it, Mowat! Where in hell have you *been*? Never mind. Catch the night train to Ottawa. Be in my office by 0900 tomorrow. See to it!" with which he hung up.

So it was that I spent my first night ashore in Canada sleepless in a crowded train. Next morning the general kept me standing at attention in front of his desk until the red-tabbed staff officer who had escorted me in to the holy of holies departed, at which point Graham favoured me with a sardonic grin and a greeting.

"You may sit down now, Mowat. Colonel Harrison sent us a radiogram saying you were on your way but you've been so long overdue it was thought you and your load of nuts and bolts must have sunk. Not such a *bad* thing if you had. *Some*body has incurred a shipping bill with the Holland-American Line for 76,000 dollars without, so far as we can see, any authorization. Treasury Board is having conniptions."

He paused to let all this sink in.

"To be frank, you and your freak show are likely to be as popular around here as the proverbial skunk at a garden party. War's over, you know. Government doesn't want to spend another dollar on it. Even the war museum wallahs want no part of your caper – afraid they might have to pay the shipping bill. Nobody will touch your stuff except some bods from Defence Research who say they'll take your rockets. But what's to be done with all the rest . . . and you . . . I really don't know."

He shook his head.

"Suppose you tell me just what you've been up too, eh?"

I told him as much as I thought he ought to know. When I finished he seemed bemused.

"Where's that shiny-faced kid who came to us in England? Turned pirate, by the sound of it. Treasury will have you hanged if ever they twig to what you've been up to. Well, me lad, you're still a Hasty P so I suppose we'll have to try and save your bacon."

By the time I got back to *Blommersdiik*, her hatches were off and unlading was well under way. The V-2 had disappeared. When I asked Roy about it, he shrugged.

"Dunno, sir. Couple of scruffy-looking civvies showed up with a lot of official papers. The stevedores got the V-2 off the boat quick as a wink and loaded onto a flat car heading for points east – or maybe west. Anyhow, she's gone."

If the boffins had been quick on the uptake, *we* were not far behind. By that evening Roy and Spike were on a train bound for Roy's home in Nova Scotia, and I had boarded one for Toronto. But not before an affecting parting from *Blommersdiik*.

Captain van Zwol took me into his cabin, poured me a glass of schnapps, and gave me a gift – a lovingly polished sextant in a teakwood case. He had received it, he told me, from the captain of a Norwegian freighter he had rescued after the freighter hit a mine in the North Sea.

"All that poor man saved when they jumped into the boats was his dog and his sextant. He gave me the sextant because he said we had saved a life – not his – his dog's! The sextant must have meant a lot to him, but his dog meant more. I have had his sextant ever since, but I have my own and I have no need of two. Take it, for when you go to sea in your father's *redningskoite*. Now, *skol* . . . until we meet again!"

My parents were waiting at Toronto's Union Station. They drove me to Richmond Hill, where a now-aged little dog, Elmer, welcomed me as if I had never been away. Home was much as it had been, and my father and mother seemed largely unchanged though slightly time-worn. I, on the other hand, felt massively out of place – a stranger in what once had been, if briefly, my own space. Years later Angus would recall my return.

"Elmer recognized you because, I suppose, you still smelled the same. Some things never change. Helen and I *pretended* we knew you but the truth was we hardly knew you at all. You were familiar in the sort of way a picture of an ancestor may be. The face is recognizable but you know nothing of who or what lurks within."

I kept no written record of my three weeks' disembarkation leave, which may have been as well because my emotions were in such turmoil that any attempt to have rendered them into words must have resulted in incoherent ramblings. My memories of that time too are vague – perhaps mercifully so.

My father's were much more focused.

"The return of the prodigal was not an unmitigated success. Your mother was in myopic ecstasy, of course, and I was happy but confused. You – well, to coin a phrase, my son, you were not yourself.

"I thought I knew what you might be going through. When I returned to Trenton in 1919 with my smashed arm still in a sling and your mother engaged to someone else, I may have had as jaundiced a view of the civilian world as yours. As Elmer might have put it, everything *smelled* wrong or, as old Sam Johnson would have insisted, everything *stank*. I felt like some sort of Rip Van Winkle who, expecting to awaken safe in his own bed after a particularly bad nightmare, wakened instead in an unfamiliar place surrounded by people who weren't as he remembered them.

"When *you* came back to *us* we put on our bravest faces. We smiled a lot though in our heart of hearts we were crying for you because, as we knew (or at least *I* knew), you weren't really with us. You were facing the chill reality that nothing was as it had been when you went away. Or ever could be again."

What I recall of those bleak days in Richmond Hill was a dreadful sensation of disassociation from everything I had known and been before the war. It wasn't the obvious differences that got to me. I could deal with the fact that most of the girls I had known were now married, about to be married, or had moved away. And that many of the boys were missing, maimed, or dead, while those who remained were preoccupied with trying to establish themselves as cogs in a structure that was essentially alien to me.

This I could handle. What I could not deal with was the realization that all the ephemeral things those of my generation had shared – dreams, ideas, objectives – had lost their power to bind me into the cohesive entity that is one's tribe.

People attempted to reassure me but, though they were well intentioned, they could not reach me where it mattered. We no longer shared common ground. I found myself becoming ever more desolately aware that soldiers who had survived the war were now something of an embarrassment to their country.

There was not even much comfort to be had from the company of others of the afflicted – other ex-servicemen and women. Although all of us were recently arrived from Mars, we were now strangers even to one another on an alien planet.

By the end of the first week of my leave, I felt that if I *had* ever belonged here, I no longer did. The temptation mounted to do what many "returned men" did do – hit the bottle. Fortunately for me an alternative distraction or, as it may be, a source of solace, existed.

A large framed photograph of *Scotch Bonnet* under full sail dominated the mantelpiece in my parents' living room. One evening I drew my father's attention to it.

"You know, Dad, I spent a lot of time over there dreaming about *Scotch Bonnet*, and thinking over what you wrote to me – that when I got back home I could take her on a voyage any place I chose and let the sea wash the war out of my system. I think I'd better take you up on that."

His measured reply knocked the wind clean out of my sails.

"Sorry to hear it, Farley. That would be a bad mistake. It would be running away, you see. What you and all the others like you need to do if you are going to survive and heal is, in a manner of speaking, go straight back into the trenches – the *civilian* trenches – and apply your energies to getting a firm grip on peacetime life. Make a place for yourself. You're twenty-four now and you've wasted enough time, or had it wasted for you. But if you work hard enough and get yourself well enough dug in, the day will come when you can safely take time off to sail away into the blue. And when that time comes, *Scotch Bonnet* will be yours."

My sense of having been let down was monumental. I did not argue with him or even discuss what he had said for fear of what *I* might say. I did what I had done in earlier years when overwhelmed by a perceived injustice: I retreated to my bedroom.

During my absence overseas Helen had preserved this room and its contents as they had been at the time I went away. She had been a meticulously successful curator. Redolent of the presence of my younger self, my bedroom showed no evidence of the passage of time, no patina of dust and cobwebs. Had it done so its effect upon me might have been less powerful. As things were, when I entered that room I fell into time's vortex.

Large photographs of the friends of my youth watched from the walls. Mutt's bright eyes, which had followed me through my boyhood, were fixed quizzically upon me. Wol, the great horned owl who had been a boon companion during my Saskatoon years, huffed at me from a balm of Gilead tree that seemed so real I could smell the fragrance of its spring catkins and taste their bitter-sweet resin.

Basil, a wood gopher I had found as a naked suckling, nursed on a bottle, and often taken to school concealed in my jacket, was there too. After his death I had tenderly skinned and stuffed him and now he stood erect and expectant on my bureau.

Marie, my first true love, smiled at me from the wall above my bed. On the opposite wall, Bruce Billings and Murray Robb warmed their hands at a campfire we had built in a prairie bluff on a January day with a blizzard raging around us.

And there were all my notebooks containing untidy scrawls and scraps of two-fingered typing; my journals; and jumbled fragments of poems, stories, and attempts at scientific reports. There were also many published books about the Others, and a good few dealing with wilderness adventures. The effect of all this was to engender a desperate hunger to live again the life that had been mine only a few short years earlier.

I spent most of the next several days in my room with the door shut against the world beyond, while downstairs my mother cooked up a storm, and both she and my father racked their brains to think of things that might distract me.

Their distress was so evident and so painful that it became more than I could endure. Several days before my leave was officially over, I told them I had been recalled and, promising I would spend Christmas with them, fled from Richmond Hill.

But where was I to go?

Because I could think of nothing better I retreated to Ottawa and re-entered the dark tunnel from which I had just begun to emerge. Abhorrent as it was, the army seemed to be the only human aggregation to which I could belong. Somebody in authority decided it would be worthwhile keeping me on staff while the foofaraw swirling around our shipload of German *matériel* was resolved, so I found myself assigned to an obscure branch of military intelligence at National Defence Headquarters; and there I went into a kind of emotional hibernation.

I did visit Richmond Hill for a few days at Christmas but despite the best efforts of my parents and friendly neighbours, I felt like a disembodied spirit casting shadows over everything in its vicinity.

Slinking back to Ottawa after Christmas, I discovered that Mike Donovan had been returned to Canada so I arranged to have him assigned as my assistant. He and I spent the first four months of 1946 swinging the lead, as the saying went, while the higher-ups continued their fruitless efforts to unravel the tangled skein of our shenanigans in post-war Europe. But Treasury Board's attempts to find who was responsible for the First Canadian War Museum Collection Team's aberrations went nowhere for we had a powerful friend in General Graham.

"It wasn't so difficult," he would later tell me. "The powers-that-be simply couldn't bring themselves to believe a mere captain could have made such a shambles of authority."

Graham was not so successful in ensuring that our collection served any useful purpose. Blindly confident that peace had come to stay, Canada's politicians were not about to spend money preparing for a possible future conflict, or even to memorialize the horrors of the one just passed. In consequence, our collection was dismembered and dispersed almost at random. The tanks and most of the German vehicles were sent to Camp Borden to be stored in an empty aircraft hangar, where they remained until it burned down, reducing most of them to scrap. A few (including a Panther tank) have since been restored and have found a home at the new Canadian War Museum in Ottawa, along with our V-1 buzz-bombs and midget submarine. However, most of our larger trophies, including almost all the artillery pieces, were sold for scrap. The majority of the smaller items met similar fates. Several tons of experimental munitions, including finned projectiles and rocket-assisted bombs, were shipped to Halifax to be dumped at sea.

The V-2's fate was a notable exception. Civilian scientists of Defence Research who had met the *Blommersdiik* on her arrival in Montreal spirited the rocket off to their base at Val Cartier, where they hurriedly disassembled it before the Americans could learn of its existence and demand it be turned over to them. The guts of our V-2, together with some other rocket engines we had collected, became the basis for Canada's own modest rocketry program, which produced two high-altitude rockets: the Black Brant and the Velvet Glove. More than fifty of these, carrying scientific instruments instead of explosives, were fired into space from a range at Churchill – less than a mile from the Black Shack in which I had camped with Uncle Frank during the summer of 1936.

In 1951 the outer shell of the V-2 was reassembled and exhibited at the Canadian National Exhibition in Toronto for one season only. Then overshadowed by the lethal products of the rocket rivalry between the United States and the USSR, it too was dispatched to limbo.

Mike and I spent our working days in the windowless cellar of a temporary wartime building with other redundant servicemen engaged in more or less meaningless activities – "fucking the dog" it was called.

Ottawa offered me little stimulation or distraction. Uniforms still swamped the city, clogging every movie theatre, café, and bar with red-tabbed staff officers, most of whom had never heard a shot fired in anger and with whom I had nothing in common.

I found the civilian scene equally depressing. Unless one was a politician, a senior civil servant, or a ranking military officer, the social ambience was as frigid as the winter weather. At this juncture, even Mike Donovan abandoned my sinking ship by getting married and losing himself in domestic bliss.

Most of my spare time was spent in my rented room, where I read a great deal, drank more than was good for me, tried (and failed) to write fiction, mourned my disbanded private army, and darkly contemplated a clouded future.

Yet a light was glowing in those depths. The voyage back to Canada had reignited my feelings for and affinity with the Others. Lying awake in the long winter nights I found myself in their company again, trekking across the rolling prairies; plunging through swamps and marshes; paddling across northern lakes and down fast-flowing rivers. Their company in these happily remembered places brought me the only comfort I knew during those bleak months in Ottawa.

At the end of January Helen took to her bed with some ill-defined affliction, perhaps arising from her concern about my state of being. At Angus's urging, I returned home to try to cheer her up, but was about as successful as a morgue attendant might have been. Finally my father lost patience with me.

"You've simply got to snap out of it, Farley. Heaven knows I sympathize with how you feel, but you can't *stay* in that slough of despond much longer. If you do you'll suffocate, and probably take your mother with you."

He demanded that I begin making my re-entry into the civilian world.

"A lot of young fellows like you are taking advantage of the veterans' education program. Getting paid to go back to school or on to university. You should damn well do the same! Not that it'll solve *all* your problems but it'll give you breathing space. Time to read, to think, to talk to your peers. Time to settle yourself down. Then you could carry on to become a professional zoologist up to your elbows in bird shit for the rest of your life if that pleased you. Or become a librarian, like me. Or a garbage collector, so long as you became an effective one. Effective! That's the key.

"You have to find your balance, before you stumble over the edge. You simply *must* regain a sense of purpose even if you have to manufacture one – as I expect you did with your war museum caper."

He was right, of course. *Scotch Bonnet*, and writing, might have provided what I needed; but neither was within present reach. I was sitting in my old bedroom one night surrounded by the memorabilia of better times when my exasperated inner self rose up and took command.

Everything changed with the force and immediacy of a right hook to the jaw. In what amounted to a revelation I suddenly knew what I was going to do with myself.

Returning to Ottawa next day I was weighed down by a duffle bag and a haversack filled with books and papers including, especially, my prairie journals – and an empty loose-leaf binder freshly labelled:

The Birds of Saskatchewan
by
Farley M. Mowat

· 15 ·

YOU CAN'T GO HOME

This time when I returned to Ottawa there was a spring in my step – from which Mike Donovan drew the wrong conclusion:

"Hey skipper! Finally get your ashes hauled?"

When I told him the real reason for the glint in my eye, he at first refused to believe I had been galvanized by a prairie bird epiphany.

"You're going to write a book about *birds*? *Real* birds, with *feathers*? You have to be effing kidding!"

Having made my decision, I wanted nothing but to get on with it so I asked for immediate "demobilization." I was refused because it appeared that the army did not want to let go of me until all the questions about the First Cdn War Mus Col Tm had been resolved. However, though I would have to wait, I could still make plans.

These centred on a new expedition to Saskatchewan (the first of many, so I hoped) to be undertaken as early as possible in the coming spring. And preferably with a like-minded companion.

I began looking for one such among those who had gone west with me in 1939. First I tracked down Harris Hord and found he had taken an early discharge from the RCAF and was working as an entomologist for the United Fruit Company in Honduras. I cabled him an invitation to join me, but he refused to take the bait.

"I've done enough risky stuff in the air force over the past couple of years to last me all the way to the old folks home," he wrote in reply. "I wouldn't go west with you again for my weight in rubies. *You* go and make a fool of yourself any way you want. I've better things to do."

Next I contacted Andy Lawrie who, after four years in the navy, was now studying zoology at the University of Toronto. Rather wistfully he told me he would love to spend the summer with me out west but could not afford to do so.

Frank Banfield was actually *in* Ottawa, where he had exchanged an army staff job for a sinecure in the federal bureaucracy. But Frank made it clear he was of no mind to risk a secure future by renewing a relationship with me.

I could find no trace of Bruce Billings, and when I finally located Murray Robb it was to find he had already exchanged *his* uniform for a business suit. He would, he said, be happy to put me up for a night or two if I happened to be in his neck of the woods.

It was apparent that the rest of the world had already taken Angus's advice so I resigned myself to making the voyage single-handed. I would have to provide my own vehicle, and the choice inevitably fell upon the ugly but indomitable Jeep.

Jeeps had served me faithfully and well throughout the war years. In Sicily one had probably saved my life by outrunning a German armoured car. I had had three Jeeps – all named Lulu Belle. Two had died in battle and the third had been reluctantly left behind when I returned home from Europe. I wanted Lulu Belle back, not just because of her toughness and versatility but to help insulate me from a civilian milieu I had no desire to re-enter.

Getting a Jeep proved a bit of a problem. The Quarter Master General's office told me I could probably acquire a used one from army surplus in six months' time. I could not wait that long so I wrote to the manufacturer, the Willys Car Company in the United States, and learned that its first civilian Jeeps would go on sale in Canada in April. They would be civilian in name only. Although painted glossy green instead of dull khaki, they would be military Jeeps right off the line. I immediately ordered one.

Preparations for the journey posed no great problem. Angus had taken good care of my camping and travel gear during my absence and all I needed to do was dust it off; but the requirements of science were more demanding. Although any enthusiasm I might once have had for killing other creatures had evaporated in the carnage of war, I knew I would still have to do some "collecting." Every species listed in my *Birds of Saskatchewan* would have to be substantiated by at least one "study skin" preserved in the catacombs of a reputable scientific establishment. So, like it or not I had to provide myself with an armoury of guns and ammunition, and with all the rest of the mortuary paraphernalia of a scientific investigator.

On April 11 I took possession of a spanking-new Jeep with LULU BELLE MK IV emblazoned in big black letters across the bottom of her fold-down windshield. The owner of the Willys dealership apologized because she was not equipped even with a canvas top. "Be pretty unprotected – windy and wet," he said dubiously.

"Gloriously unprotected!" I replied and drove happily away.

On April 20, 1946, I officially ceased to be a serving member of His Majesty's Armed Forces, and on May 2 began my odyssey.

Lulu Belle got under way at 0700 hours on a drizzly spring morning with me hunkered down behind the wheel in the old army uniform I was sentimentally wearing. We ambled westward at a sedate 40 mph, the recommended speed for cars of that era while they were being "broken in."

All went well until we reached the U.S. border at Sarnia, where two armed U.S. immigration officers warily approached. Their caution may have been due to never before having encountered a soldier wearing half-Wellington boots, khaki serge trousers, a scruffy British battledress tunic with the 8th Army crusader shoulder patches, a bright red silk scarf around his neck, and a peaked, go-to-hell military cap perched jauntily on the back of his head. The unusual colour of my Jeep may also have contributed to their unease.

"Just who might you be, mister?" one of them demanded. "Whatta ya got in that there Jeep?" the other asked.

They were joined by three customs officers, and the quintet surrounded me, watching suspiciously as, under their orders, I unloaded every blessed thing from the Jeep and spread it out for their inspection. They paid particular attention to my shotgun, to a pump-action .22 rifle, and to a smooth-bore .32 with a sawed-off barrel. My explanation that this arsenal was for collecting scientific specimens in Saskatchewan did not go over well, and I might have been in real trouble had not their supervisor, who had briefly been a liaison officer to the British 8th Army in Italy and liked "the Limeys," appeared. He was also an amateur ornithologist. The gods were smiling.

The supervisor waved me on with a friendly warning.

"If I was you, Cap, I'd get me some different duds going through the States. Some bonehead could take you for a Commie Russkie, and that would not be good."

Because I was too tired to bother pitching my tent, I spent that night in a tourist cabin in northern Michigan. The café associated with the place served me a gargantuan supper built around an enormous steak surrounded by fat sausages, giant baked potatoes, and mountains of beets, carrots, and something called succotash, the whole crowned by three fried eggs.

"Do people actually eat all this?" I asked the waitress in awe.

"Mostly they don't; but we gotta give big servings or we lose the custom."

This was something to think about at a time when meats and many other foods were still rationed in Canada, and when most of the world's peoples were going hungry. However, such profligacy did have a positive side, as I learned when the owner of the place suggested I park Lulu Belle in his pig run overnight in order to ensure her contents would be protected from thieves.

"I feed them hogs the swill from the caff," he told me. "Makes 'em big as bars and just as yeasty. They'll put the run on anything comes near their trough."

He may have meant "feisty," but he was right on the other two counts. It took me twenty minutes the next morning to get aboard Lulu Belle without losing a leg.

Trundling sedately westward, it took two more days to reach and cross the border into Saskatchewan, my Promised Land, where I was greeted by a blinding snowstorm. When I pulled up to the only garage in the village of Yellow Grass, a gaunt young man swung open a pair of double doors and beckoned me to drive on in.

"Geez, chum, you look half froze! Come and have coffee with Milt and me – he's my brother – and maybe a squirt of something into it."

The brothers Fred and Milt were veterans of the Saskatchewan Light Infantry, an outfit my regiment had served with at Monte Cassino and elsewhere in Italy. Upon being demobbed six months earlier, they had pooled their small resources and bought the White Rose station in their home town. The easy acceptance by fellow servicemen was good for my weary heart and was to be found frequently across the continent in those first post-war years.

"This place looked like a good way to start on civvy street. But last month a big shot from Regina – owns about ten thousand acres of wheat land – started building a new garage here big enough to handle a squadron of Sherman tanks. Going to give it to one of his sons, a fellow our age who run some of his pappy's farms while we was overseas. So it's going to be hard times. Don't know can we make it, but we'll sure give them stay-at-home bastards a run for their money!"

The storm got worse so we stabled Lulu in the garage for the night then drove to a wind-whipped little house where Fred's pregnant English war bride gave us supper. Later we shared memories of London during the Blitz and polished off a bottle of my rum. Before we went to bed Fred said thoughtfully:

"Funny thing. Milt and me hung in over there four goddamn years fighting for our homes and country, so they told us, and all the time itching to get back to Yellow Grass. When we *did* get back it looked about the same. Only turned out it weren't ours any more. Maybe we shoulda stayed right here to do our fighting?"

During the night the storm blew itself out and the rising sun melted the snow. As I drove on north, the long-anticipated world of meadowlarks on fence posts, tumbleweed in ditches, gophers whistling from far-spreading fields, and greenhead mallards quacking from roadside pools, revealed itself. I was back among the Others, but I was not as pleased as I should have been. I was experiencing something akin to the uncertainty of a lover hastening to a long-deferred rendezvous, apprehensive about what might await him though in a tearing hurry to find out.

I drove until late that night then caught a couple of hours' sleep while wrapped in a blanket beside Lulu Belle and at dawn was on my way again. It was May 7. On the twelfth, I would turn twenty-five and I was determined to celebrate my birthday in that fondly remembered poplar bluff near Dundurn.

It was late afternoon before I reached the deeply rutted trail leading to my old camping place. By then the darkling sky was leaden and smeared with snow flurries. The wind blew from winter, not from spring.

And nothing was as it had once been.

Although the long drought had eased, dreadful scars remained. Surrounded by dead and broken cattails flailing in the raw wind, Big Slough was nearly dry. The prairie beyond looked as lifeless as stubble on a dead man's cheek. No throbbing flocks of waterfowl greeted me, and there were few smaller birds. Even the ubiquitous gophers seemed to have all but vanished. I wrote in my journal:

> *The desolation is appalling. Even the cottonwoods in the bluff seem to be half-dead, their buds all shrivelled up. What the hell has happened to this place? Nothing green. Apparently very little alive. A couple of sad-looking magpies and sober crows and one lean and mangy coyote were all I could find. Drove Lulu all the way to the flats by the river where there used to be a stand of enormous balm o' Gilead trees. All dead now. The willows by the wisp of a river that still remains are all dead too. It couldn't look much worse if the whole place had been blitzed by the Luftwaffe.*

If nature failed to welcome me back, humanity proved no kinder. As night fell I drove to the officers' mess of the army camp on the nearby military reserve. Anticipating a comradely reception, I was instead met with suspicion from a handful of career officers who had fought *their* war in Canada.

As I was driving away, a private guarding the gate kindly told me about an empty shack a mile down the road.

"Got a stove and all. Radio says there's a storm coming and you could freeze your balls off if you pitch a tent tonight."

The twelve-by-twelve-foot shack proved to be so superior to a tent that I set up housekeeping in it in preparation for re-familiarizing myself with the surrounding country.

Next day I visited a coulee that had hosted a small stream when I had known it before. The stream had been reduced to a string of puddles, except where a dirt causeway spanned it. Here I was delighted to find a good-sized pond jam-packed with migrant ducks. At Lulu's approach they took to flight with a roar of wings.

It was the kind of welcome I had been looking for. When I jumped out of Lulu to investigate this watery oasis, I found that someone had stoppered the large culvert that pierced the causeway. I assumed the "someone" was a farmer providing a waterhole for his cattle until I heard a crack as loud as a rifle shot and beheld a large beaver thrusting its flat head above water, perhaps to see what had made the ducks take flight.

I could scarcely believe my eyes. A beaver had no business out here on the bald-headed prairie! How could such a woodland crea-ture possibly exist in this parched and almost treeless land?

It was a mystery to me until I met Bill Evans. A dirt farmer with a quarter section of land up against the reserve, Bill had been able to survive the Depression and the drought only because the military paid him to maintain its fences. Bill explained about the beavers.

"Them furry buggers! I don't know where they came from or when. They was here when I homesteaded just after the big War. Them times there was lots of poplar bluffs and willow swales for beavers to feed on and enough rain to keep things nice and green.

"When the drought come on in the thirties, it was tough going for all hands. The sloughs and cricks dried up so then the beavers took to building dams, something they'd never done here before. Never had to, I reckon.

"Well that was fine 'cause the cattle could drink at their ponds and kids could swim there. Beavers and us got along good until your war started. Pretty soon the army started all sorts of training around here. Trucks and troops and tanks running all over the country, shooting off big guns, tearing up the prairie, knocking down the bluffs.

"There used to be lots of deer around but they soon got shot off by trigger-happy soldiers. So did the jackrabbits, coyotes, and lots of other critters, including most of the beavers. By the end of the war there was just a couple beaver families left.

"One day the camp got a new gung-ho colonel. He called me in and told me to open up the culvert under the road that the beavers had plugged, in case there might be a flash flood that would wash the road away. I knew there wasn't a snowball's chance in hell of that happening and I said so. 'You just do as you're damn well told!' he told me, and so I done it.

"My boys and me spent the best part of a week with shovels and picks and crowbars unplugging that culvert. The pond drained out and the beavers was left high and dry. Not for long though. A week later the dam was back – not so good as before but good enough to hold the runoff from the only rain we had that summer.

"I'da let the new dam be but the colonel came down on me again so we tore it out. The beavers built it back. And that's how it went till the hard frosts set in and we all had to quit for the winter.

"Come spring when we busted the dam again the beavers started fighting back.

"The reserve's always been well fenced with barbed wire strung on posts of lodgepole pine brought all the way from British Columbia. All first-class stuff but now we couldn't keep fences up at all. The beavers were going for the posts tooth and nail. And not because they had any use for them. There was no bark on them for them to eat, and they couldn't drag them off to use for dams 'cause they was all bound together by three strands of barbed wire nailed into them.

"Why did the beavers do it then? I believe they chewed down every damn fence post they could find to get even with us. If 'twas revenge they was after it didn't work against me and the boys 'cause we was *paid* for putting the fences back up. And the posts the beavers cut down made the best winter firewood we ever had.

"So we had our own little war right here on the reserve. Fast as we'd put up new posts, the beavers would chop them down. It never come to blows, though it come close. One time my son Jack and me was driving our old truck across the prairie when we come upon a pack of *four* big beavers chewing down fence posts. We stopped the truck and got out and run toward them, yelling at them to get the hell out of it. They must have been really pissed off because what *they* did was come running right for us!

"We never had no guns with us so we hopped back into the truck pretty smart. I suppose we could have run them over with it but that didn't seem just right so we drove on home and left them to it.

"Last summer the camp began closing down 'cause your war was over. The colonel went away and the major left in charge didn't give a hoot about the beaver dam so we stopped pulling it apart. Right away the beavers stopped chewing down the fence posts.

"Who won? Well, I guess you could say it was even-steven 'cause them and us is both still here."

One day Lulu and I went to Proctor's Lake, which lay in an incipient desert of parched grass and blowing sand twelve miles to the south of my shanty. It turned out to be another vast alkaline slough with a wide foreshore of sun-baked mud between it and a surrounding fringe of bulrushes and reeds, but it had water in it, making it one of the few functioning waterholes for miles around.

Spring migration was then at its peak so not only the surface of the lake but also the air above it was a-shimmer with winged life. Countless ducks, geese, swans, pelicans, and gulls swam upon it, dived into it, or wheeled over it. Its mud flats swarmed with curlews, sandpipers, plovers, willets, stately avocets, and such rarities as black-necked stilts. The surrounding marshy enclaves provided a garish display of red-winged and yellow-headed blackbirds and sooty black terns, while beneath and around them grebes, moorhens, and rails slipped through the reeds like living shadows.

Proctor's Lake brought solace to my soul, though it also gave me some dicey moments. I was driving Lulu over its salt flats one day when all four wheels broke through a crust of sun-baked mud covering a slime pit of unknown depth. For a dreadful moment, I thought I had lost Lulu and might be in danger of losing myself as well, but she sank only to her floorboards, upon which she floated like a tin duck.

Putting her into reverse in four-wheel drive, I cautiously let out the clutch. Almost imperceptibly she began inching backwards, all wheels spinning, shooting geysers of mud into the air while she *swam* – literally swam – until she was able to get a grip on hard bottom and haul us out of the quagmire.

Living a surrogate life among the Others again was wonderful, but I was still lonely. One day I drove to Saskatoon seeking human company.

Although the town looked much as I remembered, it was now inhabited by strangers. I could find few friends of my youth and most of these no longer belonged to my tribe. Nor I to theirs. But I did succeed in locating Bruce Billings.

Bruce had only recently returned from *his* war. The single parent of a three-year-old son, he was now living with his parents on their rundown fox farm a few miles outside Saskatoon. He was as happy to see me as I to see him. During the next few days he told me a little about his life since we had parted in 1937.

The war had seemed to offer him a heaven-sent opportunity to escape the twin tyrannies of Depression and drought. He tried to enlist, but first the army then the air force and finally the navy rejected him because of a tractor accident suffered in his childhood that had left him with a functional but crooked leg.

Undaunted, he stole rides on freight trains east to Halifax, determined to take part in the war. The way that finally opened for him was the merchant marine and at nineteen Bruce became a stoker aboard a freighter carrying munitions from Canada to Britain.

During Bruce's second voyage, his vessel was torpedoed in mid-Atlantic. When she blew up and sank, he was one of only seven survivors, spending six winter days and nights in an open lifeboat before being rescued.

This horrendous experience did not deter him, or at least not enough to send him back to the prairies. He continued going to sea in merchant vessels until "fall of '43 I was outbound on a hard-luck Limey tanker that bust her shaft and had to be towed back to Nova Scotia. We was tied up there a couple of months and I got foolish and fell in love with a Sydney girl and married her.

"Turned out she was a goddamned tart. *Some*body had knocked her up. *Could*'a been me I suppose, but I'da been at the end of a long, long line.

"Anyway, I went to sea again and never got back to Canada till well after the kid was born. The bitch had took off for Toronto with some air force guy, dumping the kid on her old ma. But the old woman kicked the bucket so I took a job ashore and took the kid on myself, along with another bimbo I got mixed up with.

"Things went right to hell after that, and I hit the booze so hard I pretty near died. When the lights came back on, I pulled myself together for the kid's sake and figured we'd be better off back home.

"But where the hell had it got to? The old farmhouse was still here all right and my ma and pa were still alive, though both well over the hill, but now I was a foreigner hereabouts. Nobody knew me or wanted to, except a few rubby-dubs in the beer parlours. Government turned me down for a rehab grant to fix up the farm 'cause I wasn't a fly boy, a blue-jacket or, saving your worship's grace, a khaki cowboy.

"Now I'm stuck with raising goddamn foxes. I think like one and I stink like one. Not doing too good a job of it, either. First week I was back I put my mitt into the meat grinder and the foxes got to eat two of my fingers. At that I suppose I'm doing better than when I was shovelling coal on a frigging freighter with a sub ready to shove a tin fish up my ass."

Bruce accompanied me back to the shanty at Dundurn, both of us hoping to recapture something of our shared enthusiasms of earlier times.

It did not work. We stayed up all one night drinking rum washed down with beer. Next day we were fit for nothing. The day after that I drove him back to Saskatoon burdened with the knowledge that even we were now strangers to one another.

Before I dropped Bruce off at his parents' farm, he told me he had been offered a job with a construction company bulldozing a new road into the still-virginal wilderness of lakes, rivers, and forests that blanketed the top half of the province.

"Road's heading for Lac la Ronge. I'd sure like to get up there. My old man was up there with the Hudson's Bay Company when he first came out from Scotland. Still calls it God's Country. Nobody screws you around up there, he says. Sure wish I could go . . . but I got the kid, and the old folks can't do much for themselves. What the hell! I got the foxes. See you around, chum."

In the event I did not see him again for nearly half a century. In 1993, while doing publicity for a new book, I visited Saskatoon and on a whim asked my publisher's representative if she could find out anything about the fate of the Billings family. I was due to fly to Vancouver that evening, but two hours before departure she located a Bruce Billings in the city's largest hospital.

I found him in a bed in a public ward, heavily sedated. On a table beside him was a worn copy of my book *The Dog Who Wouldn't Be*, my account of my boyhood and his in Saskatoon during the Thirties.

Bruce did not awaken during my visit.

A few weeks later I learned that he was dead.

· 16 ·

GOD'S COUNTRY

By the last week of May most of the bird migrants had moved on. It was time for me to do so too. Although Dundurn was still a good place to meet the Others, it had failed to show me the way forward I was blindly seeking. So I decided to try somewhere new.

Bruce's remarks about Lac la Ronge had struck a chord. It lay only a hundred miles north of Emma Lake, where Frank, Harris, Murray, and I had pitched camp during our 1939 expedition and it was deep in the boreal forest in a world dimpled and riven by a multitude of lakes and rivers. Without roads, railroads, airports, or formal settlements it was a world in which the Others still lived much as they had always done, sharing lands and waters with scattered bands of Aboriginal people. And it was a place where human beings of my culture and stripe were blessedly still rare.

On June 1 I drove to Prince Albert where I learned that a road to Lac la Ronge was indeed under construction and might be navigable by Jeep, part way at least.

The proper way to have gone into the boreal forest would have been by canoe, but I had no canoe and I did have Lulu Belle so I loaded her up with beer and rum (Prince Albert was then the most northerly place in Saskatchewan with a liquor store) and set off.

We ran out of gravelled road just beyond Emma Lake but Lulu churned on through mud and muskeg in four-wheel drive and bull-low gear until we reached the north end of Montreal Lake (still thirty miles from la Ronge), where we found further progress blocked by a bulldozer mired to its cab in muskeg.

Off to my left was what looked like a trail of sorts so I steered Lulu into it. Deep ruts led to a small clearing on the shore of Montreal Lake dominated by a two-storey log building surrounded by a few shanties and wall tents. Slant-eyed sled dogs and dark-skinned children watched nervously as my mud-spattered green machine jounced toward them.

The owner of this establishment was Gus Stennarson, a heavy-set Swede in his early sixties who, in the 1920s, had been a deckhand in one of the last windjammers carrying wool and wheat from Australia to Europe. For reasons he never revealed to me, Gus abandoned the sea to make his way as deeply as he could get into the heart of North America.

Montreal Lake captured him and he prospered there, first as a lumberjack then as a trapper, and eventually as a trader with the local Indians and Metis.

Almost as broad as he was tall and built (as he himself put it) "like a brick shithouse," he was completely bald though possessed of a luxuriant black beard. His protruding eyes were the faded blue of willow china. A man of boundless generosity, he possessed an unplumbed affection for all mankind and a special one for womankind. He welcomed me to his log mansion in the wilds, poured us huge mugs of coffee laced with rum, and listened intently to my explanation of how I happened to be there and where I hoped to go.

"Ya. Vell, you go on and dat little green auto going to get sunkered in mudhole and maybe you with it. You vant birds? T'ick as horse-flies right here! You like rum? Never go dry yet at Stennarson's! You like eat? I am best goddamn cook in Canada! Better you stay here. Von't cost you nuttin."

Gus's arguments were so compelling that I stayed for the next six weeks, while slowly, slowly, beginning to find my way again.

Montreal Lake belongs to the arctic watershed, emptying into the Churchill River and thence into Hudson Bay. The surrounding woods were full of northern birds. White-throated sparrows, hermit thrushes, Canada jays, and half a dozen kinds of warblers reacted to my invasion with varying degrees of indignation. One day as I bent down to get under a deadfall I came face to face with a loon. Here, in the midst of a Jack pine forest and at least five miles from the nearest body of water, I found myself eyeball to eyeball with the great northern diver himself. Such a meeting was not possible, but there could be no mistaking that needle-sharp javelin bill.

Not only was this a loon, it was one with an attitude. It went for me, silently but with such alarming vigour that I stumbled back-wards and fell. The big bird was on me in an instant, thrusting its spear at the sole of my rubber boot. When I scrambled to my feet and fled, the bird gave chase!

This was not as simple as it sounds. A loon's legs are set so far aft that it cannot stand upright but must push itself forward on its breast. This one did so with amazing speed. Spotting a high stump close ahead, I scrambled up on it to become perhaps the first human in history to be treed by a loon.

It was a stalemate until I peeled off my light jacket, flung it over the loon's head, and jumped down upon the bird. Using my coat as a kind of straitjacket, I carried the loon back to Stennarson's. As I passed close to a group of young natives, the loon thrust its head and neck out and gave a sibilant warning hiss that would have done justice to an anaconda. Later, under the watchful but safely distant eyes of these youngsters and a number of adults, I fitted a numbered aluminum bird band to the captive's leg and turned it loose into the lake. It dived and vanished, leaving me to wonder how it had managed to stray so far out of its element, and the audience to wonder if I was possessed.

The effect on the local people of my dalliance with the loon was magnified when I set up shop in a large wall tent beside Gus's house and began preparing specimens. This involved wielding my formidable array of shiny surgical bone saws and shears, gleaming scalpels, intricately curved knives, serrated scissors, and an array of forceps, one of which was as long as my forearm.

The watchers, who at one time or another included most of the women and young folk (and even a few enigmatic men) from Montreal Lake's native settlements, drew their own conclusions about me. According to Gus, some thought I was merely deranged, but some concluded I was a shaman, and a number of people came seeking treatment for everything from an accidental gunshot wound to a bad bellyache.

If their ailments were of a kind that could not be fixed with iodine, adhesive tape, and a bit of gauze, Gus would get me off the hook.

"I tell them you no-good doctor on the run. Got fired because too many your patients die down south. Better they go see Indian Department doctor at Waskesiu. Ya. Even though is a long way and a lot of *his* patients dies too!"

I worked in the tent but lived in the house, sharing its amenities with Gus and with Walt, a young man whom Gus had hired (paying the salary out of his own pocket) to teach some twenty native children. The schoolroom pre-empted most of the lower floor of Gus's house. We slept on the second floor, furnished with many beds because my host extended his hospitality to all comers: trappers, mounted policemen, fur buyers, game wardens, an occasional itinerant preacher, and road-construction workers together with their attendant bootleggers and hookers.

Stennarson's Post, as it was unofficially called, was in fact a kind of northern roadhouse where one and all felt free to enjoy the moment. I sometimes returned from a day in the field to find a dozen visitors brewing up a party that might last well into the following day. On such occasions the upstairs dormitory could become a scene of such fervid activity that I would seek refuge in my work tent.

Late one night, after sustained revelry in the house had driven me to the tent, I wakened abruptly, to find Gus shaking me violently while bellowing in my ear:

"Get *oop*! Get *oop*! Angie's baby coming, but don't vant to come! So you must come!"

It took a while to clarify the issue, the essence of which was that Angela Moiestie, who lived in "the village" a few miles distant, was in labour and having difficulties. A doctor was clearly required and, since no other was to be found nearer than fifty miles, Angela's clan had decided I would have to do.

I was horrified. And thoroughly frightened. When I protested that I knew absolutely nothing about midwifery, Gus nodded.

"Ya. You know nuttin. *I* know you know nuttin. But dese people, *dey* don't know you know nuttin. So you got to come. You don't come dey blame me and den both you and me get run out of here!"

When I continued to resist he bundled up some of my skinning tools, together with a bottle of iodine, a roll of cotton batting, and a quart of rubbing alcohol. With these under one arm he shoved me out of the tent and into Lulu Belle. Finding me still reluctant, he banged me on the head with his hand and shouted, "I knock your balls off you don't go *right now*!"

The "village" consisted of nine log cabins scattered along a stretch of beach. Low-roofed, one-room affairs with a minimum of windows, the cabins were occupied by Cree-speaking people who bore surnames such as Moiestie, Nelson, Moberly, Angus, and McPherson – the names of traders and trappers of not so long ago. Regardless of their mixed blood they counted themselves Cree, were still tribal, and were still fully committed to the ancient precept of one for all and all for one.

There was little they would not do for one of their own or for friends, from whom they of course expected reciprocity. Gus was their friend so *his* friends were *their* friends and my involvement in Angela's predicament was inevitable and inescapable.

Surrounded by a group of men carrying kerosene lanterns, I was escorted (pushed would be more like it) from Lulu Belle to a cabin whose door gaped wide open, revealing Angela lying in bed with half a dozen women crowding around her. The room, about the size of a one-car garage, was lit by candles and by the glare from the open door of a sheet-iron stove on top of which pots and kettles were shooting jets of steam into the superheated and smoky air. Angela's husband, Ben Moiestie, thrust me forward, while Gus followed close behind.

Although I had never been present at any birth but my own, I had no difficulty recognizing a breech presentment. Except for Angela's gentle moaning, the room had gone expectantly silent. The next move was clearly mine.

I knew that in such a situation the baby should be turned around. But how to do it! Though I had only the haziest notion, I was sure about one thing: I was not going to engage in a hands-on attempt, for of what use would a doctor (even a pseudo doctor) have been when he had fainted dead away?

Gus tapped me on the shoulder. He was holding out the twenty-four-inch forceps I normally used for stuffing the long necks of geese. Inspiration (or maybe instinct) made me seize them: jam a huge wad of cotton around their tip, soak it in rubbing alcohol, then gingerly, *very* gingerly. . . . I have a confused remembrance of being rather sharply brushed aside by one of the women and soon thereafter of hearing the mewling of a newborn.

A few days later Ben Moiestie, accompanied by Frank Nelson, who was the de facto leader of the band, showed up at Gus's with a hindquarter of deer and a beautiful caribou skin parka decorated with beads and quill work. The meat was for Gus and Walt and me. The parka was for me alone, and Frank presented it to me, beaming.

"Baby do pretty good now. Make pretty good hunter, maybe. Angie and Ben, they call him Yeep."

Lulu Belle MK IV must have been proud!

When the visitors had gone Gus slapped me on the back.

"Any time you go down to the village now, you go right in. Stay long as you vant. Do vat you please. Ya. You got kin down dere now."

My acceptance into the community was confirmed a week later by an invitation to attend a basket social at Frank Nelson's home.

Frank's cabin was one of the largest but by the time I arrived it was clogged with relatives and friends from all around Montreal Lake. Every woman present had brought a hand-woven basket containing a lunch for two of meat, bannock, and sweets. Frank raffled the baskets off to the men, and the top bidder for each got not only the basket but its creator too. The couple then discreetly disappeared into the surrounding woods, not to be seen again until after dark when a dance started up.

Forty or fifty people had packed themselves into Frank's cabin, where the cook stove smoked and roared under kettles full of tea. Almost everyone was puffing on a pipe or a hand-rolled cigarette. The door was propped wide open and the single window had been temporarily removed from its frame without much effect on the fug within.

Somehow in the crush and confusion I found myself in possession of a basket belonging to a grinning, glitter-eyed woman whose age was impossible to guess for she was as wrinkled as a corrugated tin roof. When I declined to follow her outside to share the lunch, she took furious umbrage.

I was rescued by Frank who pulled me aside and shouted in my ear: "Don't you worry none! Sylvee won't *eat* you! She only eat *bear!*"

Life at Stennarson's Post was generally more routine. I usually spent from early morning to mid-afternoon "in the field" tramping through woods and muskegs or paddling a borrowed canoe on the big lake or its tributary streams. Returning to Gus's house, I would eat the dinner he had cooked then, with a reluctance that increased day by day, turn to skinning, stuffing, and otherwise preserving the creatures I had butchered in the name of science.

Reluctance became revulsion. I killed fewer and fewer of the Others and spent more of my time just hanging out with them.

This led to some remarkable experiences. It enabled me to closely observe a majestic pair of sandhill cranes incubating two enormous, tan-coloured eggs in a nest the size of a truck tire that floated on a muskeg pond. Although initially (and wisely) the big birds were wary, they eventually came to accept my presence with almost as much equanimity as if I had been one of their own kind, and to herald my visits to the nest site with the same sonorous cries they gave one another.

And there was the morning I came upon four downy little chicks bouncing around on the forest floor below a dishevelled nest originally built by robins but later usurped by a pair of the only species of sandpiper to nest in trees. As soon as the chicks had hatched, they had fearlessly jumped to the ground twenty feet below, and now were being shepherded by their parents toward a swamp a quarter mile distant. When I came on the scene there was panic at first, but soon the adult birds seem to have concluded I meant no harm and allowed me to provide rearguard protection for the little procession all the way to the safety of the swamp.

As my servitude to the skinning table diminished, I also spent more time in the company of my own kind. Though not effusive, Angela and Ben and their extended family (which seemed to have no limits) always welcomed me, and I grew used to being peed upon by little Jeep, who was never subjected to the indignity of diapers. I also made friends with two "white men" (as they called themselves) married to native women.

Johnny and Carl were about my own age. Both were farmers' sons from southern Saskatchewan who, even before the war, had abandoned the dust bowl and the Depression to go north in search of a better life. They had found it in the bush at Montreal Lake.

"People here kind of adopted us," Carl told me. "*We* never had much and *they* never had much, so we got along. They showed us what we needed to know about their country and the both of us found good women. We was doing good, when along come the goddamn war. I don't know why we done it – crazy as coots – but we both enlisted. Was in Italy with the SLI [Saskatchewan Light Infantry]. Well, hell, *you* know what that was like! We was lucky. Johnny got deafened by a Teller mine – still can't hear much – and I got an extra hole in my ass, but we come home in pretty good shape."

These two shared a trapline northeast of Montreal Lake, from which they made enough money to meet their families' modest cash requirements. Living on and from the land, as their relatives by marriage had done since time immemorial, they seemed an admirably contented pair, but they had their problems. One day Carl casually inquired if I would care to accompany them on a canoe trip to their trapping cabin some fifty or sixty miles into the country. He did not offer any explanation of why he and Johnny wanted to go there in summer, until after I had agreed to go along. Then, rather diffi-dently, he explained:

"Too damn many trappers around here now so things has got tight. Johnny and me is thinking we might go on north – *away* north, up around Cree Lake. Thing is we'd have to fly our outfit in and that'd cost an arm and a leg. So last winter we took a few more beaver than was on our licences so we could pay to charter a plane this fall.

"Trouble is, game wardens around here are on the warpath. We had to leave our extra beaver skins cached near our winter camp. So now we got to go back and get them, but it'd look queer if we went into the country this time of year . . . unless we was your guides helping you get those specimens of yours. See what I mean?"

I saw, and sympathized.

Their canoe was a seventeen-foot Peterborough with plenty of room for the three of us, our gear, and two weeks' grub. We had no kicker (outboard motor), which was as well for it would have been more of an encumbrance than a help on the many shallow streams and muskegs that had to be crossed between stretches of navigable water.

The country we would be travelling through was mostly low-lying and often marshy, ideal habitat for aquatic birds, especially ducks and geese. These were abundant, having probably been driven to this watery world in the forests by the prolonged drought on the prairies to the south.

July 6th

We've been two days en route, really pushing it through a maze of little lakes, ponds, marshes, and muskegs with one really rough five-mile portage to Meeamoot Lake over burned ridges covered with deadfalls from a forest fire. How in hell the boys can find their way through this maze is beyond me! There are no markers, not even a blaze on a tree to point the way. They must be doing it by smell!

They prefer to travel after dusk and before dawn, claiming this makes us less conspicuous. To whom? The only sign of anything human I've seen so far is a grave on the shore of the Bow River. Just a pole stuck into the sand with a smoke-blackened tea pail wired to it. No name. I wouldn't have guessed it was a grave until Johnny pointed to some human rib and arm bones dug up by some animal.

The first day out we slept under the canoe to baffle the flies, then pushed on at 0300, travelling across marshy ponds shrouded in morning mist, waking thousands of waterfowl, startling some deer, and getting "shot at" by beavers slapping their tails on the water to tell us to get to hell out. The morning sun began to warm us up as we came into Trout Lake, a long and sinuous body of water with lots of bays, pine-grown shores, crystal waters, and yellow-sand beaches. Made our way along its south shore through fleets of young ducks and anxious mothers. At noon stopped for a swim then ponassed a ten-pound trout we had picked up on our troll line. With tea and a hot bannock, it was a meal to remember, particularly because we had an uninvited guest — a very large black bear we assumed was male because there was no accompanying cub. He was following his nose, the end of which was wrinkling like a dog's as he sniffed fish sizzling on the coals of our fire.

We were ready to beat a quick retreat to the canoe and leave him to it, but he stopped about twenty feet away and sat back on his haunches like a trained bear in a circus, and just stared at us — hopefully, I think.

I went for my shotgun but Carl said, "Maybe he just wants a handout. Anyhow that little popgun of yours would just make him mad." With which Carl tossed him the head and guts of the trout. Mr. Bear shuffled forward, ate it, then looked like he'd like some more, so

Johnny tossed him a slab of smoking hot meat. You could tell it burned his mouth, but he glutched it down anyway.

After that he sniffed hopefully a couple of times but when no more grub was forthcoming, turned around and ambled off. He didn't say thank-ee. But if he had I wouldn't have been much more surprised than I already was.

Carl and Johnny felt we were now safely distant from Montreal Lake so we continued at a gentler pace until we reached the winter cabin. Long and low, it occupied a pine-grown point jutting into a lake that did not seem to have a name. They referred to it simply as "home lake," presumably because the cabin on its shore *was* their home for almost half of every year. Its walls were made of eight-inch logs tightly fitted and well-chinked to keep two spacious, low-ceilinged rooms cozy and comfortable in fifty-below-zero weather. It was surprisingly well furnished and equipped, considering that its contents had either been made on the spot, mainly with axe and handsaw, or laboriously brought in by canoe and dog team.

Since there was now little likelihood of being surprised by game wardens, Carl and Johnny decided to make a fast trip to retrieve the illicit fur from an outpost camp farther east. They suggested I remain behind.

I was happy to spend some time on my own moseying about the home lake in a twelve-foot birchbark canoe kept at the cabin. Everywhere I went I found myself in the company of loons, grebes, ducks, and other water birds rearing their young. They had such little fear of me that I was able to pick young loons out of the water in order to photograph them. When I put them back, adult birds would surface close alongside and unhurriedly lead them away.

A red-necked grebe and three downy little grebelets who lived in a marshy cove near the cabin became familiars. They would allow me to paddle to within a yard of them but if I came closer they would dive. The adult would go down as smoothly as a seal but the grebelets were as buoyant as Ping-Pong balls and could submerge only by seizing hold of the adult's feathers with their serrated beaks and being hauled down under by her.

The water was glass-clear, so I could watch them hanging on for dear life as their protector porpoised in the depths. Occasionally one would lose its hold (or its breath) and pop to the surface, where it might take a rest on my outstretched paddle. Such close contact with loons, grebes, ring-necked ducks, goldeneye ducks, mergansers, and their young made me feel I was living in a time before man became the universal enemy.

Then one evening the big canoe returned. It was very low in the water, and when Johnny and Carl ran it up on the landing beach I saw that four bulging packsacks occupied most of the cargo space. I did not ask about their contents and nothing was volunteered.

My companions were now ready to take life easy for a few days. Both were good cooks and we had some wonderful fish dinners after which we would sit around drinking tea and yarning.

Carl and Johnny had many stories to tell about the "real north" – stories that brought back vivid memories of my visit to Churchill with Uncle Frank. I found myself hungering for that distant world of caribou, polar bears, Inuit, and untrammelled space I had barely glimpsed. One night I wrote in my journal:

> *How bloody huge the north country is! Right now we're only in mid-Saskatchewan and there's still more than 400 miles of un-broken forest between us and its northern border. After that there's still Keewatin – another 600 miles of tundra before you reach the Arctic Ocean.*
>
> *There's hundreds of thousands of caribou up there, but so few people you might not see anybody else for months on end. A little bunch of Eskimos out on the barrens. A slightly bigger bunch of Chips*

[Chipewyans] *where the forests thin out. And a handful of white, Cree, and half-breed trappers is all. It's full of big lakes and rivers the boys say are ideal for canoe travel in summer and dog-sledding in winter.*

Though neither Carl nor Johnny has personally been much north of La Ronge they know men who've gone beyond Reindeer Lake and the northeast end of Lake Athabasca where the forests melt into the tundra. They're sure that if they can get themselves and an outfit into Cree Lake, which is halfway to Athabasca, they'll find themselves in a trapper's Eldorado.

Their enthusiasm was infectious, and I was receptive when Johnny suggested that next summer the three of us might make a canoe trip from la Ronge to Reindeer Lake, and even on out to the edge of the barrens.

According to what some old Chip told Carl there's supposed to be a canoe route west from Reindeer then south to Cree Lake. The boys would like to check that out. Carl thought it would sure and hell be a lot cheaper way in to Cree Lake than chartering a bush plane. Then he looked at me and added, "Yep, and more fun too. Might see them jeezly big caribou herds the Indians talk about. Might even see some Huskies (Eskimos). And I'll bet there's birds up there nobody's even heard about. . . ."

The upshot is we've agreed to revisit the idea when they get out from Cree Lake next spring. If it looks good we could, as Johnny says, "just try it on."

Part Four

FINDING

ˎ 17 ˏ

KEEWATIN — LAND OF THE
NORTH WIND

I was reluctant to end the canoe trip. Short as it had been, it had brought me comfort and I was beginning to have hopes of a brighter future.

This mood was not fated to endure. On arrival back at Stennarson's Post, I found some disturbing letters awaiting me. One, from my mother, informed me Angus was "in a state of gloom and doom because he feels he has failed you in your time of need." Helen went on to beg me to come home immediately and reassure my father.

A letter from Angus himself gave no indication he was troubled, but did contain a dire warning as to Helen's state of being. "Although your mother is very brave about it, your departure after such a brief time here is eating at her heart. I cannot answer for her health if you stay out west much longer."

This was such potent stuff that within twenty-four hours I had decided to cut short my journey and return to Richmond Hill.

Guilt was not the only factor. I was becoming uncomfortably aware that dedicating myself to science might not, after all, relieve the darkness of my spirit. On my final day at Stennarson's Post I wrote in my journal:

> *Do I really want to spend the foreseeable future killing every interesting animal that comes my way? Surely to God I've had enough butchery. I know it's necessary for science but what a bloody messy, dreary way to spend one's life.*

And there was something else. A remark in Angus's letter that he might be re-thinking his decision about *Scotch Bonnet*, suggested she might be available to me after all.

My departure from Montreal Lake was not easily accomplished. I was loathe to give up the beginning sense of *belonging* somewhere. Gus and the Moiestie clan (whom I had begun to think of almost as my own) did not make the parting any easier.

Gus staged a two-days-two-nights farewell party. With good reason I can't recall much about it but I remember Frank Nelson's sardonic parting toast:

"Here's big drink to best goddamn doctor we never had up here!"

Lulu and I made our way back to Ontario via the all-Canadian route which was still very much under construction. It took us three days to claw across the ancient Shield country north of Lake Superior and we broke most of Lulu's springs and all her shock absorbers doing it.

By the time we pulled into my parents' driveway in Richmond Hill, I had been absent eleven weeks in search of a place and a time that, I now had to accept, was lost to me forever.

There followed some days of overwrought emotion at the end of which my parents made a concrete offer. If I would agree to attend university, they would, upon my graduation, give me *Scotch Bonnet* together with their blessings to sail her anywhere in the world I might choose.

"Think about it," Angus insisted. "While at university you'd still have your summers free for chasing birds or whatever else you might want to do."

Helen hammered the nail home.

"We're getting on, my darling. And we do so want you to have a decent chance at life after all you've been through. We can be at peace if you find that."

My ungracious reply was that university would be a waste of time since I no longer really wanted to become a scientist and had no alternative profession in view.

"If I did enrol I might or might not even stick around to gradu-ate. I'd be just 'time serving' as they say in the army. But I'll think about it."

Afraid of where my thoughts might lead me, my parents pro-vided a distraction. They invited my western cousin, Helen Fair Thomson, to come east and join us for a late-summer cruise aboard *Scotch Bonnet* on the Bay of Quinte. Although Helen Fair was a few years my junior, we had been good companions during summer holidays spent at our grandparents' cottage in the Gatineau country.

Now she accepted the invitation with alacrity. On August 5 she joined us in Toronto and we set sail to the eastward.

My parents had stocked *Scotch Bonnet* with the best of every-thing. The sun shone, and a brisk westerly breeze sent her scudding down Lake Ontario with a bone in her teeth. Had we been setting out on a tropical cruise, things could hardly have been more idyllic.

Having reached the sheltered waters of the bay, Helen Fair and I used the dinghy to explore remote coves, go sunbathing on empty beaches, and swim wherever and whenever we wished. My parents kept very much in the background. Angus busied himself working on the vessel's gear, while my mother outdid herself in the galley.

I will never know what my parents had in mind. Were they simply hoping to distract me from my inner turmoil, or did they secretly hope that "something might come of it"? Although Helen Fair and I *were* first cousins, marriage between first cousins was not absolutely forbidden.

Nothing was ever said or even intimated until one day my parents told us they had been invited to spend the night at a friend's cottage some miles distant from where *Scotch Bonnet* lay at anchor in a snug and private little cove. Did Helen Fair and I think we would be able to manage on our own? We thought we would. And sent them on their way.

That night she and I went to bed separately but we ended up in her bunk. Since I had not brought along any contraceptives and was mortally afraid of the consequences, restraint prevailed.

I don't know what *she* thought about it at the time but a few days later when I saw her off on the train taking her home to Calgary, she eyed me quizzically and said:

"I guess they taught you how to fight in the army, Farl. Too bad they didn't teach you some other things as well. Thanks for the memories."

Early in September I enrolled at the University of Toronto – in a course that, if I managed to stick it out for three years, would see me graduate with a Bachelor of Arts degree in nothing specific. I lived with my parents in Richmond Hill that winter, commuting to classes in downtown Toronto in Lulu Belle, and spending a lot of time thinking about my experiences at Montreal Lake and about the country to the north of it. The northern virus was working in my blood.

I found little incentive to socialize with my peers at university. For the most part they were my junior by several years, and the war separated us as if we belonged to a different generation. Those who were war veterans, were mostly married (some already supporting children) and wholly committed to scholastic drudgery in their attempts to regain lost places on the economic treadmill. Neither did the city have much to offer me in the way of a social life. Unattached young women were few and far between and those still available wanted relationships leading to secure futures, which left me out of the running.

Grey days enshrouded me, so I did as I had done so often in the past – I sought comfort in a world of my own contriving. As winter closed in upon southern Ontario, I journeyed north in books and in imagination. Vivid memories of the great caribou migration – *la foule* – which I had seen on my trip to Churchill in 1935 came crowding back and I became somewhat fixated on caribou. I began to read everything I could find about the Barren Lands species, about the country they lived in, and about the other beings who shared their world.

I learned that the so-called Barren Grounds, or Barren Lands, encompassed nearly two million square miles (which is to say, most of Canada north of timberline) and that these vast tundra plains and the thin taiga forests immediately to the south provided sustenance for a plethora of living creatures. I was astonished (and delighted) by how little was actually known about the country or about the aboriginal inhabitants, the Peoples of the Deer as I thought of them. It appeared that very few outsiders had travelled through these vast reaches of taiga and tundra. One region in particular drew my attention: the interior of Keewatin territory. With the adjacent reaches of Manitoba and Saskatchewan it amounts to nearly three hundred thousand square miles, yet as late as 1947 much of it had not even been mapped.

I could find few accounts of Europeans having explored it, though, between 1770 and 1772, Samuel Hearne, a Hudson's Bay Company trader, *walked* more than 2,500 miles in the company of Dene Indians through the northernmost taiga and over the sprawling tundra from Churchill to the mouth of the Coppermine River, *then walked all the way back again.*

The next intruder of record was a young geologist, Joseph Burr Tyrrell, who was hired in 1893 by the federal government to fill in some of the enormous gaps still existing in the map of northern Canada. Joseph and his brother James were paddled by a party of Mohawk Indians (none of whom had ever seen the Barren Lands before) from Lake Athabasca north to the unknown headwaters of the Dubawnt River and through mighty Dubawnt Lake to the Thelon River and Baker Lake, where the party turned eastward and made its way to Chesterfield Inlet and the salt waters of Hudson Bay.

With winter fast closing in they then paddled south until rapidly forming winter ice drove them ashore and they were forced to make the rest of their way to Churchill (the nearest outpost) on foot. From Churchill they snowshoed eight hundred miles to Winnipeg, which they reached on January 2, 1894, having completed one of the last truly great voyages of exploration in North America.

There was, however, still much uncharted, so in July of 1884 Joe Tyrrell was back at it. This time he canoed to Reindeer Lake in northern Manitoba, and on to the headwaters of the unexplored Kazan River, following it through the Keewatin Barren Lands almost to Baker Lake. By this time winter was again upon him. Tyrrell had to break east to the coast and for a second time endure the agonies of a winter canoe voyage on Hudson Bay.

During the 1893 journey Joe and his brother encountered caribou in such abundance that, as James wrote, "the deer could only be reckoned in acres and square miles." Joe estimated that one particular herd contained as many as two hundred thousand individuals.

In addition to meeting the fabled *la foule*, the Tyrrells discovered a people unknown in the south – a thousand or more inland-dwelling Inuit living along the Kazan and Dubawnt river systems. These were truly a people out of another time for not only had most never seen a white man, they knew little or nothing about the sea and the sea-mammal culture that underlies most Inuit societies. They took *their* sustenance almost exclusively from *tuktu* – the caribou. They were still living largely unaffected by and mostly unaware of our world.

Engrossed in the task of mapping the route and studying the geology of the country, Joseph Tyrrell had little time to spare for the people he had "discovered." Nevertheless, he was much impressed by them and James, the more romantic of the brothers, wrote that he would have liked to have lived with "the Caribou Eskimaux" long enough to have understood why they seemed to be "so happily content with their simple life."

Late in December I made a momentous decision. I would seek out the caribou again, hoping the search would lead me to the people of the deer . . . *if* any such still existed.

Uncertain how to get myself there, I asked Jim Baillie if he knew of any upcoming expedition heading into Keewatin Territory. One day in mid-February Jim called me.

"I've just heard from a zoology prof in the States who wants to spend a summer on the Barrens collecting whatever he can find. He's looking for a Canadian associate. There's no pay, but if you went with him we'd buy any specimens you could collect, at our usually princely rate."

Pursuing this lead, I eventually found myself constituting half of something called the Keewatin Zoological Expedition. The other half was Dr. Francis Harper, a scientist of my father's generation, later described to me by one of his peers as having "a strong antipathy toward socialism, labour unions, and civil rights." He hardly sounded like my cup of tea, nor was I thrilled to learn that his expenses would be covered by the U.S. Office of Naval Research, whereas I would be expected to pay half the expedition's costs out of my own pocket. Nevertheless, I concluded that if I was to get to the Barrens at all that summer I had better take what was available.

We planned to fly into central Keewatin in a ski-equipped plane before the spring thaw began, then establish a base camp at some suitably remote place where Harper and I could spend the summer collecting animals and plants.

This, at any rate, was Harper's plan. I, however, had no real desire to devote my time to enlarging collections of bird and mammal mummies. *I* wanted to find and travel with the caribou; hoping to meet any remaining people of the deer and to learn what I could about the lives of both.

On May 17, 1947, Francis Harper and I boarded the north-bound Muskeg Special to Churchill. There I arranged with a bush pilot to fly us some 250 miles north and west to a little-known lake Samuel Hearne had visited almost two centuries earlier, called *Nuelthin-tua* – Sleeping Island Lake – by the Chipewyans. Here we hoped to find the cabin of a white trapper who was reputedly in touch with survivors of the so-called Caribou Eskimos.

Luck was with us. Against heavy odds, we located the cabin and managed to land on a still-frozen arm of Nueltin Lake, as it is now called. The cabin, at the mouth of Windy River, was then inhabited by three half-Cree, half-German brothers, the oldest of whom was twenty-one-year-old Charles Schweder. The brothers were very surprised to see us but, like all northern people, they made us welcome.

Thereafter, while Harper busied himself shooting and trapping whatever wild creatures came within reach, Charles and I embarked on an epic canoe journey of more than a thousand miles that took us north to the country of the inland Eskimos; then south to the trading post at Brochet, on Reindeer Lake; then back to Nueltin; and finally east to Hudson Bay, and so eventually to Churchill.

We encountered many caribou during our travels but also grim evidence that their numbers were in steep decline. For years white trappers had been slaughtering them for human and dog food, and using them as bait for traps and sets. We also met most of the few remaining Inuit people of the deer (*Ihalmiut* – People from Beyond – they called themselves) and visited some of the surviving *Idthen Eldeli*, the Chipewyan people of the deer.

That summer was a transcendental experience during which I developed a consuming desire to learn more about the peoples of the deer and, if I was lucky, about their inner world. I also became deeply perturbed and angry at the way the indigenous peoples and the other natural denizens of tundra and taiga were being savaged by my kind – by the interlopers.

By summer's end I was seriously considering dropping out of university in order to spend the coming winter roaming the tundra by dog team with Charles and his brothers. Then, when summer returned, I could canoe the countless lakes and rivers getting to know the deer and the deer people with a view to – perhaps – championing their cause.

Although this was no more than a half-formed notion, the idea of becoming a defender rather than a destroyer was irresistibly attractive. But if I intended to become a self-appointed champion of the Barren Lands, I had better have some allies.

Returning to Toronto in mid-September I resumed sporadic attendance at university, while spending much of my time trying to organize a new expedition to the Barren Lands – one that would include a photographer and a trained biologist.

I persuaded Andy Lawrie to come along as the "expert biologist," at least through the summer of 1948; Bill Carrick, another pal from the Toronto Ornithological Field Group, agreed to bring and man the cameras.

Against the odds (for I was without standing in the scientific world), I managed to persuade the prestigious Arctic Institute of

North America to provide a grant-in-aid of a thousand dollars, a formidable sum in those days and one that would go a long way toward covering outfitting and transportation costs.

All in all, things were looking rosy. They became even rosier after I met a classmate in Botany 2A who was unable to see anything through a microscope and was effusively grateful when I described for her the things she could not see for herself.

Frances Thornhill was a blond, blue-eyed, twenty-three-year-old veteran of the Wrens (Women's Royal Canadian Naval Service) recently demobbed and, like me, now enrolled in a pass arts course to, as she wryly put it, "pass the time away" until something better appeared. She too was ill at ease in the university milieu. Not surprisingly, we drifted together, and I soon found myself in courting mode.

She did not respond with any marked enthusiasm until one warm and sunny October day I took her birdwatching in the wooded glades of High Park, where she joined me in "making angels" in the windrows of fallen leaves. We wound up making love under a blanket of them.

Since we were fully clothed this was a fumbling and unsatisfactory encounter, but we made up for that a few days later when we visited *Scotch Bonnet*, cosily moored for the winter in a lagoon on Toronto Island.

Things moved rapidly after that. On a day late in October, after I had known Fran for little more than a month, I was with her in one of the Royal Ontario Museum's specimen storage vaults proudly showing her examples of my previous (and perhaps future) scientific endeavours when she turned suddenly on me, white-faced and tense, and demanded:

"You've got to marry me!"

In the language of the times, this meant she was pregnant.

Once my panicky first reaction had simmered down, the prospect was surprisingly easy to accept. Marriage would mean escape from the vale of loneliness, would ensure ongoing sex, and (so I assumed) would bring me all the rest of the promised rewards of married life. Even when it turned out (as it soon did) that the pregnancy was a false alarm, I made no attempt to avoid a commitment that was already in train.

Before enlisting in the armed forces, Fran had been a student at Bishop Strachan School, one of Toronto's most prestigious private schools for girls. She was now determined to be married in BSS's impressive chapel and as soon as possible.

Her parents, Reuben and Florence Thornhill, had migrated to Toronto in the 1920s from a disintegrating rural community in western Ontario. A young couple without money or resources, they had been hoping to find the proverbial better life in the big city. In classic style, Rube worked his way up from the shop floor of a factory to become a successful salesman able to buy a heavily mortgaged semi-detached house and a new Ford car.

Rube was satisfied with these achievements, and so was Florence – up to a point. The "point" was her daughter's future and Florence's aspirations for her. Even though the Depression was by then draining the economic lifeblood from people in the Thornhills' circumstances, they somehow managed to put their only daughter into Bishop Strachan School and maintain her there for several years. Had the war not intervened, Fran would doubtless have graduated from BSS and, if her mother's dreams had been realized, would have married well above her station to live in affluence ever after.

BSS took its time replying to Fran's request for us to be married in the chapel. The reply, when it came, was a singularly curt refusal. Fran was devastated and I was angry. I demanded explanations and eventually we were granted an audience with the head mistress. This regal lady (I have forgotten her name) coolly informed us that being

211

married in the school chapel was a privilege reserved for graduates only, and there could and would be no exceptions.

My response was roughly this:

Leading Seaman Thornhill and I are both veterans of the recent war. Both of us left school to *volunteer* for action in the armed forces, in which we served a total of seven years helping to defend this country and its institutions – of which Bishop Strachan School is a prime example. We think we've done *our* bit. How come you won't do yours and give us dispensation from your damn fool regulation?

Frances Thornhill and I were married by a former army chaplain on December 19 in a Toronto church at some distance from BSS.

We spent our honeymoon at a summer cottage in northern Ontario where the temperature fell to thirty-five degrees below freezing and the only really warm place was in bed. On December 23 we took up married life in two rooms of my parents' house in Richmond Hill.

A few weeks later the axe fell.

As a matter of form, the Arctic Institute had sent a copy of my proposal and the institute's offer of support to the federal Minister of Mines and Resources, whose department administered the Northwest Territories. This material ended up in the hands of a recent graduate in zoology whom the Department of Mines and Resources had just hired.

He was Frank Banfield, of the Dodge sedan and one of my companions on the 1939 Faunal Survey of Saskatchewan.

Frank scrutinized my proposal, then, having elaborated on it somewhat, took it to his chief and convinced him that, not only was a study of the Barren Land caribou an urgent matter, it was too important to be entrusted to a pair of undergraduates and a freelance photographer. Frank strongly recommended the job be done by the department and volunteered to take charge of it himself.

Andy and I knew nothing of this when, early in the new year, we were invited to Ottawa for an interview with the deputy minister of Mines and Resources, who was also deputy commissioner of the Northwest Territories and the effective monarch of that vast region. Greatly excited, for we thought we had been summoned in order to receive the imprimatur on our plans, we travelled to Ottawa, where with due ceremony we were escorted into the sanctum of a portly Colonel Blimp-type who was deferentially introduced to us as Commissioner Gibson.

R.A. Gibson did most of the talking. Having informed us that "his" department was undertaking a comprehensive survey of the status of *Rangifer arcticus* (the scientific name for the Barren Land caribou) and of the "native tribes associated with the animal," he delivered our *coup de grâce*.

"You understand, of course, that a proposal such as yours is now redundant and cannot be supported by the department. We have so informed the Arctic Institute of North America who might otherwise have sponsored you. Furthermore, I must advise you that an Explorer's and Scientist's Permit to undertake field studies in the Northwest Territories on your own cannot be issued to you."

He paused to let all this sink in, then added: "However, Captain Banfield, who is in charge of the survey, believes he might be able to find employment for you."

Captain Banfield (the use of military titles was *de rigueur* in Ottawa) was waiting for us as we slunk out of the commissioner's imposing office.

Frank took us to the cafeteria of the Lord Elgin Hotel for lunch and attempted to cheer us up.

"Sorry about all this, you chaps, but it ain't necessarily so bad. Bill Carrick's out but I have the authority to hire both of you. You'd sign on as student biologists in training – at a pretty small salary I'm afraid, but you'd get the chance to do a lot of things you wanted to do. Your base camp could still be the Schweder cabin at Nueltin

Lake. The department would provide everything you'll need, including a canoe, outboard motor, air transport . . . even a short-wave radio. And you could hire your young half-breed friend as a guide and general factotum."

He paused for a long moment. "I don't want to push you, but time is short. I have to have your answer by tomorrow morning."

Andy and I spent the rest of that dismal day in a cheap hotel room trying to come to terms with the bitter reality that we really had little choice but to accept Banfield's offer.

Our train for Toronto was due to leave at eleven the next morning. By then we had formally submitted ourselves to servitude as part-time government employees. This was especially hard for me to swallow because I had sworn that, having freed myself from the morass of bureaucratic imbecilities in which the army had immersed me, I would never again subject myself to such a fate.

As the train trundled us homeward, the only solace I could find lay in the private thought that, having avoided becoming a zombie in the army, I might be able to avoid the same fate as a government employee.

· 18 ·

SLEEPING ISLAND LAKE

Spring had come to Ontario. Birds were streaming northward and soon I would be too. Frances and I felt it might make the coming separation easier if we had a second honeymoon before I departed. On my twenty-seventh birthday we drove Lulu Belle back to the place we thought of as Icy Cottage and spent five glorious May days soaking up the essence of spring while making love and making plans.

Surprisingly the university had agreed to let Andy and me do most of our next year's course work extramurally, requiring only that we return to Toronto in the spring of 1949 to write formal examinations. In consequence, he and I planned to spend the coming year attempting to follow the Keewatin caribou herds by canoe and on foot wherever they might lead.

We would try to live with the deer on the tundra until the autumn of 1948, then follow them to their wintering grounds in the vicinity of Reindeer Lake. Frances would join me there and we would set up housekeeping (if we could find a house or cabin) in the tiny settlement of Brochet at the north end of the lake. In the spring of 1949 all three of us would return to Toronto.

Fran and I had very little idea of what we might do after that. The uncomfortable truth was that I had nothing substantial in view for the future. The abandonment of my *Birds of Saskatchewan* project followed by my disillusioning experiences as a neophyte zoologist under Dr. Harper's tutelage had combined to kill any remaining inclination to become a professional biologist.

Although I had been a "writer" since childhood, I had never thought about it as anything more than a pleasurable avocation. Now I was beginning to wonder if I might be able to earn a livelihood at it.

Frances encouraged me, suggesting that I might someday write a book about our travels. The idea took hold and as I prepared to go north again I began keeping an extensive journal.

May 18th. A grey day in Ottawa, this grey-minded city of bureaucrats and bullshit. A mist swirls over the airport. Out on the tarmac looms a massive Lancaster bomber recently demobbed from war to peace. In the foreground stands a small green jeep from which two figures swathed in heavy arctic clothing make their way toward the big RCAF plane, rifles in hands and heavy packs upon their backs. Alongside the jeep a third figure, a small one in a blue naval raincoat, with a gaudy kerchief tied around her head, watches them go. The sky seems to glower and a wet, sulphurous wind sweeps in from the Ottawa River.

An odd assortment of other passengers climbs a ladder into what had formerly been the bomb bay. They include two private soldiers from the Three Rivers Regiment nursing monumental hangovers; a handful of U.S. enlisted men and officers from somewhere south of the Mason-Dixon Line on their way north for the first time in their lives; a middle-aged Newfoundland nurse escorting an Eskimo child who has spent two of its three years of existence in the Hamilton Tuberculosis Sanatorium. The nurse is herself returning to another year of exile at a lonely post on Hudson Bay. And there is a smattering of civilians looking slightly ashamed, as civilians tend to do when in the military presence.

Our steward, a saturnine, gum-chewing RCAF corporal, waves Andy and me to our seats – wooden benches against the plane's sides. If I strain my neck I can just manage to peer through a tiny window behind me and see Lulu Belle at the distant edge of the field and huddled beside it the small figure of my wife. A signal light flashes from the tower and the Lanc begins to vibrate alarmingly as all four Rolls-Royce motors bellow. We begin to roll . . . become airborne. Ottawa looms in view for a moment or two then is lost as we climb into a dirty overcast and the world disappears.

Of the flight, which takes us a thousand miles in a little less than seven hours, there is not much to say. There was not much to say or do aboard either. The thundering engines precluded conversation and there was hardly enough light to read by. Like cattle, we could do little but ruminate. A civilian meteorologist beside me stretched his long legs half way across the plane and dozed with mouth gaping and prominent teeth bared as if in the rictus of death. As on any long journey where human beings are crammed together in a confined space, an aura of frowziness soon gathered over us. Faces grew slack and an oily film seemed to overlie the skin. Only the Eskimo child seemed untouched by the slow decay which seemed to assail the rest of us. It slept contentedly for most of the journey.

The bomb bay was not pressurized and there was no supplementary oxygen so we flew at only a few thousand feet, immersed in cloud and unable to see anything outside the plane. Three-quarters of the trip passed before we escaped into clear skies over the bizarre country that lies southwest of Hudson Bay. Not long emerged from an ancient *polar sea, this vast coastal plain seems half-submerged. Bereft of trees and filled with bogs, muskegs, ponds, and meandering streams, it appeared to Andy (as he yelled into my ear) "good for sweet fuck-all except ducks." Most of the other passengers gave this, their first view of the sub-arctic, an appalled glance then gloomily returned to staring blankly at the inside of the plane. But I was fascinated by the palette of Dutch Masters' colours and the infinite variety of sinuous watery shapes. I thought that if an ancestor who had been alive when the earth was very young was to see it, he would greet it familiarly and call it by a name we will never know.*

In late afternoon we swept out over still-frozen Hudson Bay, its old ice dark and forbidding. The corporal/steward appeared, to yell a laconic "Twenty minutes!" Passengers began to stir, scuffling about for lost scarves and gloves. Combs came out amongst the soldiery and hats were cocked at rakish angles as we came in sight of an immense concrete grain elevator looming like a mountain titan over the scattering of shacks still half-buried in winter drifts that is Churchill.

We spent an infuriating week in Churchill dealing with matters Captain Banfield had failed to arrange, such as the hiring of Charles Schweder. The Schweder brothers had made their way to Churchill by dog team late in the winter and I had since been in touch with Charles, but now when I ran him to earth he gave me the bad news that the "officer from Ottawa" (Banfield) had refused to pay rent for the cabin at Windy River and, in consequence, Charles's father refused to let his son accompany us. Instead, Charles had been put to work on a local construction site to help support his father's family.

This major disappointment was followed by a second when we called at the home of young Gunnar Ingebritson, who had been chartered to fly us to Nueltin in his old, ski-equipped Norseman. We learned he was in Winnipeg getting his airplane repaired and by the time he returned to Churchill the season would be too advanced to fly us in on skis. We were advised to relax and enjoy the "amenities" of Churchill until the thaw brought open water to the lakes and made it practicable to fly float-equipped planes into the interior. When we asked how long that might be, the discouraging answer was "Mid-June, or maybe later."

At this juncture Churchill inflicted a severe attack of food poisoning on me.

The gods finally took pity.

Late on May 22 Gunnar's Norseman stuttered over the sleazy hotel where we were staying. An hour later this laconic son of a Norwegian fisherman joined us to announce that next day he would attempt to coax his plane, laden with us and our ton of supplies, off the disintegrating ice of the nearby tundra pond where he had just made a "dicey" landing.

The sky next day was heavily obscured by fog and snow flurries. The Norseman laboured mightily to get airborne, its skis sending up fountains of meltwater as it plunged across the rotting ice. Somehow Gunnar jockeyed it into the air, and we turned northward along the coast only to find ourselves pinned down by the fog to thirty or forty feet above a ragged jumble of sea ice.

I was for returning to Churchill, until Gunnar shouted into the intercom:

"We turn back now and you guys have lost it. Might be a month before I can fly on floats."

I glanced at Andy. Cheerfully he waved us on.

Somewhere near the mouth of Seal River we swung inland, thankfully leaving the fog behind. The weather still held us down to five hundred feet as the coastal barrens were replaced by rolling highlands whose massive black rock ridges slashed across the softer reds and browns of muskeg glittering with meltwater. Great eskers (the reversed beds of one-time glacial rivers) ran their dry courses beneath us, gigantic yellow serpents overriding the ponds, rock barrens, muskegs, and living rivers that lay in their path. Caribou trails laced the muskeg, but we saw only one herd, a small one, and I was afraid we might have already missed the main northbound migration of *la foule*.

I tried to follow our course on a chart filled with white voids containing the cryptic word "Unmapped."

"Never you mind the maps," Gunnar shouted, noticing me peering at mine. "Can't trust the buggers! Steer by the sun and the stars and by the feeling in your gut. Never failed me yet."

Two hours after leaving the coast of Hudson Bay, the Norseman was abreast of a singular black basalt outcrop that Gunnar thought marked the entrance to Nueltin's northwestern arm. Soon we were flying at deck level above unbroken ice toward the mouth of Windy River, where the Schweder cabin stood.

Gunnar made such an abrupt landing that the plane skidded and slithered for several hundred yards before he was able to ease it to a stop. With scarcely enough fuel remaining for the return trip and with ominous black clouds rolling in from the west, he was not about to waste any time.

"Get your fucking stuff outta my plane!" he shouted as he flung open the doors. "You got five minutes before I'm off!"

Andy and I threw everything onto the ice, and five minutes later waved the plane away into the darkening sky. Only then did it register on us that we were half a mile from shore.

A cock ptarmigan on a nearby islet called mockingly. Two ravens circled overhead, hopefully perhaps. I looked shoreward and saw a two-legged object bounding toward us. Soon it resolved itself into the sturdy fur-clad figure of a man I recognized from the summer before, an Inuit named Owliktuk.

When we three had finished beaming at one another and shaking hands, Owliktuk let us toward the empty cabin. Later we would learn he had walked down from the Ihalmiut camps near the Kazan River some sixty miles to the north, bringing five white fox skins he had hoped to trade with Charles Schweder. Finding the cabin abandoned, as it had been for months, Owliktuk searched for but found no useable supplies except a few pounds of tea. There being nothing else for it, he had exchanged his pelts for the tea and set off for home but had gone only a mile or two when he heard the Norseman.

Now he led us into the dank and dismal Schweder cabin where, with difficulty, we managed to get a fire going in the rusty old cookstove. As we waited for the tea water to boil, Owliktuk explained that his people had endured another starvation winter (their third in five years). Although the migrant deer were now returning north, the people were unable to hunt because the Schweders, their only source of ammunition, were still absent.

We would learn that in February the surviving Ihalmiut, numbering forty-seven men, women, and children, had come to the cabin in search of help. Finding none they had nevertheless remained close by, hoping Charles would soon return. They had sustained themselves chiefly with what they could scavenge from the frozen carcasses of wolves and foxes skinned then tossed aside by Charles and his brothers, and on the bones, guts, and hides of caribou the Schweders had killed the previous autumn.

All but four of the Ihalmiuts' remaining dogs had died of starvation during the weeks of waiting for Charles to return – and had been eaten. There had been just enough sustenance to keep the people alive through March when they had straggled back to their own camps hoping to kill some caribou with bows and arrows at natural defiles. They had in fact been able to kill enough to keep themselves going.

Owliktuk viewed our arrival as the salvation for his people and was desperately anxious to take the good news and ammunition back to them. Despite this, he agreed to remain with us for a few days to help us get our gear ashore before the ice weakened. He did this even though the creeks and rivers across his homeward path were already flooding with meltwater and he knew if he delayed too long he would have to wade shoulder-deep or even swim many of these obstacles.

Making use of some old dog sleds the Schweders had left behind, we hauled everything to the nearest point of land – Cache Point, we came to call it – and stored it under canvas there until we could find time to move it to the cabin. When we began opening some of our crates, we came across two items of special interest. The first contained our supply of cigarettes and pipe tobacco. This find triggered ecstasy in Owliktuk. The second held an Inuit-English dictionary, which was as good as a Rosetta stone to me.

A third, government-packed crate plastered with red FRAGILE labels contained a battery-operated short-wave radio with which we were supposed to keep in contact with our employer. But instead of the ten-watt model we had been promised, we had received a mere toy of 2.5 watts' power.

Nevertheless we rigged it up, attached the battery, and made our first attempt to communicate with the outside world. We were unable to get a response from anyone, including the powerful Churchill Radio, which was supposed to be our point of contact. When our voice transmissions went unanswered, I tried using Morse code, but this too failed to elicit any response. All we could hear in the earphones was the manic chuckle and whistle of static. When anxious efforts to report the dire situation of the Ihalmiut succeeded only in draining our batteries, we decided to give up the attempt for a few days in hopes atmospheric conditions would improve.

The thaw was now well under way, which meant it ought soon to be possible for us to travel by water. We had planned to bring a canoe in with us lashed to one of the plane's pontoons but on arrival at Churchill had been told a "collapsible boat" had been substituted for the canoe.

We had seen no sign of such a thing until, at Windy River, we began unpacking some peculiarly shaped packages tightly swathed in sacking. These turned out to contain intricately shaped pieces of plywood which, when finally assembled (with much cursing and bad temper), proved to be a kind of boat.

I wrote this about it in my journal:

> *It is evidently Banfield's version of the 18-foot freighter canoe we asked for. If it floats, it might prove useful for something but God help us if any of the little snap-fasteners that hold it together let go. And it sure and hell won't support an engine, which leaves us with a fine new 5-horsepower outboard and a boat that won't have anything to do with each other. Maybe we can use it for a bathtub.*

By the end of our first week at Windy Cabin the thaw was well advanced.

> *There's an exhilaration in the air. You can almost feel it as an electric buzz in every nerve and muscle. It makes you feel so goddamn full of life you want to climb a mountain, swim an ocean, or screw an entire chorus line. There are priceless moments sitting on the skinned log we use for a john with the rising sun on your face, looking out over the Windy Hills scarified by ten thousand caribou trails; listening to the first flies of the season trying to get their wings unthawed; hearing the rumble of ice beginning to move in the river; and watching the tumbling flight of a pair of ravens celebrating the most important things in the whole bloody world – the coming of spring and the need to make love.*

One morning Andy and I were startled by what felt like a minor earthquake. Alarmed, we ran out of the cabin to find the river ice grinding and roaring as it tore loose from the bottom, thrusting up enormous cakes four to five feet thick. Soon pans from upstream were piling up on those in front, forming a dam right across the valley. Behind it the river quickly became a lake.

Before long the water, thick with ice crystals, was almost up to the cabin door. Frantically we scuttled about building a dyke of snow and ice against it, though our efforts were pitifully inadequate. We would surely have lost the battle *and* the cabin with all its contents had not the dam fortuitously burst and spewed ice pans with thunderous violence for more than a mile out over the still-solid surface of the bay, sending them spinning and crashing into one another like fun-cars in a giant midway ride.

Spring was now on us with a vengeance. Noon temperatures shot up into the seventies (though they generally fell to below freezing at night), and it seemed to us the country had become one vast water-soaked sponge, impassable to any four-legged animal except, perhaps long-legged deer.

We were wrong about that.

Today I climbed the high gravel ridge north of camp and spotted what I thought was a bunch of deer galloping toward me. I watched them lope along until it dawned on me that the creatures splashing across the tundra like water buffalos were people. As they got closer they began waving their arms like crazy and making a hell of a row. I was relieved to recognize Owliktuk leading a charge of seven men, who turned out to be the heads of families of the Kazan band.

They'd been out of tobacco all winter so the first thing they did was empty my pouch into their stone pipes and light up. Then they all followed me back to the cabin gabbling like jay birds. When we poured in on Andy he looked as if he might have a fit but rose to the occasion and began making tea for all hands like a good hostess should. The cabin literally bulged with Eskimos. There was much hand-shaking (no nose rubbing, thank God), introductions, and friendly beaming but it took a while and gallons of tea before we could make much sense of things because of the language problem. We gathered that Owliktuk had told everybody we had come to catch caribou and wanted their help to do that, so here they were, and pretty damn anxious to go to work.

We staked them to a bag of flour, baking powder, lard, and tea, and they happily set up camp on the ridge behind the cabin. They had a dog, one of the few survivors from the winter. We gave it the bones and scraps from a deer Owliktuk had killed for us before his departure and it ate until literally it could hardly walk. Same with the Eskimos, who ate most of the rest of the deer then cooked the whole bag of flour into bannocks and scoffed them down. They really were starving.

Owliktuk, by the way, has shed the skin clothing he was wearing when we first met him and in our honour is wearing a tattered old shirt Charles must have given him and something that looks vaguely like a pair of ancient breeches that are worn right through at the knees and ass. When he was dressed in clothing made of caribou hides he looked like a man to be respected. In white man's castoffs he looked like a hopeless bum.

Supper over, we had ourselves a party. What a blow-out! Nine of us crammed into a space about as big as an average bedroom, with the stove roaring away as it boiled a river of tea. Most of us not having had a bath since God knows when, you could've sliced the air with a knife. Thank God for the smell of tobacco, though the smoke did make it hard to see what the gang was up to.

Fun and games was what. Ohoto, a squat little guy with a grin like a cat, seemed to be the chief clown. He did imitations of white men (namely Andy and me) that brought the house down. Then he found

a bag of our onions and started juggling them. I swear he had a dozen
aloft when he lost control and they flew everywhere. I found a couple
in the five-gallon pail we were using to make tea, but they only added
spice to the flavour.

A guy called Mikki produced an Eskimo drum, which is a hoop
covered with caribou gut, and they took turns singing and dancing for
us. Then we had to do our stuff. Andy tried dancing a hornpipe while
I did my bagpipe imitation. Our efforts were well received, perhaps
because we had slipped a few slugs of caribou juice (90% proof alcohol
intended for preserving specimens) into the tea.

Our visitors remained several days and were a great help ferrying supplies from our temporary cache and collecting firewood for
us. We especially appreciated the latter because there on the edge
of the Barrens the trees were tiny – seldom taller than ten feet – and
usually few and far between. Furthermore, those within easy reach
of the cabin had mostly been felled and burned long since.

When not working with us, our visitors tried to teach us their
language and learn ours. Then one evening they announced they had
to return to their families. They asked nothing from us except ammunition, which they offered to pay for with white fox skins next winter.

Unfortunately we had few shells of the calibre they needed and
so had to refuse all except one man, a big, smiling fellow named
Hekwaw, who owned a beaten-up .30-30 carbine. We gave him
several boxes of ammo for it, with the stern stipulation that everything he shot had to be shared among all the people. Hekwaw
seemed surprised by that, for of course this is what he intended to
do anyway. It was what the Inuit *did*.

Owliktuk, Ohoto, Mikki, Hekwaw, Ootek, Onekwa, and Halo
departed next morning, each toting a heavy backpack supported by
a rawhide band around his forehead. We were left alone to get on
with our job, which promised to be difficult.

Because the arrangements made by the department had delayed our departure until break-up, the pregnant does were now far to the north, hurrying to reach their fawning grounds near the arctic coast. Most of the bucks had also gone by, leaving only occasional sick or wounded strays in our part of the country.

In consequence I assumed I would not be able to proceed with one of my special projects – studying the home life of wolves – for I concluded that if there were no caribou in the vicinity of Nueltin there would be no wolves.

I was dead wrong about that.

I woke this morning feeling really low, partly because of being some-what worried how this separation may be affecting Fran. Partly because although I think I got an SOS out on the radio last night to Churchill about the terrible winter the Eskimos have had, I couldn't get a clear acknowledgement. And partly because we've missed the spring migration of the deer.

Without the deer we're up shit creek without a paddle. Or – what's more like it – with just a paddle.

I decided to see could I do something about that. Using bits of old packing cases I spent a day and a half strengthening our folding boat and making a frame to hang the outboard on the stern of it. Andy thought I was nuts, or suicidal. But it worked!

The motor fired at the first pull. The boat stood the strain and none of its buttons popped. In a fit of bravado I ran her up the rapids at the mouth of Windy River, then back down again. C'est bon! We are no longer stuck in one spot. Once the ice on Nueltin melts we'll be able to go anywhere, perhaps even the Kazan River, though right now Windy Bay is only barely showing open water around its shores.

I beached her on Cache Point and was waiting for Andy, who'd said he'd join me (he'd wisely decided against taking part in the initial run on the river), when I heard queer noises from away to the eastward: yaps, and yelps, and whimpers like a bunch of dogs playing. Andy failed to join me so I ran the boat across the bay and climbed a ridge on the far side to see what was up. Nothing was, but the noises continued so I climbed two more ridges and came upon a sight I'll remember to my dying day. Poised on the crest of a yellow esker, sharply outlined by the setting sun, was a big white wolf. In that clear light it looked as big as a polar bear. My neck hairs crawled then damn near stood on end as the wolf threw back its head in a full-throated howl. This was echo'ed from further down the esker and when I swung my binoculars that way I could see two more big wolves, and a scurry that looked like pups at the mouth of a black hole in the side of the esker. It had to be a den!

About then it dawned on me that I didn't even have a firecracker with me. Though I knew wolves aren't supposed to attack human beings, did they know it? Truth to tell, I slunk back to the boat and went speedily home, where I had several shots of caribou juice before going to bed happy as hell.

I know what I'm going to be doing for the next little while.

· 19 ·

INUIT AND OTHERS

Two days after my discovery of the wolves' den, the energetic Ohoto reappeared. Wet as a muskrat after spending several days wading across overflowing streams and through swollen muskegs, he bounced into the cabin to announce he would be our tuktu catcher, adding that, since there were no deer about at the moment, he was ready to take on any other project we might have in mind.

I seized on the offer to make him my assistant (and, as it turned out, chief instructor) in my study of *amow* – the wolf.

The first thing we did was to establish an observation post about a quarter mile from the den. We pitched a very small tent camouflaged with spruce boughs outside of which we set up a powerful binocular telescope I had "liberated" from the German army. Inside we installed a Primus stove so we could brew tea while taking a break from wolf-watching.

While we were setting up our spy camp, the big white wolf kept us under close observation. He stared so long (and, it seemed to me, speculatively) that I was tempted to reach for my rifle, until reassured by Ohoto:

"*Amow* not eat white men. Taste bad!"

I spent much of my time during the next several weeks at this observation post, accompanied at first by Ohoto, later by Ootek.

Before dawn this morning Ohoto showed up from his little camp (a bit of canvas stretched between two spruce stubs) and he and I headed for the wolf den in Banfield's Bathtub. Made tea when we got there, then lay on our bellies watching the wolf den, but there was damn little action. I think we got three quick glimpses of wolves for a day-long vigil. We got well chilled and well bored, and the mosquitoes have thawed out so we got well bitten. too. For a break, Ohoto went off prospecting and came back with about a ton of iron pyrite, which he hoped was gold. All my fault for trying to tell him how white men get rich quick.

Knocked off at dusk and on the way back to the boat found a lemming mooching around under a dried-up deer carcass. An incredible little guy built like a brick but cuddly as a teddy bear, very prettily coloured in reds and browns, and absolutely unafraid of us. To the contrary, Owinak (his Eskimo name) greeted us like old pals and when I picked him up spent about ten minutes licking my fingers (for the salt?). So we took him home to add to a battalion of red-backed mice who, uninvited, share the cabin with us.

After supper Andy and I worked at learning Inuktitut with Ohoto as teacher. He's really good. Patient, understanding, and with a racy sense of humour. We teach him English in exchange. I wonder if we mangle his language as badly as he does ours? Together he and I composed a song in both lingoes about how we would like to screw Pommela's two wives.

When he figures we're getting bored, he does tricks to amuse us. Yesterday he did back flips over a ten-inch butcher knife stuck, blade up, in the sand outside our door. Scared the bejesus out of me. He never seems to sleep. Can keep going all day and all night. These people must do all their sleeping in the winter.

Tonight I tried to work our stupid little radio again. Could hear snatches from Churchill Radio, but they couldn't hear us and we couldn't make sense of their transmissions. Hope to hell my message last week to Ottawa about the terrible condition of the Kazan Eskimos got through and help is sent before it's too late.

I don't know what Ohoto makes of our struggle with the radio but he seems to have figured out what the snatches of voices in the earphones are, though sometimes he may get it wrong. This night he was listening to the static when suddenly he jumped to his feet, wild-eyed and frantic, and rushed out the door. We hurried after, wondering what the hell, and caught him half way to the river. He was gibbering like a maniac and fairly bouncing up and down.

"Ino . . . Ino . . :," he howled, spinning around like a top and pointing all around the horizon.

We got him back inside and sat him down. I took his pulse and his heart was going like a trip-hammer. After a lot of confusion we discovered Ino is some kind of bad spirit who had just paid us a visit. Apparently Ohoto heard Ino voices and glanced up to see one – it looks somewhat like a man – go floating slowly by the window beckoning to him to follow. Ohoto says he had to follow, and if we hadn't caught him he would have followed the Ino into the river.

There was no doubt he was scared half to death. He wouldn't go out again on his own so we let him spend the rest of the night in the cabin. When, at about 0100, the place suddenly shook as if a dinosaur had grabbed it, Andy and I damn near panicked too. We sidled outside with rifles cocked, but there was nothing unusual to be seen. All was *still in the half-light, and there wasn't any wind. Earthquake? Maybe.*

When the cabin shook, Ohoto just about went bonkers. We dosed him with a heavy shot of our alky and he finally seemed to go into a coma. Then he seemed to have a fit. At one point he swallowed his tongue and his face was turning black before Andy managed to hook a finger around his tongue and free up his windpipe. After that, he finally went to sleep and so, thank God, did we.

No deer left around here, not even a straggler now so with Ohoto's help we set two nets at the mouth of the river, which is still in spate and running like a millrace. This morning we took out two suckers, a grayling, and two lake trout running about ten pounds each. We won't go hungry!

The big excitement this day was when Ohoto saw a freshwater seal on the rocks off Cache Point! There was no doubt about what it was. It must have come from the group Charles and I saw on the Thlewiaza River last summer, though it would have had to travel more than 300 miles inland by river route from salt water. Well, why not? What gives us the right to think we are the only animals interested in exploration?

The world around us has really come to life. Every pond and swamp has Old Squaw [ducks], mergansers, loons, and phalaropes nesting on it. Every little bush poking its head up above the tundra seems to have a Harris, white-crowned, or song sparrow nesting in it. So far we have logged 74 species of birds and the crazy buggers sing all day and all night such as it is. Spring is a short season up here, but sure and hell a merry one. All this sex frenzy is driving me nuts. I can't even get a message to or from my girl, so all I can do is dream — well, almost all I can do. . . .

Ohoto left yesterday [June 21], carrying a bundle of grub for his wife and kid. I baked a huge batch of bread this morning and while the stove was hot heated up six pails of water for a much-needed clean-up. Andy and I stripped to the buff then turned the cabin into a small Niagara filled with foam and fury. I found I couldn't lie down in a ten-gallon pail so I sat in it, but when I got up, it got up with me. Après moi le deluge!

We were splashing nakedly around when the door opened and a startled Inuk poked his head in. It was Halo. He tried to retreat but we hauled him in and sat him on a bunk while we completed our ablutions. He was dreadfully embarrassed by the sight of two naked kabloonas and kept his eyes shut and his head between his hands until we were clothed again. The bath was not entirely a good thing. I could now distinctly smell our guest, whereas before we all stank alike so nobody smelled the others.

Three more visitors arrived in the afternoon: Yaha; Ootek; and a young lad also named Ohoto, but no relation to our Ohoto. They were pretty hungry but we had made a good catch in our nets and so could stuff them up. They brought two young dogs to give us because they could no longer feed them, even though these were just about the last of their dogs. We took them, but only temporarily because the people will need them badly if they are going to make it through another winter.

We are getting to understand each other a lot better. They told us a lot more about how things are at the camps. The situation at Inuit Ku, River of Men, as they call the Kazan, is truly grim. Because they had no ammo to shoot deer when the big herds went through this spring, they couldn't get deer skins to cover their kayaks and so couldn't spear deer crossing the rivers as they do every spring. They had eaten the old kayak coverings last winter to keep from starving. Now the deer have gone further north and since they have no useable kayaks they can't even set nets for fish, even if they still had any good nets, which they don't.

We have given them most of the grub we can spare but there are 47 of them, young and old, and we can't begin to feed that lot. The men with us now are catching enough fish so they are saving what flour we can give them to take home to their families. Truth is, they're completely destitute. Although I radioed for help the first week in June, there's been no reply. I'm writing a blistering report to the Minister to go out on the first plane, and if that doesn't get results the newspapers are going to get a story that will put him on the hot seat.

Ohoto has had to go home to look after his family but Ootek has offered to work for us in exchange for food for his wife and child at the Kazan camps. We're happy to have him. Though all the Ihalmiut we have met so far are friendly, personable guys, Ootek stands out. He's maybe thirty, alert, very bright and obliging, lightly built, with a mobile, expressive play of features, very little reserve, and is somewhat puppyish in his friendliness. He is also a shaman or medicine man of considerable repute.

Today I set off with him to look for another wolf family we've heard howling in the Windy Hills south of us. Charles sometimes called those the Ghost Hills. He told me they were impenetrable, so rough nobody but a ghost could get around or make a living there.

We crossed the Windy River near camp and started climbing. Although steep, these hills don't have peaks – just false crests that recede as you climb toward them. They are covered with an indescribable confusion of frost-shattered granitic boulders, some as big as houses, and pretty well all with sharp edges that lacerate your feet. In some places we had to go two or three hundred yards at a time leaping from edge to edge like bleeding mountain goats. Though I was wearing heavy miner's rubber boots, my feet got badly bruised. Ootek was wearing only kamikpak – thin deerskin boots. I don't know how he stood it.

It took us three hours to make about a mile to the top, which was so covered with rock shards you could nowhere see the ground. To the

east and west the world looked like a war-torn version of the moon —
a place only a bird could navigate.

To the south was something else! Surrounded on all sides by
mountains of grey rubble was a valley maybe half a mile wide with a
massive golden-yellow sand esker a hundred feet wide and fifty high
winding its serpentine way between clear ponds and lakelets whose
banks nurtured stands of spruce which would have been impressive
five hundred miles to the south. And the whole place, except for the
golden esker and the sapphire water, was green with berry bushes and
low-lying plants. A gold and green heaven surrounded by what looked
like the ash pit of hell itself.

There seemed to be no exit or entrance at our end of this hidden
valley, except maybe by a couple of rock-clogged gullies away off to
our left. Ootek was now limping badly and I wasn't in much better
shape so, though I was dying to explore, we couldn't face trying to
make a descent into the valley. We limped back to the boat and went
home, both of us beat out.

June 25. Ootek and I tried again to get into the hidden valley in the
Windy Hills. I wondered if the gullies we'd seen to the east might be
reachable from South Bay so we went off in the bathtub to find out.
Sure enough, we found what looked like traces of an esker there. We
landed and walked a mile inland to where we could see two cols
between looming rock piles. I picked one on spec, and we climbed
hopefully into it over half a mile of shattered rock and then, thank
heaven, found the esker itself. Following it down into the hidden valley
was as easy as walking along pavement, easier on the feet because the
sand was firm but soft.

Following the esker, which runs as level as a well-engineered
railway embankment, we came to a stand of spruce trees that were
veritable giants for this far north. Nestled in amongst them we found

the ruins of two logs cabins, one about twelve feet long and the other somewhat smaller.

They were very old. Nothing remained of their roofs, and the walls had collapsed. The floors were buried under a rich growth of plants. Their shape was odd – instead of being roughly square they were long and narrow, like very large grave enclosures. They made Ootek nervous. He muttered something about Ino, then retreated to the ridge of the esker, leaving me to poke around on my own. I found some very old cuts in a big spruce that looked indicative of human activity, but was uncomfortably surprised to find a fresh hole in the thin soil near one of the cabins, with dirt around it and paw prints of a big bear.

There aren't supposed to be bears around here. Too far south for the Barren Land grizzly and too far north for black bears. So what was this? I tried to get Ootek's opinion but when I called out the word akla – bear – he shook his head, shouted back something about paija, and withdrew even farther. When I joined him on the esker he acted as if he had ants in his pants. I gather paija is a singularly nasty kind of spirit.

Walking on down the esker in calm sunshine we grew hot, though a cold wind was whistling through the rock hills above us. We sat in the lee side of the esker overlooking several pretty little ponds and I took my shirt off for the first time outdoors this summer. We munched bannocks and cold chunks of fried trout for lunch. Miracle of miracles, there were no mosquitoes!

We weren't the only folk to use the esker. Along its crest, which varied from a few feet to several yards wide, was a well-worn path. Although pretty well packed down, we could find recognizable tracks here and there. Caribou, wolf, and fox, but no bear and nothing remotely human. This seemed to reassure Ootek, though he still kept a sharp look out and insisted on carrying my rifle.

We walked about five miles in that lovely place and couldn't see the *end of the valley. I'm going to be dreaming about it for a long time. A Barren Land Shangri-La! You could hide out there forever and chances are nobody would ever find you. Probably lots of meat and fish, plenty of berries, certainly the finest kind of trees for building and firewood, and a quiet neighbourhood. The sort of place where a biblical troglodyte might happily live out his days. . . .*

June is drawing to an end and Ootek and I are spending long hours at the wolf OP. We are picking up each other's lingo and I'm learning a lot about wolves and the Ihalmiut, but there's damn-all news from home. No incoming messages on the radio, or at least none we can understand. Curse the goddamn thing! If we didn't have it, we'd never miss it. But having it and unable to use it is driving us nuts. I'm for trashing it or drowning it in the river, but Andy still has faith in the Machine. He spends hours glued to it with the headphones on, though all he gets is static.

Coming home tonight I stopped the kicker in the middle of the bay and without preamble told Ootek to take over. He's never touched a motor before. His eyes bugged, but he wiggled aft, sat himself down and, repeating every movement I had made, started the kicker and we were off. I pretended unconcern as he ran us about at top speed like a teenager in a souped-up car, but he did everything just right. I'm convinced he understands that engine as well as he understands one of his sled dogs, though he's never touched a kicker before we came along. Wonder what he'd do with a Sherman tank?

It had been our original intention to establish a base at Windy River from which to study the caribou herds as they emerged from the taiga forests on their northward migration into the tundra plains. After they had passed by, and after the spring thaw had opened the lakes and rivers to canoe travel, we had planned to follow the deer north to the Ihalmiut camps, there to study the interactions between deer and people. Later, when the herds moved on to their summering grounds we had hoped to be airlifted still farther north to rejoin *la foule*.

Our late arrival at Windy, together with the lack of a suitable canoe had made nonsense of these plans. In mid-June, taking advantage of a rare opportunity when the radio seemed to be functional, I sent another SOS message on behalf of the Inuit, to which I added a request that the relief plane also bring us in a proper canoe and enough extra gas to fly us and our gear from Windy direct to Angikuni Lake.

We had heard nothing in reply but, on July 1, a strangely misshapen Norseman came thundering over Windy Bay to splash down off Cache Point. It was Gunnar's, with a seventeen-foot freighter canoe lashed to one of his plane's floats. We were in no way ready for it but we jumped into the Bathtub and hurried out to query Gunnar, who greeted us with his usual mocking grin.

"Surprise . . . surprise. You guys sure musta stirred up the shit in Ottawa. They've sent me in on special charter with a load of crap for them Huskies up on the Kazan. Huskies'll have to come down here to get it though 'cause I can't fly it on up to 'em. The drag of that fucking canoe made me burn more gas on the way in here than a hundred-mile-an-hour headwind. I'll be lucky to make it home."

"What about our trip to Angikuni?" I asked anxiously.

"Not to worry. That's laid on. Be back in a couple weeks. Right now, get your Husky pet to help unload this junk."

While Ootek put the freight ashore, Andy and I hastened back to the cabin to fetch our outbound mail. Included was a long letter I had written to the minister detailing the perilous condition of the Ihalmiut. Before sealing it, I scrawled a postscript pointing out that the relief supplies we had just received – white beans, flour, five sheet-metal stoves, a dozen galvanized iron pails, six shovels, twelve lumberjack axes, and two dozen fox and wolf traps, *but no ammunition and no fishnets* – were unlikely to solve either the immediate or the long-term problems of the Ihalmiut.

Gunnar had also brought us a bundle of personal mail which we had had no time to read before he took off on his return flight to Churchill. My share included several letters from Fran. I opened and read these as soon as I could – and felt as if I had been kicked in the stomach.

She was seriously unhappy, envisaging a future of perenial choices between accompanying me on long and arduous expeditions to the back-of-beyond or of remaining in Toronto and seeing me only in passing.

Although her letters filled me with distress and apprehension, there was nothing I could do for the moment except get myself into a state. Andy admonished me:

"You can't do damn-all to straighten things out 'til Gunnar comes back, maybe in a couple of weeks, so hustle back to your wolves and do some work."

I took this advice and immersed myself in the comings and goings of the four adult and four juvenile wolves who constituted the family at Wolf Knoll. *Their* world at least seemed to be unfolding as it should.

Soon after Gunnar's brief visit, Ootek returned to his family, to be replaced by Ohoto, who arrived at our cabin a few days later in poor shape, having eaten nothing for three days except one small, rotten sucker he had found dead beside a stream.

He brought bleak news. The migrating caribou, which by now were well north of the Kazan camps, could provide no more meat. The spawning run of fish in the rivers was coming to an end and, without kayaks, the people could not fish the lakes.

Andy and I tried our best to transmit another SOS to Churchill. When there was no indication our signals had been received, we sent Ohoto back to the Kazan camps with orders to bring the people to Windy Cabin, where we would give them all the grub we could spare and provide a canoe and nets with which they could fish Nueltin's deep waters, where lake trout and fat whitefish abounded.

On July 10 all but one of the able-bodied Ihalmiut men and youths arrived on our doorstep. They told us most of the old folk and children were now too weak to make the journey so the women had stayed behind to care for them. We also learned that Ootek's wife, Howmik, was too ill to look after the couple's sole surviving child so Ootek had chosen to remain with them.

He had, however, sent us a present – a black-and-white male puppy. Yaha delivered the scrawny little creature, explaining that, having failed to keep the rest of the litter alive on a diet of fish scales and bones, Ootek hoped *we* would be able to save this last pup's life. We named him Tegpa and fed him so much canned milk that for the first few days he threw up as much as he was able to keep down.

After a day at Windy Cabin, mostly spent eating and sleeping, all the men except Ohoto headed for home again, laden with as much of our food and fish as they could carry. As I watched them go, I was filled with fury on their behalf – and with shame, for was I not a *kablunait*, one of the invaders of their land?

In the cabin that evening I tried to explain to Ohoto how I felt. He listened in silence then, as he went off to his own small tent, touched me lightly on the arm and softly spoke a single word:

"*Ayorama*" . . . it cannot be helped.

· 20 ·

PEOPLE OF THE DEER

As I awaited Gunnar's return I had to decide whether or not to go out with him to Churchill, and perhaps on to Toronto, to deal with my personal problems and to raise what hell I could about the Ihalmiut situation.

In the end I decided not to go. As far as Frances was concerned, I hardened my heart. Surely, I thought, she could possess her soul in patience until October when we would be reunited at Brochet. To help her accept the situation, I prepared a packet of encouraging letters, journal notes, funny poems, and sketches that Gunnar could mail to her.

I also wrote a long and scathing report on the Ihalmiut situation to be forwarded by registered mail to the commissioner of the Northwest Territories.

Gunnar finally appeared (more than a week overdue) and landed with his usual panache. Although we were greatly cheered to see him, we were angry to find he had nothing for the Ihalmiut. According to his account, the Churchill RCMP detachment (which was responsible for "native administration") had received no authorization to release relief supplies.

I scribbled an angry telegram about this for Gunnar to dispatch to Ottawa. There was no time to do more since Gunnar was anxious to get us to our destination and return to his base before daylight ended.

Hastily we loaded our gear and ourselves (including an apprehensive Tegpa) aboard the Norseman. Without the least hesitation, Ohoto, whom we had persuaded to accompany us, climbed into the co-pilot's seat nodding his understanding of Gunnar's pantomimed warning not to touch any of the controls.

Overloaded with supplies for six weeks, an extra forty-five gallons of avgas for Gunnar's return to Churchill, and the new canoe lashed to the starboard float, the Norseman at first refused to fly. Roaring down the bay at full throttle, we were perilously close to the Duck Islets before Gunnar was able to rock it free of the water. I thought we were goners as we passed over the islets with only inches to spare, but Ohoto, leaning as far forward as his seatbelt would allow, was ecstatic.

"Dwoeee! *Dwoeee!*" Faster! *Faster!* he shrieked with delight.

Gunnar flew at about five hundred feet, a height from which Ohoto could see for several miles horizontally while still being able to recognize familiar detail directly below us. Under his guidance we rumbled north into a world that seemed more aquatic than terrestrial – an amoeboid water-world gleaming with uncounted lakes, streams, and rivers and pocked by varicoloured ponds, bogs, and muskegs.

We had been flying over this watery confusion for about an hour when Ohoto began bouncing in his seat. Suddenly he gave a shout we could hear even above the thunder of the engine.

"*Inuit Ku!*"

This was the great River of Men Joseph Tyrrell had known by its Chipewyan name, Kazan. But, try as we might, we three white men could not pick it out among what looked like a million glittering shards of broken mirror blindingly reflecting the light of the westering sun.

The Norseman laboured up to 2,500 feet. Despite Ohoto's anxious attempts to point us in an easterly direction, Gunnar now took a northwesterly course. From close behind Ohoto's shoulder, I watched what seemed to be a distant haze gradually become a water horizon of such magnitude it seemed oceanic.

Shaking his head in exasperation, Ohoto pointed at it:

"*Angikuni Nowk . . . No . . . Tulemaliguak!*"

Tulemaliguak was the Inuit name for the largest body of water in the Barren Lands – the vast lake we now call Dubawnt.

Gunnar glanced at the crumpled map spread across his lap.

"Could be. Look at the size of the fucker! So where the hell's Angikuni?"

When I shouted the question into Ohoto's ear he replied by jabbing a finger eastward and downward. Gunnar nodded. The plane banked in that direction and began losing altitude. Twenty minutes later Ohoto turned to me, his broad face made broader still by an enormous smile.

"There! Angikuni! The Great Lake! My people's place!"

Gunnar set the Norseman down in a little cove backed by a naked headland near which, so Ohoto proudly told us, he himself had been born.

In a tearing hurry to be rid of us, for it was growing late and he would have to find his way back to Churchill in semi-darkness, Gunnar remained in the pilot's seat, keeping the engine ticking over while the three of us launched the canoe and ferried ourselves and our gear to a tiny gravel beach.

We had not seen any Caribou during our flight and their absence had made Andy and me distinctly uneasy for, despite Ohoto's assurances that vast herds *would* appear, we could not get on with our investigations of their lives while they were absent.

While Andy and Ohoto pitched our two tents, I climbed the long slope of the brooding hill behind the cove for a closer look at the country. The view from the crest was stunning. To the north, west, and east the tundra rolled into infinity like gigantic billows in a frozen sea.

Although old caribou trails were everywhere, neither the deer nor any of their normal consorts – wolves, wolverines, ravens, gulls – were to be seen. The almighty sky was empty of wings; the glittering surface of Angikuni Lake was itself unmarred by any living being. The entire enormous panorama appeared devoid of life except for two tiny human figures and a puppy down by the cove, diminished by distance to the size of insects . . . and, ah yes . . . except for insects.

When the blessed breeze eased for an instant, a roiling mass of blackflies and mosquitoes lifted from the mosses and lichens like a rising tide and enveloped me. They were understandably insatiable because, until the deer returned, there was precious little good red blood for them to eat.

Our camp was on an ancient gravel beach fifty feet above the current level of the lake and, thankfully, exposed to every wind that could blow bugs away. The site also commanded a superb view over Angikuni's principal southwestern bay, and of a great lumpen hill called Kinetua several miles to the westward, from which the people who once lived here had taken their local name, Kinetuamiut.

We anchored our large wall tent and one-man pup tent with heavy stones for it was impossible to drive stakes into the rocky and permanently frozen ground. The big tent, which had a more-or-less bug-proof door, became a refuge for all of us and provided sleeping quarters for Andy, me, and Tegpa. By his own decision, and for reasons he did not reveal, Ohoto chose to sleep in the pup tent.

Nearby we built a stone fireplace for use when the flies permitted and when we could scrounge enough twigs, moss, and berry bushes for fuel. Otherwise we cooked inside the big tent on a stinking, roaring gasoline stove whose fumes the blackflies could not tolerate.

Because Barren Lands lakes are subject to ferocious and almost instant storms, we took particular care of our precious canoe, hauling it well above high-water mark and lashing it down to heavy boulders.

In the absence of caribou and wolves I tried to discover what I could about the Kinetuamiut. When Tyrrell arrived among them half a century earlier, they had been so numerous they had given his two canoes an escort of *twenty-three* kayaks. His sketch map of Kinetua Bay showed five "camps" on its northern shore.

Rather reluctantly Ohoto accompanied me on my first exploration, which was to the nearby cove where he had been born. At first I could see nothing to indicate that the grassy bench behind the beach had ever been occupied by human beings. Then Ohoto peeled some moss away from what proved to be a ring of boulders twenty feet in diameter that had once anchored a deerskin *topay* – a tent.

The topay which had once stood here had belonged, Ohoto said, to his grandfather Utuwiak and both Ohoto and his father had been born in it. Poking around the rest of the site I found seven more tent circles, all apparently of about the same age. Together they may have housed fifty or sixty people.

Where had all the people gone? What had become of them?

I turned to Ohoto, but he was not his usual helpful self. He would tell me nothing except to mutter a few words about "the great dying." And he was very anxious to be gone from this place of his ancestors. When I started scratching around inside one of the circles, he abruptly abandoned me and trotted off toward our own camp, paying no attention to my attempts to persuade him to return.

Annoyed, I continued on alone around the shore of the bay past a series of paired stone pillars that had once supported kayaks and came upon an even more extensive settlement site of more than two dozen tent rings, some as much as twenty-four feet in diameter. The tents raised over them must have been the size of small houses.

This camp was protected on the landward northern side by massive granite outcrops frost-fractured into a chaos of angular fragments and studded with odd-looking protuberances. When I climbed up to investigate these I found they were rock-built graves. Although originally roofed with flat stones, many had been opened by wild weather and wild animals. Human skulls gaped up at me from the mossy depths of some.

Unnerved by so many dead (I counted thirty-one clearly recognizable graves among many more reduced to mere piles of rocky rubble), I returned to our outpost, but found little comfort there. Andy had just returned from a long trek across the plains to the north and gloomily reported having seen neither caribou nor recent signs of any. Ohoto was in a despondent mood from which he emerged only long enough to assure me he would not go near any more old encampments of his people. Tegpa alone seemed cheerful, and it was in his company that I continued my attempt to discover what I could about the empty camps – and the full graves.

Although examining the graves was an unsettling and unsavoury business, I hoped the tools, weapons, and ornaments placed in them for the use of their occupants in the afterlife might be revealing of how these people had lived.

One thing was evident: they had not suffered from any shortage of material goods. Many well-made hunting and household artefacts of flint, soapstone, bone, and wood, together with trade goods including guns, iron snow-knives, steel hatchets and knives, and copper cooking pots accompanied most of the dead.

The majority appeared to have perished during one relatively brief period. The first to go had been buried in well-constructed graves farthest from the camp and provided with ample grave goods. Later victims had been interred ever closer to the tent circles, in increasingly makeshift graves, and with fewer grave goods. The last burials hardly deserved the name. One that I literally stumbled across was no more than a jumble of human bones (of an adult and a child) scattered *within* one of the tent rings, suggesting that no one from this tent had survived to bury them.

Starvation could hardly have been the killer since the many stone-built meat caches sealed with heavy rocks standing in and around the camp were full of animal bones, suggesting that the meat which had once clothed them had gone uneaten except by worms.

Neither was there any indication of assault by other human beings. The bones of the dead were not broken or cut, nor had the graves been pillaged. Furthermore, kayaks and dog sleds (among the most precious possessions of the deer people) had not been taken. I found the decayed remnants of at least seven kayaks crumpled between stone pillars that had once raised them out of harm's way.

The evidence was unequivocal – many people had once lived around the shore of Kinetua Bay.

Now there were none.

In the mid-eighteenth century, when Europeans first began exploiting the central Canadian Arctic, the Barren Lands were home to inland-dwelling Inuit who had very little knowledge of or congress with the sea and with Inuit whose way of life was dependent on sea mammals. The inland people relied almost exclusively on caribou.

These people bore a number of tribal names but shared a common way of life vigorously and successfully maintained until 1867, when Father Gasté, a Roman Catholic priest of the Oblate order, set out by dog sled from a mission at Reindeer Lake to proselytize "some pagan savages" whose existence in the Barren Lands to the northward he had heard about from some of his mission Indians.

Gasté persuaded some of the latter to guide him to the headwaters of the Kazan River. There they encountered a group of "Esquimaux living more than three hundred miles from the sea where is the natural home of this people." Although the "Esquimaux" were friendly and hospitable, Gasté was quite unable to interest them in Christianity. Defeated, he retreated back into the forests, happy to have escaped from the "Barren Lands, that dreadful wilderness."

Although he himself never again ventured to the Kazan, Gasté's visit resulted in a trade link being established between the inland Inuit and the outer world. A few of the most enterprising Ihalmiut began daring the two-hundred-mile winter journey south through mostly Indian territory to trade white fox furs with the mission or at a Hudson's Bay Company post of Reindeer Lake.

Contact had been established; nevertheless, the world of the Ihalmiut remained essentially unaltered. Only a few Ihalmiut of each generation undertook the long and arduous journey south and, until just before the turn of the nineteenth century, no white strangers followed Gasté north.

Then, in 1894, Joseph Tyrrell and his Iroquois canoeman came paddling down the Kazan.

Tyrrell was astonished to find twenty-three populous villages (he called them "camps") on the river's upper reaches. In his official reports he estimated the big, conical skin tents in these camps were then home to five or six hundred Eskimos. However, shortly before his death in 1949 he told me he believed that at the time he came among them the Eskimos of the Dubawnt and Kazan systems together may have numbered *as many as two thousand* men, women, and children.

Confirmation of that estimate exists in the reports of another

Oblate missionary, Father Turquetil, who between 1901 and 1906 ventured into the Barren Lands from the west coast of Hudson Bay and made brief contact with the Ihalmiut. Turquetil estimated that "850 souls" then lived along the Kazan and that the inland Eskimos of Keewatin numbered between one and two thousand.

In their heyday these people of the deer may have constituted the most numerous and cohesive Inuit group anywhere on earth. Unlike their coastal-dwelling relatives they were *not* nomads but a people of relatively settled residence, mostly at or near major caribou routes and crossing places where huge herds of *tuktu* regularly *came to them.*

As wealth was measured in Inuit society, the inland dwellers were rich and, for the most part, blessed with all they required in the way of food, clothing, and shelter. Fleet kayaks and sturdy dog sleds enabled them to travel swiftly almost anywhere they chose, at any season. The summers of the Long Day were times of leisure and abundance. The winters, far from being times of dread and hardship, provided opportunities for feasting, story-telling, dancing, singing, and love-making.

Above all, they possessed an abundance of that most precious of commodities – time itself. They had ample time to remember their past, to celebrate who and what they were, to dream, to work with words and thoughts, and to play.

Despite living in what *we* might consider extreme discomfort – even bitter adversity – *they* appear to have been well content.

Such was the world of the Ihalmiut in the second decade of the twentieth century, when the Great Dying came upon them.

Death burst out of an Ihalmio returning from a trading trip to Reindeer Lake and leapt from camp to camp along the Kazan with appalling swiftness, emptying the topays and filling many graves. By the time the caribou returned that spring much of the Ihalmiut country had been virtually denuded of human kind.

Word of what had happened was slow to reach the outside world. Not until two years later did Father Turquetil, in charge of a mission at Chesterfield Inlet, learn that a burning and fatal fever (which he thought might have been influenza) had decimated the inland people. He estimated that "between five and six hundred Esquimaux of the interior perished in this great dying."

Some of the Ihalmiut survivors sought sanctuary where the Kazan debouches out of Ennadai. But the Kazan River – Inuit Ku, the River of Men – was now a river of the dead.

The survivors of the Great Dying knew only brief respite. By the turn of the twentieth century white fox pelts had become the white gold of the north and when it was discovered that the so-called Barren Lands were inhabited by multitudes of white foxes a tide of *kablunait* trappers flooded in. By 1920 some had reached Ennadai and the Kazan.

These interlopers were servants of commercial behemoths that battened on fur. Now the Ihalmiut became serfs to the servants. They found themselves impelled, if not compelled, to spend the bulk of their time and energy killing inedible little animals which they then exchanged for high-powered rifles and other marvels that vastly increased their ability to kill caribou.

The white trappers penetrating the Barren Lands typically ran traplines of enormous length (a hundred miles was not exceptional), servicing them with teams of up to fifteen huskies. One such team could consume an entire caribou carcass every day or two. In addition, the bait used for trapping foxes, wolves, and other furbearers was almost always caribou. *And* the trappers fed themselves and their dependants on caribou. During the peak period of the white fox bonanza many Barren Land and taiga trappers routinely slaughtered four or five hundred caribou a year: a profligate butchery of large mammals on a scale not seen upon this continent since the virtual extinction of the prairie bison.

Little wonder that the river of life which had sustained the peoples of taiga and tundra since time immemorial began drying up.

The harried deer abandoned ancestral migration routes and their behaviour became so erratic it was difficult to know where, and when, the remnant herds might be encountered. During the autumn of 1924, only a scattered few caribou came within reach of the remaining Ihalmiut. And that winter one outpost trader recorded the deaths from starvation of fifty of "his" Inuit. As many as two hundred others are thought to have perished along the Kazan and Thelon rivers that same hungry winter.

The diminution of the caribou and the disruption of their age-old migration patterns struck a deadly blow at indigenous human life both in the northern forests and on the Barren Lands. The Inuit (and Chipewyans) became more and more dependent on the fur trade for survival. Then, in the late 1920s, the already beleaguered world of the Ihalmiut was invaded by a new and singularly rapacious wave of white trappers.

The new intruders seldom employed steel traps, which were expensive, heavy to transport, and cumbersome to use. They preferred poison. Every autumn they would slaughter caribou over as large an area as possible, and later seed the far-flung carcasses with strychnine or arsenic.

Some white trappers preyed even more directly on the Inuit by engrossing native traplines, robbing native meat caches, and, in general, taking whatever they pleased, including women.

One such white trapper entered the camp of Igluardjuak (one of Ohoto's uncles) and at gun point took a dog team, a sled, and Igluardjuak's wife. Doubtless he believed the "huskies" would not dare retaliate. Next day Igluardjuak borrowed a team and drove off into the winter darkness. He returned several days later with his wife, the stolen team, and the sled. He never spoke of what he had done during his absence but when spring came the bloated body of the white trapper was found bobbing among the melting ice pans on Ennadai Lake.

Roaming at will over the Barrens, white trappers took most of the available fur, leaving little to sustain the people of the deer who had now become trappers themselves. The caribou slaughter continued unabated. During the decade following the First World War the Inuit population of the entire Canadian Barren Lands fell well below four hundred, of whom perhaps a hundred and fifty were Ihalmiut.

When in 1929 the Great Depression overwhelmed most of the Western world, white fox pelts became virtually worthless. Most free traders decamped, as did the majority of white trappers. Many outposts, even of such old established trading firms as the Hudson's Bay Company, were abandoned.

The Ihalmiut became people of the dole. And it proved woefully insufficient to hold body and soul together.

Although the remaining Ihalmiut now retained unchallenged possession of their country, its nature had been fatally changed. The seemingly infinite multitudes of caribou had been savagely diminished. The silken fur of the white fox fur could no longer provide a substitute. Famine and disease became almost permanent residents in the few remaining Ihalmiut camps.

At the beginning of the Second World War, the Ihalmiut numbered just 139 men, women, and children.[*] During the ensuing five years, even these few disappeared from the peripheral vision of the outside world. If anyone in authority gave the Ihalmiut a thought, it was to assume they had become "non-existent."

---

[*] Many of these population figures are derived from old records kept by Hudson's Bay Company post managers (some of which I myself found at an abandoned post); from diaries and other documents kept by the Schweders; and from interviews with surviving Ihalmiut in 1947 and 1948 and during subsequent visits to the region.

The assumption was not far from the reality. During the autumn and winter of 1943, forty-four Ihalmiut starved to death. During the summer of 1946, the survivors were smitten by what may have been diphtheria and fourteen children and young adults died. That winter, twelve more perished of starvation.

By the time Andy and I came to Kinetua Bay, only forty-seven Ihalmiut still survived in all the wide reaches of a land that had once been vividly alive with men and deer.

ᛌ 21 ᛌ

THE WESTERN WATER WAY

The continuing absence of caribou had made us very restive. Ohoto had taken to spending most of the daylight hours roaming the tundra far to the northwest, from which direction, so he doggedly continued to assert, tuktu would soon come. Although Andy and I certainly hoped he was right, all we really knew was that great herds had come this way in times past. While descending the Dubawnt River in 1893, Joseph and James Tyrrell had met no caribou until July 30 when, about seventy miles east of where we now were, they had been engulfed by multitudes of southbound deer.

James later wrote:

"There were so many great bands, literally covering the country over wide areas, that the valleys and the hillsides for miles appeared to be moving masses of caribou . . . whose numbers could only be reckoned in square miles."

Joseph, leader of the expedition, conservatively estimated the numbers seen that day at between one and two hundred thousand.

On returning from one of his fruitless overland quests, Ohoto suggested we break camp and travel west, where we would surely meet great herds streaming south past Tulemaliguak (Dubawnt Lake).

Andy and I were easily persuaded. We had kept company with the dead at Kinetua Bay long enough and, caribou aside, I very much wanted to explore the unknown and unmapped country lying between Angikuni and Dubawnt. Furthermore, we were all four of us ravenously meat-hungry.

We set off on July 26 hoping to find a water route to the westward but with no real idea where to look. All we could do was hold as close as possible to the island-shrouded shore of Angikuni in hopes of coming upon a river flowing in from the west.

The morning of our departure was calm, hot, and seething with flies as anxious for the return of the deer as we were. They had been making life hell for us, especially for Tegpa, whose almost-naked little belly was so badly bitten that I sometimes carried him under my summer parka when we went walking. This amused Ohoto, who claimed it confirmed the Inuit belief that white men and dogs had the same mother.

We left the big tent and much of our gear behind, taking with us the small tent; one gun; a few pots and pans; a trolling line; and a grub box containing ten pounds of canned bacon (our "fat" supply), a bag of flour, some baking powder, tea, and sugar.

With everything aboard, we pushed off and I tried to start our shiny new outboard motor. It at first refused to go, and when it finally did kick over, pissed a stream of gas into the canoe through a hole in the fuel tank.

While Andy and Ohoto paddled manfully to distance us from the pursuing cloud of flies, I dismantled the tank, found the leak, and plugged it with a wad of chewing gum. Then, under a blazing sun, we fled the flies until we found ourselves entering another of Angikuni's great bays.

This one was so obscured by points, islands, and shimmering mirages it was impossible to make sense out of it. Like rats in a maze we poked around, never knowing whether distant shores were the mainland or more islands, or whether the next opening was a strait or the mouth of the river we hoped to find.

During my long canoe journeys with Charles Schweder the previous year, he had taught me how to "read water." Now as we threaded our way through the tangle of islands I kept watching for any indication of current. In mid-afternoon I found what I was looking for: a barely discernible slick in a channel between two of the innumerable islands. We followed this slick into a masked narrows where an actual current became visible, leading us toward a barren island upon whose crest squatted a stone beacon – an *inuksuak* – semblance of a man.

Passing close below this evidence that other human beings had passed this way, we spotted a strange anomaly on the shore of an island to the northward. It turned out to be an enormous cast-iron cook stove complete with floral castings and nickel-plated ornaments. The presence of such a fuel-guzzling monster here in the heart of the treeless barrens seemed an absolute absurdity. Andy and I were baffled but Ohoto thought he knew the answer.

He deduced that this rusting giant had been the property of a legendary and long-since-dead Kinetuamiut shaman named Kakumee who, many decades earlier, had made a famous winter journey out to the coast of Hudson Bay, where he had met and traded fox pelts with white men. These men may have been traders, but were as likely to have been Yankee whalers wintering aboard their ships. Whoever they were, their affluence so impressed Kakumee that he decided to become an equally Big Man in his own country.

Either through trade or as salvage from a wrecked whaler, he acquired this massive symbol of *kablunait* wealth and set out to cart it home on his dog sled until, caught by the spring thaw, he had been forced to cache the stove where we had found it. As to why he had never returned for it, Ohoto offered no explanation.

It was a momentous find for us since it indicated the existence of a travel route to the westward. When we climbed to the peak of the island and looked west, we saw the glitter of rapids marking the mouth of a river which Ohoto thought might be one he had heard about in his childhood but had never seen – one that could be followed to Dubawnt Lake.

We headed for the river mouth with high expectations and found it clogged with boulders. Indeed, its lower reaches seemed to consist of an almost continuous shallow rapid, impassable to a canoe the size of ours.

When I asked Ohoto the name of this aquatic obstacle course, he told me *Kuwee* – Little River. At which I said to Andy:

"*Little?* It's no bigger than a goddamn sewer. We haven't a hope in hell of getting up *it* to Dubawnt!"

I was wrong. We managed to scrabble up its formidable lower reaches in ice-cold water, towing the canoe as we waded hip-deep, slipping and falling on mossy rocks and batting hopelessly at clouds of mosquitoes and blackflies.

After hours of this torment, we thankfully emerged into a stretch deep enough to float the canoe. This eventually brought us to the shore of a vast watery maze which stretched thirty or more miles to the northward, cradling an indescribable confusion of islands, points, channels and bays and sprawled across an area that, on our map, showed only blank white space.

What I wrote about it in my journal that night may have been somewhat overblown:

To be off-the-map is as thrilling though as disconcerting as peering into the core of some primeval world through a hole in the veil of time and place. I feel irresistibly drawn but scared silly. Like a dumb little dickey bird facing a hungry snake.

Because Ohoto had no personal knowledge of this new water-world and we had no map to guide us, we could only guess which way to go. Where, along hundreds of miles of convoluted shores masked by unnumbered islands, twists, and turns were we to re-discover Kuwee?

The day was almost over and sensibly we should have camped for the night and made our decision in the morning. However, even my usually cautious partner seemed to have been infected by the explorer's itch.

"Hell's bells," said Andy cheerfully. "There's open water stretching west from right where we're at. Let's just go see what's on the other side."

We were in the middle of a broad opening in this unknown lake when a vicious nor'wester struck us. Within minutes the canoe was shipping so much water that even with Andy and Ohoto bailing furiously we could barely keep afloat. I was kept busy trying to protect the engine from flying spray for, had it stalled, we could easily have broached into waves breaking four or five feet high.

Somehow we managed to claw up upon a gravel reef partway across the big opening. But the waves pounded the canoe ferociously upon the reef and we were forced to drag her over, launch her on the other side, and again take our chances in open water.

We were near to sinking by the time we clawed our way into a cove on the western shore. There, finally, was a deep, vigorous rapid. Surmounting it, we looked around and saw not one but *three* inuksuak ranged along the ice-scoured bank above us.

Tegpa scrambled ashore desperate to relieve himself. Ohoto followed, waving his paddle at the inuksuak in greeting, or perhaps in gratitude. We had found Kuwee again. Or Kuwee had found us.

We camped below the inuksuak that night and they were very much on my mind as I went to sleep. Those little piles of stones (no more than slight realignments of the bones of the land itself) reassured us that other men had passed this way. Where they had gone, we too would go.

Next morning we ascended Kuwee under power. Using a kicker for upstream canoe work can be exciting. The motor has to be run at full throttle to keep the canoe fish-tailing up an unseen incline into a surging torrent. Should the engine fail or the propeller strike a rock and shear a pin, the canoe is likely to be swept broadside and capsized among the river rocks.

We made painfully slow progress. When we halted for the night, cold and soaking from struggling with the river, Andy and I warmed up by climbing a hill to see what we could see.

We were awed to behold, some miles to the west, a mighty expanse of open water stretching to the horizon.

Could this be Tulemaliguak?

We hurried back to camp to ask Ohoto. He could not identify our discovery for he had never seen Tulemaliguak himself. "*Imaha*" – perhaps – was the best he could offer.

It rained that night and next morning, and the chill air carried a warning that frost would soon be whitening the tundra. A peculiar inertia seemed to settle over us. Tegpa kept his nose under his curled tail, refusing even to open an eye to greet me as I crawled out of my sleeping bag. Andy and Ohoto were taciturn and seemed depressed. As for me, I had slipped into a mire of black thoughts about my marriage. Perhaps we were all in the grip of the oppressive realization of just how alone we were.

The desire to reach the big lake and our hopes of finding the vanguard of the great herds put us back on the river. Rapids followed rapids. Most were too shallow and shoal-filled to allow us to use the kicker, so we turned to lining – breasting the current while hauling on a tow rope – to drag the canoe inch by inch up interminable runs and chutes against an implacable torrent. Andy and I were wearing rubber-soled boots, which gave us traction and some protection for our feet so we did most of the river work. Ohoto, who had only moccasin-like deerskin *kamikpak* – thin as chamois – kept pace along the shore, holding a line made fast to the bow with which to take the strain in case we slipped and the river began to sweep the canoe away. To Andy's and my own amusement, Tegpa elected to ride in the canoe.

"Inuit dogs pull man," Ohoto remarked a trifle grimly. "*Kablunait* men pull dog."

Progress was painfully slow as we battled a series of heavy rapids. One of these included a chute through which the constricted river flowed too furiously to permit lining up it. We hauled the canoe ashore, and while I went off to look for a portage Andy and Ohoto fished the pool below the rapid, using hooks baited with bits of shiny tin cut from an empty can. Up to this point we had seen no sign of fish in Kuwee and had no idea what we might catch, but we were not about to be choosy. We were tired of flour-and-water bannocks and ready to eat anything with flesh on it.

My search for a portage route took me across a vast bog sloping almost imperceptibly upward. Squelching along, I eventually reached the shore of a lake whose size unnerved me, as did its emptiness. I saw no evidence of life – not even a high-flying gull. The only sound was the threatening mutter of Kuwee's rapids far behind me.

Looking back, I could see we had been crossing an enormous basin extending out of sight to the north, east, and west, but bounded on the south by high land resembling a distant shore. We did not know it then but we had been travelling across the remnants of an inland sea that a mere ten thousand years earlier had been filled to overflowing by glacial meltwater.

Intimidated by the magnitude of this world of rock and water, I slogged back to the canoe, to find my companions had caught no fish. According to Ohoto, the river spirits were not pleased with us. He seemed so sure of this that Andy and I accepted his demand that we pitch camp for the night. It was the right decision. Early next morning Ohoto gladdened our hearts and stomachs by hauling a ten-pound lake trout out of the pool below the rapid. Roasted over a small fire of moss and willow twigs, it made a splendid breakfast.

With full bellies and restored optimism we returned to the river which now became a veritable *chevaux de frise*, not of iron spikes but of frost-riven boulders through which even a seal would have had trouble finding a passage. Resignedly we hauled the canoe ashore and began a long portage across the saturated tundra. Eventually we reached the shore of the great lake we had earlier seen, to find it surrounded by a palisade of boulders ten to twenty feet high bulldozed from the bottom by massive ice floes driven ashore by spring storms.

We got the canoe and gear over this barrier and set off under power to coast the northern shore, staying in the lee of the rock dyke for we had not forgotten the malignant wind that had struck us a few days earlier. The height of the dyke almost completely concealed the land to the north, giving me a disquieting sensation of being at the edge of the world, though far to the south we could see smudges on the horizon which could have been either islands or mainland.

During the next two days we found only five breaks in the rocky barrier where we could safely beach the canoe. When we did get ashore, we were dismayed by the bleak aspect of the wastes beyond. All the Others seemed to have abandoned this part of the world. Most ominously, the tundra was unmarred by the intricate network of deer trails imprinted almost everywhere else across the Barren Lands.

Andy and I both became so oppressed by the feeling of being sucked into a lifeless void that we were independently contemplating a retreat to Angikuni, though neither of us was willing to voice his fears aloud. As for Ohoto, he had almost ceased to talk. As time drew on, he withdrew so far into himself as to be virtually unreachable. Our sojourn in a land that even the deer seemed to avoid was plunging him into deep depression.

One day we were hit by a fearsome squall that almost instantly whipped the lake to white fury and might have smashed the canoe had we not been lucky enough to find a break in the boulder dyke through which we could haul her up to safety. Leaving Ohoto to pitch camp, Andy and I set off on foot seeking a vantage point from which to get our bearings. No prominent hills were within reach but the ground sloped slightly upward away from our camp. After squelching across it for several miles, we finally opened a view to the north and west.

We could see now that the shore of the lake we had been travelling upon curved away to a range of shadowy highlands far to the south, and that only a narrow isthmus separated our lake from what seemed to be its twin to the west. Both lakes were big, but not big enough to be the one we sought. However, in the far distant northwest we could just discern what appeared to be a watery expanse so vast it had to be Dubawnt – the Inuit's Tulemaliguak.

Hurrying back to camp we found Ohoto had killed a *sic-sic* – a ground squirrel – and was boiling it up with rice for dinner. Although the little creature weighed no more than a pound or two, it was the first fresh meat we had had for many days and it raised our spirits.

We were elated, too, when Ohoto concluded that the enormous body of water to the northwest had to be Tulemaliguak. Furthermore, he also concluded that the lake we were on must be the one known

as Nowleye, and its close companion was Kamilikuak which drained
into Tulemaliguak.

Coasting Nowleye's northwestern shore we happily watched the
rock dykes fade away revealing the nature of the land beyond. We
were delighted to find it reticulated and patterned by a multitude of
caribou trails, both old and new, and to see real trees at both ends
of the narrow isthmus separating the twin lakes. There were not many
trees, nor were they large, but they tempted us to go ashore where we
soon had a big and wasteful fire crackling and the tea pail boiling.

The strip of land separating Nowleye from Kamilikuak extended
from north to south for six or seven miles and at its narrowest point
was about a mile wide. It was the only dry land between the Kazan
and Dubawnt river systems.

This low and boggy isthmus was a natural causeway across
which migrating caribou had funnelled during their great annual
treks spanning countless millennia. In many places their passing
had churned the peaty soil to mire and worn ruts down to deeply
scarred bedrock.

Ohoto was ecstatic at the sight of the tangle of tuktu trails.

"Kinetuamiut often talked about this place – the deer's way. My
father, Elaitutna, came here many times as his father had done, and
his father, because tuktu never failed to come here too, travelling
between the salt water in the north and the forests in the south.

"Soon, they will come again. . . ."

· 22 ·

MASTER OF THE
BARREN LANDS

We pitched our tent on a slight rise in the middle of the isthmus –
a vantage point from which Kamilikuak stretched westward to the
horizon, bounded by high hills to the south and rock-strewn plains
to the north. The southern portion looked less forbidding so we
launched the canoe on it and set off to explore.

We stayed close to shore. This vast lake was clearly no place to
be caught out upon by one of the country's instant gales. An hour's
easy paddle brought us to the mouth of a deep bay on whose eastern
shore we came upon a sandy beach dominated by three tall wooden
columns standing like bizarre sentries. We landed beneath a trio of
rough-hewn pillars. Each was about a foot square, ten or twelve feet
tall, with a prominent V-shaped notch cut across its top.

I turned to Ohoto for an explanation, but he had nothing to
offer, apart from assuring us the columns were not his people's

work. We were all puzzled. These wardens of the beach looked like nothing we were familiar with except for a loose resemblance to uncarved Pacific coast totem poles.

They were guarding the mouth of a valley behind the beach. We ventured into it along an overgrown trail that led us to the largest trees any of us had ever encountered in the Barren Lands – some of them forty or fifty feet tall and two feet in diameter. We found a number of stumps, but of the felled trees there was no sign until we emerged into a cleared area of high ground and were faced by six even more imposing columns.

These towered twenty or more feet high and must have extended another three or four feet into the sandy soil of the ancient esker. They had been roughly squared with an axe and, like the smaller ones on the beach, each had a deep V-shaped notch cut across its top. Four of these massive pillars stood as corner posts of a rectangular space enclosing a ruined structure that looked to me like some kind of habitation, but which Ohoto feared was a grave.

The remaining two columns were sited in front of the enclosure. Inside were the remains of a log cabin whose walls and roof had collapsed to form a dense layer of broken scantlings, rotted sphagnum moss, and the hair and fragments of skin from uncured deer hides.

Ohoto watched nervously from a safe distance as Andy and I poked about in the debris. We identified the remains of a pole bed, a rough-hewn plank table, a broken chair contrived from caribou antlers, a rusty sheet-iron stove, and a battered trunk. Weather and wolverines seemed to have destroyed almost everything else except a few tins containing remnants of flour, rice, and tea. The trunk was broken, and its contents had been reduced to a jumble of water-soaked and mouse-ravelled cloth and paper. Nearby we found a glass Mason jar still firmly sealed and half full of white powder.

Andy cautiously tasted the contents – spat vigorously – and announced it was arsenic, the mainstay of Barren Lands white trappers.

Our interest in rooting about in the debris cooled when we turned up a well-chewed long bone that *might* have come from a caribou but which bore an ominous similarity to a human tibia. Memories of the Kinetuamiut cemeteries at Angikuni flooded back upon me and by unspoken agreement we withdrew from the wreckage of what had apparently been one man's transient, but maybe final, home.

An ominous haze in the western sky and the first skirl of wind gave notice that a storm was brewing. Turning our backs on the inscrutable sentries, we launched the canoe and hurried to regain the security of our camp before the storm could break.

My first real lead to a solution of this mystery surfaced forty-five years later when I heard that Charles Schweder, my companion and mentor in 1947 during my first major venture into the Barren Lands, had died, and shortly afterwards one of his relatives sent me several little black notebooks in which Charles had kept a perfunctory record of his life.

Leafing through these I came across the following entry for January 16, 1946.

> *Been gone from home* [Windy Cabin] *ten days and come to end of my trapline. Got 32 foxes so far two eat by Wolverine. Short of dog feed so have to turn back. Wish I could go on because pretty near the place Eskimo Charley supposed to hide hisself away. Sure would like to seen it and what its like.*

Reading this, I recalled that somewhere in my files I had a sketch map of Charles Schweder's trapline. On a hunch I dug it out. Beginning at Windy Camp, a dotted line meandered northward to an unnamed lake forty miles south of the cryptic wooden pillars Andy, Ohoto, and I had come upon on the shore of Kamilikuak.

Forty miles was an easy day's sled travel. Could Eskimo Charley – a legendary Barren Lands trapper about whom I had heard many strange stories – have been responsible for the strange structures we had found?

The search for an answer to this question would involve me in a ten-year quest that ranged from central Europe, west and north to Alaska, then east across the top of the world to the Keewatin Barren Lands, south to the Gulf of Mexico, north again up the Atlantic coast to Montreal, and finally back to the Barrens.

I was able to discover little enough about the early part of Eskimo Charley's story. The bare bones seemed to be that, about 1885, a boy by the name of Janez Planinshek was born on a farm in Slovenia. While still in his teens, he set out to make his fortune in the New World. Arriving in New York in classic immigrant fashion without money, friends, or prospects, he worked his way across the United States to San Francisco. Then, following the lure of gold, he went north to Alaska, where he was charged with being an accomplice in a murder.

He fled across the unmarked border to Herschel Island in the Canadian Arctic, where he signed on as a deckhand aboard a Yankee whaler. The old wooden vessel carried him a thousand perilous miles eastward in arctic waters until it drove ashore and was wrecked near the mouth of the Back River.

Most of the crew apparently made their way back to Herschel in the ship's frail whaleboats but Charley (as Janez now called himself) chose to remain behind (or perhaps was left behind) in the territory of the Back River Inuit, where he was the sole intruder from the white man's world.

Slightly built, Charley's narrow face was dominated by his fierce black eyes. In the words of an old fellow Keewatin trapper, "he was a queer-looking bird. Make your flesh creep if you looked at him too long. Tough as a wolf trap and just as touchy! Nobody couldn't get close to him. Not that many wanted to."

Charley Planinshek seemed to make a point of avoiding human beings – unless he could impose his will upon them, something he was more successful in doing with native people than with his own kind. Charley spent about a year imposing upon the Utkuhikilingmiut (Soapstone People) of the Back River. When his welcome there began to grow perilously thin, he commandeered a dog team and drove two hundred miles south and west to try his luck among the Thelon River Inuit, who were neighbours and relatives of the Kazan River Ihalmiut.

Here Charley struck gold – white gold, in the form of pelts from arctic foxes – and became a Barren Lands trapper. He took to his new trade with enthusiasm, helping himself to foxes caught in traps set by the Inuit and on occasion taking over their entire traplines by threatening to loose evil spirits on the owners and their families.

He next appeared in the taiga/tundra border country, which constituted a kind of no man's land between the Ihalmiut and the northern Idthen Eldeli. Charley built a cabin in the thinly forested country, near a smaller lake that still bears his name, between Kasba and Ennadai. Here he set about making himself something of a middleman between the outer world and the Ihalmiut and Idthen Eldeli.

He succeeded in doing this through threats, bribery, and violence – including shooting the natives' dogs so the people could not transport their furs to distant trading posts and by shooting at least one Ihalmio who refused to let Charley do his trading for him.

Charley "bought" pelts for whatever value he chose to put upon them and sold them to legitimate trading companies farther south for whatever the traffic would bear. An astute businessman, he also ran his own extensive traplines. He seldom set steel traps, preferring to use strychnine and arsenic, which killed anything and everything that took the bait, including ravens, eagles, wolves, foxes, dogs belonging to the natives, and, on occasion, starving human beings. He was not at all perturbed by the fact that, before succumbing, his victims were often able to drag themselves so far away from the bait stations that they were lost to him. In those times fur-bearers were still so abundant that such losses did not signify.

Charley did very well until the collapse of fur prices during the Great War reduced white gold to dross. By then Eskimo Charley, as he had now become known to his own kind, had done so well he could afford to take a prolonged holiday in the forested country of the Cree peoples some three hundred miles to the south of Charley's Lake.

Here he found himself a young Cree woman and here he encountered and established a wary relationship with Fred Schweder, father of my friend Charles Schweder.

Engaging in a variety of shadowy, not to say shady, enterprises, Eskimo Charley stayed "down south" until the Great War came to an end and the value of white fox pelts began to recover. Then he went back to the "real north" and openly set himself up as a free-trader in opposition to such long-established firms as the Hudson's Bay Company. He did this to such effect that the HBC, the greatest commercial power in the Canadian North, proscribed him, and Charley found himself blacklisted at most legitimate trading posts in Keewatin Territory and the adjacent northern regions of Saskatchewan and Manitoba.

Although the mercenary details of the struggle were of little interest to me, I was fascinated by the rumours and legends that swirled around Eskimo Charley as, during the 1920s, he abandoned all pretence of living within the law – within *any* law except his own – and tried to turn the world of the Ihalmiut into what amounted to his own personal fiefdom.

By the middle of the decade he was such a scourge to the remaining People of the Deer (Ihalmiut and Idthen Eldeli), taking from them whatever he wanted, including fur, food, and women, that it had become only a question of when and how they would rid themselves of him. They tried setting fire to his outpost cabins. When this failed, he and his dog team were lured onto dangerous ice in a narrows of the Kazan River from which he made a hair's-breadth escape that was taken as indisputable evidence he really did possess occult powers. Finally Ooliebuk, an Ihalmio whose wife and daughter Charley had sexually abused, took a shot at him. The bullet missed.

Not long afterwards the bodies of Ooliebuk and one of his cousins were found on the shore of Ennadai Lake. Both had been shot.

Charley withdrew into the Cree country south of Reindeer Lake, where he spent the next several years sustaining himself and his several children (whose mother had died) "by hook and by crook" while gestating the most grandiose enterprise of his entire life.

Eskimo Charley was ready to set out on a journey he believed would win him immortal fame, and a fortune. Together with Frank O'Grady, a recently arrived, impressionable, young Irish immigrant, Charley proposed to make a canoe-and-dog-sled journey south from the Arctic Circle to Cuba and the Tropic of Capricorn.

The Expedition from Arctic to Tropic, as Charley called it, was to include two of his two children – eight-year-old Inez and six-year-old Tony – together with four Eskimo sled dogs. Transport was to consist of an eighteen-foot canoe and a fifteen-foot dog sled, either of which could carry the other.

In March of 1929, the expedition left Chesterfield Inlet on the frozen shore of Hudson Bay with the canoe lashed on top of the sled to serve as a carriage for the children, luggage, and supplies. The two men took turns breaking trail for the dogs or, when the going was good, walked or ran behind the sled.

It was late June before the ice melted sufficiently to let them launch the canoe. Loading the sled and dogs aboard they paddled south and east to Lake Winnipeg and up the Red River to its headwaters where the dogs again came into play, hauling the canoe over land on a sled temporarily fitted with old bicycle wheels, to the Mississippi, down which they paddled to New Orleans and into the Gulf of Mexico.

They followed the Gulf coast east to Florida but, concluding it would be pushing their luck to attempt a canoe crossing to Cuba, went to the Bahamas, landing at Nassau to complete an outward voyage of some eight thousand miles.

En route they had staged shows in church halls, schools, small theatres, barns, anywhere a paying audience could be assembled – shows that included performances by *Two Eskimo Children in Full Native Costume and Four Huge Arctic Wolf-Dogs*. The star was *That Renowned Northern Explorer, Baron Charles Planinshek*, whom O'Grady always introduced as "The Master of the Barren Lands."

However, despite their best efforts, recognition and rewards resolutely eluded them. When they reached Nassau (after a harrowing crossing from Miami), they found themselves regarded as drifters and pariahs.

The Great Expedition had failed utterly to catch the world's eye. Now it began to dissolve. One of the dogs was traded for a keg of rum, and when Charley announced that they would now return to Canada O'Grady jumped ship and disappeared.

The Master of the Barren Lands and the two children persevered, paddling laboriously north along the Atlantic seaboard of the continent through terrible winter weather until one spring day in 1932 they came ashore in Montreal.

The great voyage was finished, and the man who had been introduced to more than 150 audiences as "King of forty thousand

Eskimos" was nearly finished too. He was admitted to a Montreal hospital as a welfare patient while his children and two remaining dogs were adopted by local families. They were now and forever out of Eskimo Charley's life.

When summer came and he was discharged from hospital, he drifted west to the long-abandoned cabin near Pelican Narrows. The place was in ruins; when Charley set to work to clean it up and uncovered the skeleton of its last occupant spread-eagled on a collapsed bunk bed he moved on, making his way to Reindeer Lake; along the Cochrane River; down the Kasmere to Nueltin Lake, to eventually reach his long-derelict cabin at Charley Lake.

The king had returned but the few remaining Ihalmiut would have no part of him nor would the Idthen Eldeli. The few white men in the country gave him a wide berth. His only sustaining contacts with living beings seem to have been with his dogs and occasional brief visits to the Schweders, who were then managing a small outpost of the HBC at Windy Lake.

Charles Schweder told me his namesake was convinced that "all the natives was out to murder him."

Believing himself to be in deadly peril, Eskimo Charley took protective measures. He trained his dogs to attack all strangers, but generally kept them with him inside his cabin, where they could not be poisoned by skulking enemies.

He always carried a cocked .30-30 rifle in the crook of his arm when he went outside and did not hesitate to snap off a shot in the direction of any untoward sight or sound.

"Father told me," Charles remembered, "never you go near to that man's place 'less you lets him know you is comin', from a good ways off."

His most bizarre guardians were the dead. He systematically robbed native graves; especially Inuit graves, which were always built above-ground and so were easily located and readily accessible.

Charley took only skulls, favouring those of relatively recent dead to which scalps and hanks of long black hair still adhered.

He brought the skulls to one or other of his lairs (he maintained several widely dispersed cabins, but never stayed long in any one of them) and affixed them to the tops of stout poles so that they formed a perimeter of grisly guards around each cabin. When he moved from one cabin to another, the skulls went with him.

"They was a sure-fire *Keep Out* sign. When them skulls was up, nothin' would go anywheres near Charley's place . . . not even a wolverine!"

According to Charles Schweder: "He'd kill anything that walked, flew or swam 'round his cabins. He had poison and traps and snares scattered every which way. Seems like he had a special hate for wolfs. Never bothered skinning them – said he hated their stink. But he sure like to kill 'em – any time, any place. He used to smash up old bottles and stuff deer guts with the pieces and scatter them any place he see wolf tracks around.

"Told my father he cut up old clock springs into pieces, sharpened the ends of the pieces, coiled them up tight and fastened them with deer sinew. Then he freeze them inside chunks of meat and leave the chunks where wolfs could find them. They melted inside the wolfs and the spring opened out and tore the hell out of the wolf's gut. Charley claimed that trick never failed.

"He was pretty near as hard on the deer. Joe Highway from Brochet used to trap up our way sometimes. Told me he come on a deer-crossing place on the Putahow River where Charley had shot off a case of .30-30 into one of the big fall herds. Joe said you could smell rotten meat a couple miles away. Charley never had no need to do that."

In mid-summer of 1941, Fred and Charles Schweder arrived by canoe with their winter's fur at the HBC post on Reindeer Lake. They brought word that Eskimo Charley had not been seen for almost two years. This news filtered out to the RCMP detachment at The Pas and during the winter of 1942–43 a constable and a "native special" went north by dog team to investigate. They were directed by an Idthen Eldeli (who refused to accompany the patrol himself) to the south-ernmost of Charley's several cabins. The searchers concluded it belonged to Eskimo Charley even though the tall poles surrounding it were not crowned with skulls. They banged on the door and, when nobody answered, broke it down. According to Charles Schweder, who had the story from the native special constable:

"They got one hell of a surprise when they seen what was inside. Bones all over the place. Looked to them fellows like Charley must've died in there and there being nobody to feed the dogs was in there with him, I guess they ate him. Some people thought the dogs killed him . . . because of the kind of a man he was."

That would have been wishful thinking. When the patrol searched the cabin they found this note:

April. I guess it is the twelfth.

For four days I am feeling rotten. I can neither eat or sleep. I have paines in my chest. For four days I havent been able to pass water or bowel. I have no laxitive. I had some epsom salt but I cannot find it. Last night I passed out for some time. I guess this is the end. . . .

Charles told me something more – something that does not appear in the police report.

"There was a bunch of people skulls in there. One was pretty well chewed up but most was in one piece. The Indian was there said they took all them bones, dogs and all, and buried them all together to save trying to figure out who in hell *any* of 'em *was*. Figured it would just have been a waste of time.

"I guess if anyone ever digs up old Eskimo Charley's bones they're going to wonder . . . what kind of a thing *was* he, anyhow?"

There remains a question as to why *all* the skulls were found *inside* the cabin. I think it was because Eskimo Charley had been preparing to take them with him to his ultimate refuge at the lake called Kamilikuak when Death forestalled him.

· 23 ·

TUKTU

Although our explorations of the twin-lakes country revealed no deer the country was by no means lifeless. Loons were abundant. Three kinds shared the lakes – red-necked, black-throated, and yellow-billed – and they were everywhere. We could hear their cries at all hours of the long days and short nights.

There were few ravens (we supposed because most would have been travelling with the deer herds) but many raptors. Rough-legged hawks circled close overhead waiting to pounce on ground squirrels whose insatiable curiosity about us had brought them out of their secure burrows. Peregrine falcons and long-tailed jaegers hunting for lemmings sometimes made use of us as involuntary "beaters." And we had a spectacular encounter with a pair of ghost-white gyr-falcons who had an eyrie on a shoreside cliff. Their nest held three almost full-fledged young. The adults would not allow us a close approach, diving fiercely upon us.

Although we saw no living deer, shed antlers and white bones testified that, in due season, this was very much their country. At some time in the not-too-distant past they had shared it with even larger creatures. Twice we found muskox skulls, one with its curved horns still intact. And once we came upon the skull of a Barren Lands grizzly, the largest carnivore on the continent. The incisors were almost three inches long, curved and pointed like scimitars. I took a bear's tooth back to camp and gave it to Ohoto, who accepted it with reverence, slipping it into a deerskin amulet bag he wore around his neck.

Andy and I were still asleep early one morning when Ohoto came bursting into the tent shouting that the deer had come. We scrambled out in time to see him with our .30-30 in hand running along the isthmus toward the northern skyline, where seven does with seven fawns stood silhouetted. We dressed and hurried in pursuit but long before we could reach him he had begun shooting. Three does and a fawn went down.

I might have called Ohoto to account for such butchery had I not been aware he could claim to have killed on our behalf – to help Andy and me in our mysterious purposes, one of which was "to procure and dissect at least fifty caribou to provide scientific data upon which plans for the future management of the herds" could be based.

So three does and a fawn lay bleeding on the tundra while two surviving fawns stood a few yards off, grunting in their peculiarly plaintive way, not knowing whether to follow the fleeing remnant of their little herd or stay close to their slaughtered mothers.

While Andy was busy measuring the corpses and Ohoto was skinning and butchering a doe for meat, I tried to chase the surviving fawns away. They went reluctantly, perhaps aware (as I certainly was) that their chances of survival on their own were slim indeed.

Returning to camp laden with bloody bundles, we squandered our hoarded firewood to fuel a roaring blaze, thrust enormous chunks of meat into the coals, hauled them out again when they were charred, scraped off the charcoal, and gorged ourselves on the pink and steaming flesh beneath.

Having subsisted too long on a diet of flour, tea, and lean fish, our craving for red meat was exceeded only by our craving for fat. At this season of the year, does carried very little fat but there was still marrow in their leg bones. So we roasted the long bones, cracked them open, and gulped down steaming hot strips of juicy marrow.

It was astonishing how much meat we were able to eat. During the subsequent forty-eight hours, the three of us and Tegpa consumed most of an entire doe, including the heart, liver, kidneys, and tongue.

As "senior scientist," Andy was responsible for dissecting the carcasses, a task that kept him busy with scalpels, knives, scissors, and forceps for two full days, looking for parasites and pathogens while turning the patch of tundra where the deer had died into an abattoir of bloody fragments.

Ohoto scavenged what meat was useable, some of which he buried in the permafrost beneath the moss, where it would remain fresh for many days. The rest he sliced into paper-thin strips and spread over the upper branches of bushes to dry in wind and sun. This was *nipku* – jerky – which, he assured us, was excellent and would keep for years.

Although I spent most of my time looking for live caribou, the great flood of southbound does and fawns Ohoto had assured us was just beyond the horizon failed to materialize. When I asked him why, he explained reasonably enough:

"*Schweenak* [bad] to camp in the deer path. Tuktu may wait for us to go away. Or look for way around. Better we move."

He suggested we shift camp to the southeast shore of Nowleye, but Andy and I felt it would be more convenient to stay put.

During the next few days a scattering of fawns and does drifted past us. They were wary and skittish but we were encouraged to stick to our decision by flights of ravens soaring in the pale skies and by occasional glimpses of wolves – signs we took to be indicative of the near presence of *la foule*.

Wolves being my particular scientific responsibility I busily collected wolf feces, old or new, and analyzed their contents; which proved to be mainly fragments of caribou bones embedded in a stiff matrix of caribou hair.

Ohoto watched intently as I dissected the wolf "scats," and I could imagine the sardonic pleasure he would get from someday telling his friends how deeply the *kablunait* were enamoured of wolf shit.

When there was nothing better to do Ohoto would make string figures for my entertainment. Using both hands, he would weave and interweave a loop of string between his fingers to create representations of plants, spirits, and animals. He made these abstract forms move in weirdly lifelike ways, each illustrating some particular aspect in the lives of the creatures represented. The figures were compelling, both in themselves and for what they had to tell me about wolves, lemmings, caribou, people, and other inhabitants of the Barren Lands.

Andy considered string figures child's play and thought them frivolous, but I was becoming increasingly sceptical about the ability of science to define, explain, and illuminate the nature of nearly everything. When I defended the string figures as a valid source of information Andy would have none of it. "Only facts can reveal the truth" was his unyielding dictum.

August was now well advanced and the scarcity of deer had become our major worry. One day Ohoto confronted Andy and me with the blunt accusation that the absence of great herds was *our* fault. If we had not insisted on camping on the isthmus, he told us, the herds would certainly have come that way. We had blocked their chosen path so they had probably gone south across the plains behind our Angikuni camp. Ohoto insisted that if we were to find the herds we must return to Angikuni.

We did not require much persuasion.

Tuesday: Up and away at 0700 heading back to Angikuni. Dead calm day, hot and clear, though there was a frost last night. I sat in the bow with plane-table and compass, mapping the south shore of Nowleye while to save gas Andy and Ohoto paddled. Tegpa snoozed in the sunshine. It was a bit like a Sunday picnic excursion to Toronto Island, only without girls or booze. Alas.

Near the east end of Nowleye Ohoto spotted a big buck on shore. First buck we've seen and he had a magnificent spread of antlers. Andy wanted him so Ohoto took him with one shot and I was sorry. He looked so magnificent against a crimson evening sky. There was no pleasure in seeing him suddenly fling himself into the air then crumple backward on his haunches with bloody foam flecking his wide nostrils. But I have to admit to the pleasure of sinking my teeth into a strip of his back meat, with an inch of fat on it, roasted poneass-style on an open fire after Andy had got his measurements and checked his guts for parasites. He tasted a hell of a lot better than the maggoty nipku I'd been chewing on all day.

We went ashore to check out the first big Kuwee rapid, which we had portaged on the way west. The main chute is about 250 yards long and 40 wide. A stinker, full of white water and three-foot back waves. Ohoto wouldn't run it and didn't want us to, but Andy and I were in a what-the-hell mood. We unloaded most of the gear for Ohoto to carry around the rapid, then pushed out into the slick current at its head. As was usually the case when once committed, doubt and irresolution vanished and we shot into the spume in a state of high excitement that lasted till we were spat out at about 20 mph into the pool at the foot of the rapid. Ohoto, watching, shook his head and pointedly didn't congratulate us.

Thursday: Up at dawn, to find a major miracle has taken place. The flies are gone! Utterly vanished! There seems no logical explanation for this. It's a dead-calm day, hot and clear and no frost last night. I timidly stripped off and took a bath in a pond. Still no flies so I spent about an hour splashing about in the nude while Tegpa and Ohoto both tried to get me to come out. Neither Eskimos nor Eskimo dogs believe in swimming or in bathing.

Ohoto has been keeping a diary. He and I have this in common — both of us have trouble reading what we write, but I have the edge because I'm using the Roman alphabet. He's apparently using one he made up himself.

Andy doing another autopsy this evening. Not many deer around but heavy tracks on both sides of Kuwee show where they've been crossing. In some places the banks are churned into muck for hundreds of yards. And below some rapids the hair shed while swimming is matted so thick along the shore you can shovel it up with a paddle. No doubt about it, for whatever reason the big herds of cows and fawns avoided the isthmus this year and crossed Kuwee instead. Too damn bad we missed them, but Ohoto says not to worry, the bucks are still to come and once back at Angikuni we'll be on hand to greet them.

A piping hot pile of marrow bones for supper, with steak and kidney stew. Ohoto says that Eskimos eat five meals a day and snack in between. On the trail they get by with only three meals! He mentioned that a good way to get next to a girl is to give her a bundle of marrow bones. He says results are usually immediate and satisfying, which is more than we kablunait can claim for bouquets of roses.

We came down Kuwee like shit through a goose, running all the rapids, sometimes with the kicker going full blast to give us steerage way in the tight spots. Scary stuff! But wonderfully stimulating, though Ohoto looks worried and shakes his head and Tegpa sticks his head under a packsack when the going gets really wet. Ah well, boys will be boys and we are on the home stretch.

We still had some gas so we decided to use it up finding out how big the nameless lake northwest of Angikuni is. Well, we never did find out. It goes on and on, one stretch of water leading into another. It was such a maze it was impossible to map it or figure where we were, but we must have got to within a few miles of another huge lake Tyrrell heard about from the Eskimos and stuck on his map in dotted lines: Tulemaliguetna – Little Dubawnt. There's supposed to be a river from it running north to Baker Lake and we could maybe go out that way to Hudson Bay if we have to. There seems to be no bloody end to where you could go in this country in a canoe if you had the time and inclination.

Last day on the trail. At dusk we paddled, because now out of gas, through the strait separating Tyrrell Bay from Kinetua Bay, and our old wall tent came into view. It looked as insignificant as a splash of gull shit against the awesome backdrop of the Angikuni plateau but was sure and hell a more encouraging sight than an empty tent ring!

We spent the next morning settling in but after lunch I climbed the escarpment behind camp to see if there might be deer on the plateau. *Might* be? When I looked west it seemed as if the entire wide sweep of tundra had come alive! *La foule* was here at last.

The deer were mostly bulls in strings of a dozen to a hundred or more, but so many strings oozing implacably southward that the entire countryside appeared to be rippling in slow motion. My range of vision was about ten miles and everywhere within view, west, south, and north, deer were drifting along, grazing as they went. Every ridge line was roughened by their antler-crowned silhouettes, and the lowlands were scarred by flagellation of intertwining paths.

It was such a compelling sight that only with difficulty could I break free and race back to camp with the electrifying news. Then the three of us trotted up the escarpment; Andy and I to record the spectacle and Ohoto simply to revel in it.

Andy counted 1,347 bucks passing within a mile of us during half an hour's observation. They seemed to be moving at slightly more than a mile an hour. We calculated that between eight and ten thousand were in sight on the entire sweep of tundra at any given moment and estimated that as many as thirty thousand were probably passing through our field of view every twenty-four hours.

After a time I grew tired of calculations and slipped away by myself to a distant rock pile where I could watch the passing show close up.

A superb day with a pale opal sky, a blinding sun, a light breeze to cool me off, and not a single blackfly. This world seemed freshly reborn with the arrival of the deer.

Those I met en route to the rock pile showed little interest in me. Not quite correct – a typical reaction of those passing at close range was to take a wide-eyed look, snort incredulously, then, spreading both back legs in a most undignified sort of half-squat, have a huge piss. They might then circle me fifty or a hundred feet distant until they got my wind. At which they sometimes sneezed then, loping off a few yards, would ignore me. At no time did they appear to have any fear of me. The experience was humbling.

One yearling seemed to think I might make an acceptable companion and followed along close at my heel. I hadn't a clue what was on his mind but was afraid he might draw too much attention to me so I tried getting rid of him by howling at him, wolf-style. Whereupon,

I swear, he edged even closer. Finally I pelted him with handfuls of bog, whereat he snorted and departed in high dudgeon.

So I wandered through the grazing herds, to take a seat amongst the boulders of the rock pile and remained there until dusk, moving as little as possible . . . watching, smelling, and hearing the passage of la foulé.

Smelling? Yes, because the gentle breeze carried the sweetish odour of cow barn. And all the time I was hearing the soft rumble of caribou guts digesting moss and lichens and gently farting, all to the rhythm of a steady click-clack made by their ankle joints. The truth was, the caribou were not just part of the landscape – they were the landscape!

The immense antlers borne by the bigger bucks seemed impossibly ponderous, swollen by the velvet coating which most of them had not yet shed. Younger bucks with lesser antlers made way for their elders. Some individuals noticed my presence and came right up to the rock pile, thrusting their big muzzles toward me and snuffling wetly. One young buck essayed a tentative lick and when I waved him off, leapt back on all four legs at once with a great who-o-o-o-f of astonishment or indignation.

There was a tiny pond nearby and all the while the deer were streaming past and around it (sometimes pausing to drink), a pair of old squaw ducks and eight or ten half-grown young swam about as contentedly as if they and the deer all belonged to one big happy family.

Clouds began rolling in from the south and when the sun was briefly obscured by a thunderhead, paralysis seemed to grip the deer. Each became motionless, standing statue-like, heads down and all facing north as if in some obscure act of obeisance. Most held their positions until the sun shone out again, at which they resumed their southward plodding and grazing as if nothing had happened. It all seemed most peculiar and somewhat ominous, although when I swept the horizon with my binoculars I could see nothing untoward.

Occasionally an individual broke out in an insane sort of gallop, running at top speed, weaving and twisting, sometimes slipping and falling down, only to leap to its feet and be off again. At least I knew what this was all about. Although too far away for me to see, I knew a bumble-bee lookalike, a warble fly or botfly, was trying to lay its eggs on some victim, which fled from this little nemesis in panic terror. Justifiable terror, for I have found a fist-sized mass of botfly maggots clogging the throat and nostrils of an emaciated and exhausted deer, and have counted as many as a hundred bullet-sized holes in a deer hide: holes drilled through the living skin by the emerging larvae of warble flies.

As the evening drew down, the strings of bucks dissolved into individual animals spreading out on every side. A short-eared owl flew by, bat-like, and so close to my head that I felt the wind of its passing and it roused me from what must have been a nearly hypnotic trance.

Stiffly I got to my feet and headed back to camp carrying an indelible vision of la foule. *I wonder, though, will these enormous herds survive even in the memory of the next generation of mankind? Maybe by then* la foule *will become as mythical as the earth-shaking multitudes of prairie buffalo have become. As for me, I'm convinced the Eskimos have got it right when they claim tuktu gives the world a special aura of vitality – one that enters into the being of every watcher, man or beast, and makes the hearts of all beat stronger.*

Two days later there came a lull in the flow of deer across the plateau behind our camp so we paddled to the inlet of the Kazan where, on an earlier visit, we had found evidence of a major caribou crossing of great antiquity.

It was again in use.

Both banks had been freshly torn to shreds by deer hooves but few deer were to be seen so we pushed on upstream under the slopes of Kinetua to Tyrrell's Turning Lake. Here we met the herds again. They were crossing the Kazan in a nearly solid stream and the effect was as if two rivers, one of water and one of flesh and bone, were intersecting.

We landed well below them and went ashore where a solidly massed phalanx of about a hundred bucks was doing what looked like close-order drill, bunched together so tightly their antlers seemed to interlock.

Anxious to shoot some close-up photos, Andy and I crouched behind some boulders and sent Ohoto around behind the herd. When he leapt out at them they stampeded so directly for us that if we hadn't stood up and yelled and waved our arms madly they could have overrun us. It was scary enough to send us back to the safety of the canoe.

Relative safety because now Ohoto decided to demonstrate how the Ihalmiut hunt caribou at river crossings. They do it from kayaks — we did it from a much-less-manoeuvrable seventeen-foot canoe. They use short spears about four feet long fitted with broad, knife-like points but we had no such weapons.

At Ohoto's instruction Andy and I paddled the canoe into the midst of a herd of swimming bucks, which began milling about un- certain whether to continue across the river or retreat to the north shore. We were soon surrounded by flying forefeet, plunging bodies, and great, swinging antlers. Yelling lustily, Ohoto thrust the blade of his paddle at the backs of the nearest bucks, aiming close to the spine and just behind the rib cage. The paddle did no damage but had it been a real spear it would have cut a rent through skin and flesh to collapse the deer's diaphragm. A deer so speared will quickly drown. But the ones Ohoto whacked with his paddle seemed more likely to pound the canoe into slivers so with one accord Andy and I paddled us out of the melee and downstream, while Ohoto laughed like a mad fool.

It was a vivid demonstration of something I would not want to try in a kayak, but then I am not an Ihalmiut.

The superb late-summer weather continued and the biting flies remained mercifully absent so one hot morning I decided to have a sun bath. Wearing nothing but boots and binoculars I climbed the escarpment to stretch out on a warm rocky outcrop and dream about my distant wife. The reverie was short-lived. Glancing inland I was startled to see a big white wolf accompanied by two almost black ones trotting across an adjacent ridge. .

Many strings of deer were scattered about on the plateau so this seemed like a heaven-sent opportunity to observe the interaction between prey and predator. As the wolves slipped over the ridge and out of sight, I grabbed my binoculars and hared off in pursuit, *au naturel*.

This part of the plateau consisted of a series of low ridges separated by grassy swales in each of which groups of caribou were grazing their way south. It was ideal country for my purpose. I could keep watch from the ridge crests while the wolves crossed each valley, then, when they dropped from view over the next ridge, could sprint to the next elevation and watch them traverse another valley.

Sweating with excitement and exertion I breasted the first ridge expecting to see frenzied action as the wolves came down among the caribou. It was disconcerting to witness a scene of perfect tranquility. About fifty bucks were in view lazily grazing while the two black wolves and their white leader sauntered by as if they had no more interest in the caribou than in the rocks. The deer for their part seemed unaware that death walked among them. Three familiar dogs crossing a farm pasture might have provoked more reaction from a herd of domestic cattle.

As I watched incredulously, the wolves trotted to within fifty yards of a pair of young bucks lying down. The bucks turned their heads negligently but did not get to their feet. To me their apparent disdain for the wolves seemed suicidal. My bewilderment increased when, as the wolves swung up the slope and disappeared over the next crest and I jumped up to follow, the apathetic bucks scrambled to their feet, stared at me in astonishment, and galloped away.

Cresting the next ridge I almost ran into the wolves, who had gathered on the forward slope for some nose smelling and tail wagging. They did not see me duck behind an outcrop and, the wind being in my favour, did not scent me. After a few minutes of what looked like aimless social intercourse but which undoubtedly had meaning for them, the white leader led them off again.

As they meandered down the slope into another valley where scores of deer were grazing, the wolves stopped occasionally to sniff clumps of vegetation and sometimes to pee on them in passing, but showed no particular interest in the caribou.

For their part, the deer evinced an almost equal lack of interest in the wolves. When the pack (or family, as it probably was), now travelling in line abreast, came within fifty or sixty feet of it a deer *might* snort indignantly before trotting off a few yards to one side of the wolves' line of advance, but that was all.

I followed the wolves at a discreet distance for several miles as they wove their way among scattered groups of caribou. The reactions of the deer amounted to little more than casual interest verging on indifference, unless one or other of the wolves happened to stray too close, in which case the deer would unhurriedly move away from the wolves' line of march. There was none of the stampeding-under-threat that our stereotypical imagery of wolf and deer demands.

So far almost all the deer the wolves and I had encountered had been bucks. Now we began meeting small numbers of does and fawns, and the behaviour of the wolves changed.

When the wolves came close to a particular fawn who had strayed some distance from its mother, one of the black ones made a sudden dash toward it. The fawn fled full tilt with the wolf in hot pursuit – both behaving as I had always imagined prey and predator normally behaved. My heart began to thud in anticipation of what looked to be a certain kill.

It did not happen.

The wolf ran all-out for about a hundred yards without gaining perceptibly on the fawn . . . then abruptly broke off and casually trotted back to rejoin its two companions, who *had sat themselves down to watch the chase*!

I was dumbfounded. I had been certain the fawn was doomed, as it assuredly would have been had the wolves lived up to the mythic reputation of their kind. During the next hour each of the wolves made similar feints toward fawns, but in every case soon broke off the chase, leaving the putative victims to stop, turn their heads, and stare briefly at their departing pursuers before placidly resuming the endless task of grazing reindeer moss.

It did not occur to me at the time that what I was witnessing was a kind of lupine shopping technique – that these wolves I was following were engaged in testing potential dinners in order to ascertain if any were ripe for the eating – in other words, were ailing or disabled. I had yet to learn that any caribou of whatever age – even a fawn as young as a week or two – could, if in good health and condition, almost invariably outrun even the most athletic wolf. The wolves, of course, were only too well aware of this.

Being ignorant of this salient fact, I was exasperated by the wolves' unproductive behaviour. I had not run several miles cross-country and exhausted myself just to watch a passel of wolves playing silly buggers. As they ambled off to disappear over yet another crest, I lost my cool.

I went charging after them with blood in my eye. I am not exactly sure what I had in mind, but I wanted action. I may have intended to try chasing down a fawn myself, just to show these lazy dogs it could be done. Whatever. When I came pounding over the ridge, I almost ran headlong into the little pack.

Evidently they had been taking a breather lolling about within a few feet of one another, when a naked human burst in upon them like a bomb. Wolves blew off in three directions, ears back and tails stretched straight out behind them. . . .

And all the herds of deer within sight *now* began erupting in the stampede I had been anticipating.

Only – and this I realized with some chagrin – the wolves were not responsible for this rout of caribou.

I was the villain whose unseemly behaviour had spooked the denizens of the tundra plains.

OF WOLVES AND WOMEN

There was a sharp frost last night and we woke to the tent being banged like a drum by an easterly gale with driving rain and freezing sleet. Piss-willy weather! Nevertheless, we spent most of the day out in it gathering whatever burnables we could find, mostly willow twigs and moss, to pile on top of the escarpment to fuel a smoke signal to help Gunnar find us. He is due anytime. And none too bloody soon! Summer gives way to winter without much transition in this country and summer is surely over. In case G. doesn't make it we've built a stone cairn here with a letter in a bottle, giving our plans for going out down the Kazan. But remembering how Charlie Schweder and I had to dice with the devil on Hudson Bay last August, I'd rather Gunnar flew us out.

This is the last week Gunnar said he might be able to make it. It's overcast and windy with the cloud deck dropping lower by the minute.

We didn't think there was a chance in hell he'd come today. But just before noon Ohoto heard an engine.

"Tingmeak!" he yelled and went haring up the hill to light the beacon. Pretty soon a little speck came out of the grey sky and homed in on the smoke. A few minutes later the old red Norseman plopped down on the bay like a big fat duck and waddled in to shore with Gunnar hollering at us out the pilot's window:

"Pull the plug, you lazy fuckers! If we don't get our asses out of here right now we'll be here 'til spring!"

Twenty minutes later we were airborne. Below us Kinetua Bay was veiled with snow scud. We left it as it had been when we came to it – bleak and desolate.

Relief at seeing Gunnar did not last long. I had barely squeezed into the Norseman's overloaded cabin when he passed me a bundle of letters. Two were from Fran. I ripped them open and the bottom fell out of everything. Both were poignant distillations of misery and despair whose burden was that our marriage had been a mistake and was effectively over. The last letter ended with the naked accusation: *You have abandoned me.*

The black fates that subvert us all were not yet finished. Emotionally pole-axed as I was, I had to listen to Gunnar explaining through the stutter on the intercom why once again he had not brought in relief supplies for the Ihalmiut.

"No freight scheduled for the trip . . . nothing from your bosses . . . Mounties said they was looking after the Huskies . . . like shit they was . . . Mountie plane been down south all summer . . . I landed gas at Windy on the way here and your pal Ootek was there looking for ammo . . . said his folks wouldn't make it through the winter without they soon killed a bunch of deer . . . couldn't do that 'cause they got no ammo . . . can't even get no skins to cover their kayaks . . . got no nets left either . . . fucking government's screwed up as usual."

Shouting in order to be heard, Andy and I wrestled with the problem of what to do about the Ihalmiut. We decided that one of us must fly out with Gunnar and try to get some action. Desperately anxious to deal with my impending marital disaster, I wanted to be the one to go. We agreed that Andy would remain at Windy and hoped Ohoto could be persuaded to stay with him until I returned.

I did not even step ashore at Windy. While the others ferried our gear to the beach, I sat alone in the cockpit deeply depressed. However, during the ongoing flight, anger at the failure of the authorities to do anything for the Ihalmiut distracted me somewhat from my personal anguish.

The first thing I did on reaching Churchill was to send a telegram to my nominal boss, R.A. Gibson, deputy commissioner of the Northwest Territories. I warned again of imminent disaster threatening the Ihalmiut, concluding with a peremptory demand for aid. Thirty-six anxious hours passed before an answer from Ottawa reached me. It was forthright and unequivocal, stating that "native problems" were not my affair, that the RCMP would deal with any difficulties concerning Inuit, and ordering me to "return immediately to Nueltin Lake and carry out the duties previously assigned to you."

I went to the office of the Churchill detachment of the RCMP, where I was assured a police patrol would be flying to Windy soon.

"How soon?" I demanded.

"A week. Possibly two. Our aircraft is in Winnipeg for an engine inspection right now."

I offered to stand by at Churchill until the plane returned, then accompany the patrol as a guide and as a source of local information, but the offer was dismissed with a brusque "Not really your business, is it? We'll manage, thank you."

Since there appeared to be nothing more I could do for the Ihalmiut at Churchill, and my own problems loomed large, I decided to go absent without leave and head for Toronto, where Fran and I might be able to deal with our difficulties face to face, and where I might also be able to stir up some public concern for the Ihalmiut.

That evening in the bar of the Hudson Hotel, I was lucky enough to meet an RCAF pilot who was scheduled to ferry a DC-3 to Toronto the following day.

Fran's reception of me was equivocal. Although she embraced me passionately, she could not conceal her fear that marrying me had been a mistake – not because we did not love one another but because she felt she could not rely upon me.

"Who knows where you'll go next and how long you'll be gone? I can't stand that. I wanted to settle down with you. Here in Toronto, I hoped. That's where I belong. Is that so bad?"

When I replied that the caribou project was a one-time commitment, she clearly did not believe me.

I had no idea how to deal with this situation. More out of desperation than anything else, I tentatively suggested that, instead of joining me in the autumn at Brochet as originally planned, she return with me now to Windy Cabin where we could try to work out our difficulties and where we would at least be together. To my immeasurable relief, she accepted and underwent a sea change, becoming cheerful, almost ebullient at the prospect of something I had been afraid would horrify her.

There was very little opportunity for her to change her mind. Within forty-eight hours I had bought a pair of horrendously expensive one-way tickets on a Trans-Canada Air Lines flight to Winnipeg and we had assembled an outfit which, haphazard and incomplete as it was, I hoped would suffice to see her through an initial period of wilderness living.

I had expected us to fly from Winnipeg to Churchill but there was no commercial flight available, so we boarded the old Muskeg Special instead. This turned out to be a good thing for it gave Fran a lively and useful introduction to northern life.

I was delighted by her response to the people on the train, but apprehensive about the situation awaiting me in Churchill. While in Toronto I had tried to involve the media in the Ihalmiut cause but my attempts had been met by a massive lack of interest. Starving Inuit seemed to be as distant from the concerns of Torontonians as starving Martians might have been. I could only hope that during my absence from Churchill the RCMP had done what so badly needed doing.

It turned out that they had done what they conceived to be their duty.

Five days after my departure, Andy had hurried out of the cabin to greet an incoming Norseman, which he assumed was bringing me back. It turned out to be the police plane carrying an RCMP corporal on patrol.

"He told me," Andy recalled, "he had been sent to investigate rumours the natives near the Kazan River were in trouble. He questioned the two Ihalmiut men who happened to be in camp and, since he didn't know the language, I had to do what I could as interpreter.

"It was a total screw-up. The Eskimos didn't have a clue what the guy was after so, anxious as ever to please a white man, they mostly just said *eema* [yes] to everything he asked . . . most of which I didn't know how to put into their lingo anyhow.

"After about an hour of this babble he called a halt and told me there didn't seem to be any evidence of starvation and our Huskies – that's what he called them – seemed like a pretty shiftless lot, probably just looking for handouts. He said it was second nature for natives to cry poor and we shouldn't be taken in by it. Anyway, it was no concern of ours, he said, and we should leave that sort of thing to the proper authorities.

"He hadn't brought in any relief supplies. After a couple of hours he and his pilot took off again. Not for the Kazan to look at the camps there but back to base. Mission accomplished."

Fran and I found ourselves stranded at Churchill. There seemed to be no way we could get to Windy River short of chartering an airplane – something I could not possibly afford and something I could hardly ask the Department to do on my behalf.

I delivered a message to the Churchill radio station for transmission to Andy, telling him I would be back as soon as I could find transport, and that I was bringing Fran with me. Then I took my wife to the snug home of the Ingebritson family, where Gunnar's parents greeted her like one of their own, and Gunnar assured me he would somehow find a way to fly us to Windy without bankrupting us.

Gunnar also told me the RCMP patrol had not delivered any supplies to the Ihalmiut. When I visited police headquarters to find out what had happened, the sergeant in command of the detachment tried to mollify me by explaining that he had now assembled a load of relief supplies but had been unable to deliver it because the Force's Norseman was somewhere in the western Arctic. However, assuming I would be flying to Windy on a government charter, he offered to entrust the shipment to me. Then he fired a thunderbolt.

"One thing. . . . These are *relief* goods only. Mostly flour, beans, baking powder, and the like. There's no ammunition and no rifles. The territorial government won't spring for anything like that."

There now remained only one possible card for me to play – the army – an organization I had assured myself I would never again have anything to do with. That afternoon I borrowed Gunnar's old truck and drove across the tundra to the sprawling U.S./Canadian military base known as Fort Churchill.

I went there emboldened by a report that the Canadian base commander had served in my old outfit – the Hastings and Prince Edward Regiment. Fortunately the report was accurate. Colonel Donald Cameron listened intently while I described the plight of the Ihalmiut and emphasized the grim prediction that without an adequate supply of ammunition for their decrepit old rifles, many of the people would probably not survive the coming winter.

Cameron never hesitated.

"I'll do what I can," he said crisply. "You can depend on it."

Within the hour he had arranged for Gunnar's Norseman to be fuelled with enough RCAF avgas for a return flight to Windy River, at no cost either to Gunnar or to me.

And he did more – much more.

Risking severe consequences for misusing government and military property, he arranged the immediate delivery to the Ingebritsons' home of twelve .303 service rifles together with an entire case of ammunition. And, in the event these might not reach the Inuit in time to ensure an adequate supply of deer skins, he added forty brand-new woollen battledress trousers and jackets.

"Won't keep them as warm as caribou skin," he apologized, "but better than a kick in the arse from those buffoons in Ottawa."

It may well be that the Ihalmiut survived the winter that lay ahead of them that year because of Donald Cameron.

Frances had very little opportunity to acclimatize herself to Churchill. On September 9 Gunnar roused us early and we hastened out to Landing Lake, where the Norseman waited, fully fuelled and loaded. We lifted off in fair visibility but within twenty minutes clouds had forced us down to less than a thousand feet. A cautious pilot would probably have turned back. Not Gunnar. We pressed on, catching only blurred glimpses of a world of rock and water close below us.

Nervous enough on my own account, I was apprehensive about how Fran would react. To my relief and admiration, she took it in stride. Holding my hand tightly and leaning close she yelled into my ear: "If Gunnar goes any closer I'll pick a flower!"

For the first time since suggesting that she come north with me, I could believe it had been the right decision.

Three hours after takeoff, the Norseman slid over the crest of the Caribou Hills to splash down in the cove at the mouth of Windy River. Fran never afterwards revealed what her feelings were as I popped open the cabin door and she peered out at the rain-swept vista of rock, water, and tundra surrounding us.

Not having received my radio message, Andy had no forewarning of our arrival. He and Alekahaw, one of the younger Ihalmiut, had been upriver fishing when the distinctive snarl of the Norseman's engine brought their canoe belting downstream so recklessly they barely avoided colliding with the plane.

Draped in soaking-wet, patched, and filthy *attigi* (summer parkas), they were a hard-looking pair, wild-eyed and long-haired. Fran eyed them tentatively while we hurriedly ferried gear, freight, and ourselves ashore.

The exterior of Fran's new home was unprepossessing enough, but the inside must have truly appalled her. At the best of times Andy was not much of a housekeeper, and during the past two weeks he had been entertaining a throng of hungry Inuit visitors. The dark and dank interior looked and smelled almost as much like a bear's den as a human habitation.

Tegpa did his best to brighten the moment by deciding he had been born to be Fran's dog. He set out to prove it by furiously licking her face, which I think may have been as wet with tears as with rain and dog spittle.

Alekahaw also accepted Fran unreservedly. In fact, he was so smitten by the first white woman he had ever seen that within twenty-four hours he had intimated a willingness to exchange wives with me. At least that is what I, with my imperfect knowledge of his language, thought he had in mind. Fran's response when I told her about the offer was that perhaps we ought to get to know each other a little better first. I concluded she was making a good adjustment to local mores.

Andy's reception of her was polite but reserved. Her unexpected and uninvited arrival posed all sorts of problems for him, but these he decided to set aside for the moment.

There was work to be done.

We had first to ready the relief supplies for distribution to the Ihalmiut. The supplies consisted principally of a fifty-pound drum of powdered milk, two hundred pounds of flour, some lard, and two bundles of clothing. To our distress the milk powder proved to be so old and rancid as to be inedible. Much of the flour had been water damaged and had set as hard as stone. The two bundles of "clothing" contained tattered underwear apparently salvaged from some government institution – possibly a prison – before being consigned to the RCMP for distribution to needy natives.

We destroyed the milk and made a pile of legless, armless, torn-and-worn underwear from which the Inuit could help themselves if they so chose. Few did.

These disappointments were offset by Colonel Cameron's magnificent gift of twelve gleaming, well-oiled army rifles and the supply of ammunition that came with them. Alekahaw was rendered speechless by such largesse. Watching his face, I concluded that whatever might befall the Ihalmiut in the future, this coming winter was *not* destined to be their last.

Next morning Alekahaw hurried off to the Inuit camps to spread the news that I had returned with rifles and shells enough to ensure the success of the autumnal deer hunt. He assured us he would be back at Windy in a few days accompanied by all the men.

We put that interval to good use making our home habitable. Andy and I laboured long and hard cutting wood and getting water then, with the old stove heated almost red hot, we turned the cabin into a kind of northern steam laundry. While I scrubbed a lifetime's accumulation of dirt and grease off the split-log floor, Fran scraped and washed our sparse collection of battered cooking utensils, tin cups, plates, and cutlery. Then she boiled the towels, socks, and anything else that still looked strong enough to survive immersion in hot water.

Once a degree of cleanliness had been achieved, Fran spread some caribou hides on the floor and on the benches that served as beds and seats, organized the "kitchen corner" to her liking, and hung up a few flowered dishtowels she had brought from Toronto, to serve as window curtains.

I spent most of one day constructing a seat for the backhouse (a simple two-by-four no longer seemed adequate) and in contriving a sort of door for this well-ventilated structure. Then Andy and I devoted a day in a freezing drizzle to waterproofing the cabin roof with tarpaper I had brought in from Churchill. This was especially needful over the cabin's back room (which was to be Fran's and my bedroom) because, although it had originally been roofed with caribou hides, these had become so porous that rain and snow easily found a way through them.

This windowless back room, originally the Schweders' storeroom, was ankle deep in decaying pieces of hides, mildewed scraps of clothing, rotting fragments of cardboard cartons, and unidentifiable muck and mush. The stink was almost palpable. I forbade Fran even to enter until I had cleaned it out, rigged up a double bed of sorts, and attempted – none too successfully – to mask the stench with a sprinkling of carbolic acid. If Fran had rejected this nuptial chamber out of hand, I would not have been at all surprised. I *was* surprised, and happily so, when she mustered a somewhat wan smile and pronounced it to be "quite cozy."

Having surmounted the first hurdles facing her, she now faced the challenge of coming to terms with the land. This was made easier by the onset of a spell of good weather following a sharp frost. Overnight the shrubbery on the Barrens flamed with autumnal colours almost as spectacular as those of the hardwoods of Ontario. Moreover, the frost seemed to have triggered the southern migration of the caribou, and forerunners of the great herds soon appeared at Windy River.

One fine day Fran and I took the canoe to visit the wolf den at Smith House Bay. She proved adept with the paddle and was curious about everything around her. Although nobody was home at the wolf den, the vast sweep of plains to the northward was crawling with serpentine lines of caribou. Fran was spellbound by them.

"The *ground* seems to be moving," she said in a hushed voice. "Almost as if it's alive. It's really worth coming all this way to see it."

This appreciation of a world so foreign to her seemed confirmation of my hopes that our future together might not be as uncertain as it had seemed only a few days earlier. My optimism grew during succeeding days as we explored the edge of Hidden Valley, fished for grayling in Windy River, spied on a dun-coloured arctic fox not yet in his white winter coat, captured live lemmings, stalked ptarmigan, and made love on the soft lichens in a hidden cleft in the Caribou Hills.

Fran was interested in the work Andy and I were doing though repelled by the killing it entailed. She could not accept that so many deer had to be butchered for, as Andy put it, "the good of the species."

"Can't you find out what you need to know by *watching* them?" Fran asked. "We don't kill people to find out what makes *them* tick, do we?"

I avoided a direct reply but Andy accepted the challenge.

"Suppose science did limit itself to studying living animals in their natural state, we would need hundreds more scientists to dig out all the data we need to set up effective management programs and protect the caribou herds. We don't have that many trained zoologists so if we have to kill some deer in order to get the data . . . well, Fran, that's just the way it has to be."

Although she may not have been fully convinced, Frances showed no compunction about cooking or eating caribou meat. In fact, she took over the cook's job so effectively that within a week she was even baking bread, something she had never done before.

I had feared Andy might resent her arrival but he showed no sign of doing so. To the contrary, he was exceptionally sympathetic to her problems.

I was less sympathetic to his, wilfully so. I did not let myself consider what his inner feelings might be at finding himself, a sexually vigorous young male, the odd man out in a potential but unrealized *ménage à trois*.

Fran's problems were of a different kind. During the early hours before one bitterly cold dawn, I was awakened by what I thought were raindrops penetrating the roof to patter onto our shared sleeping bag. I reached for a flashlight and by its pale shimmer discovered we were being subjected to a living rain of small white worms – maggots no less. It took me only moments to realize they were blowfly larvae that had been prospering in the rotting deer hides on the roof until an especially cold night had driven them to seek a warmer haven down below.

I did not find the sight of them particularly repulsive, and might even have felt sorry for them had not Frances chosen that moment to awaken. Although she neither screamed nor panicked, she was not well pleased. I shepherded her into the main cabin, where she spent the rest of the night in the bunk there that had formerly been

mine. Andy, bless him, got up, lit the stove, and made her a sooth-
ing cup of cocoa.

While we had been settling in, Alekahaw had carried the word
to the Ihalmiut that I was back, with a white wife and a planeload
of treasures. Every able male in the camps immediately set off for
Windy Cabin. Ohoto was the first to arrive. He brought gifts: two
wolf skins for me and a precious deer tongue for Fran, which would
have been the Inuit equivalent of a box of Swiss chocolates.

Ohoto and Fran established an instant rapport. That very
evening he began teaching her how to make pornographic string
figures, while she responded by brewing gallons of tea for him.

Next day Fran and I trekked far out into the Barrens to watch
herds of buck deer go drifting by. Their enormous racks of antlers –
now free of velvet – gleamed as if polished and clicked and clacked
against one another with a sound like castanets. The rut was about
to begin, and soon the plains would echo to the sound and fury of
a spectacularly horny multitude.

While we watched the passing parade of caribou, a human
figure appeared over a distant ridge and trotted toward us. It was
Ohoto's cousin, Halo, also bearing gifts, including a *tuglee*, a delicately carved woman's hair ornament of antler bone that he shyly
gave Fran. He told us most of the other men were close behind.

By midnight the cabin was bulging. In addition to Ohoto and
Halo, Fran found herself entertaining Alekahaw, Ootek, Onekwa,
Yaha, and Yaha's six-year-old son, Alektaiuwa. The stove glowed as
Fran produced a torrent of tea, not just steeped but boiled in a five-
gallon pail and served in whatever mugs, pots, and old tin cans
could be found. Andy and I provided tobacco, and every Inuit,
including young Alektaiuwa, lit up a stone pipe.

For a young woman from a middle-class Toronto milieu, Fran
not only appeared surprisingly at ease, she seemed to be having the

time of her life. Despite the fact that she spoke not a word of Inuktitut, and none of the Ihalmiut but Ohoto had a word of English, she and our guests got along so famously that the Great Inaugural Tea Party, as we later called it, lasted until dawn, when we finally packed our guests off so we could catch a few hours' sleep.

As more Ihalmiut arrived, they also became Frances's admirers, guests, and helpers. Ohoto and Ootek took over our fish nets and every morning brought in more trout and whitefish than all of us could use. Others roamed the plains, armed now with new rifles and ample ammunition, and saw to it that our larder was overstocked with meat. Youngsters scoured the Windy River valley for wood to keep the big cook stove glowing and so ensure there would always be tea "on tap."

Our social life became positively hectic. Every evening (and at frequent intervals during most days) the cabin would become crowded; tea would flow, and conversation, story-telling, Inuit drum-dancing, *kablunait* singing, laughter, and high spirits would erupt and continue until, having had enough, we would shepherd our ebullient guests out the door and thankfully crawl into our sleeping bags. The Ihalmiut proved themselves indefatigable party-goers.

The boy Alektaiuwa became Fran's inseparable companion. One day he took her to nearby Soapstone Point to demonstrate his expertise as a hand-line fisher. Using a spinner I had given him, he hooked a twenty-three-pound lake trout that he did not have the strength to pull ashore. He and the fish engaged in a desperate tug-of-war. The fish fought silently but Alex shouted so loudly in his incongruously gruff voice that everyone within hearing turned out to watch the duel.

Alex eventually dragged the great fish to within a few feet of shore where, in a last act of desperation, it snatched the line right out of the boy's hands. Without hesitation he plunged into the river to grapple with the fleeing fish. When his chilled fingers proved incapable of maintaining a grip, he sank his teeth into its tail and, sitting shoulder-deep in the fast-flowing and icy water, held on for dear life.

At this juncture Fran fearlessly waded in and stunned the fish with a rock and together, they hauled their prize ashore. Thereafter, boy and woman became such fast friends that on occasion I had to chase the lad out of our room to keep him from sharing the bed with us.

Life for Fran as the centre of attention from ten males (including Tegpa) seemed to imbue her with an energy and vivacity I had not seen before. However, as September drew on the days began to darken. All our Inuit visitors departed for their own camps, armed with new rifles and anxious to get on with the hunt upon which their survival depended. They would have no more time for visiting until late November, when their meat caches should be full and the tuktu herds would have abandoned the Barren Lands.

By then we, too, expected to be gone. The original plan had been to have Gunnar fly us south to Brochet early in October, to take up quarters in the heart of the caribou winter range. But as time passed we began to wonder if this plan could be realized. Since our little radio produced only ominous silence or bursts of crackling static, we had no way of knowing what was happening "outside" and when, or even if, the Department intended to implement the plan.

Andy and I knew that unless we were flown out before freeze-up we would be stranded at Windy Cabin until the ice on the bay could support a ski-equipped plane.

So while trying to avoid alarming Frances, we began making surreptitious preparations for a prolonged stay. We spent weary hours in the little copses scattered along the river valley cutting and stacking wood to be hauled back to the cabin on hand sleds once sufficient snow had fallen. Closer to home we netted scores of trout and whitefish. These we gutted, split, and racked to dry or freeze in an outhouse in which we also hung haunches of deer meat and strings of ptarmigan.

Impelled by primal instinct we, like all the Others around us, were working compulsively to ensure survival during the dark and hungry times that would soon be upon us.

We could not conceal what we were doing from Frances and she grew increasingly uneasy. The absence of other human beings, the disappearance of the deer (together with most other visible forms of life), and the imminence of arctic winter heightened her anxiety until she began slipping back into the quagmire of depression that had engulfed her before my visit to Toronto.

She was not the only one of us with problems.

Andy had about had his fill of "studies in the field" and was itching to return to university to process his data and get on with acquiring his degree. Furthermore, he and I were increasingly at odds over my growing suspicion that science was *not* necessarily the absolute source of truth and understanding. During one of our disagreements about what I had begun to disparagingly refer to as the New Religion, I accused my friend of becoming a "fact addict." To which he heatedly replied that I was allowing myself to be led astray by "sheer emotionalism and an addiction to fairy tales."

Whatever his reasons (sexual frustration may have been one of them) the gap between us widened until a day late in September when he announced he would not go to Brochet but would return to Toronto when Gunnar came for us.

I ought to have felt bad about this, and how it might affect our friendship but I was more worried that Fran would want to return to Toronto.

As autumn slid precipitately toward winter, Fran took to spending more and more of her time in bed, seemingly immersed in one of our few books. Occasionally I was able to persuade her to go for a short trip in the canoe or a walk over the ridges behind the cabin, where hundreds of cackling ptarmigan were assembling before heading south. However, such interludes gave her no real relief. Only Tegpa seemed able to lighten my wife's inner darkness.

Andy was now spending most of his waking hours out on the land gathering data about food available to caribou in winter. When at the cabin he isolated himself, doing analysis of tissue samples or identifying and preserving caribou parasites. I chiefly occupied myself with camp chores and with my journals, while remaining ever alert for the distant whine of an aircraft engine.

Meaningful communications among us almost ceased. Tegpa seemed to understand that his little pack was in trouble and did his best to rectify matters. Playing no favourites, he made himself available to each of us on equal terms, providing a conduit between us.

Early in October, after several days of sleet squalls and snow flurries, a clear, bright morning provided an excuse to put some distance between myself and Windy Cabin. Claiming that I needed to examine the inside of the wolf den at Smith House Bay now that they had moved out, I donned my parka, gathered my gear, and launched the canoe. We had no more gas for the kicker but an exhilarating paddle took me to the shore of Smith House Bay, where I landed and walked half a mile to Wolf Knoll, the high sandy esker that held the den. No wolves were about, nor was there any recent evidence of their presence from which I concluded the den had, indeed, been abandoned for the season.

Setting my rifle aside, I shed parka and sweater, got out a measuring tape and a flashlight (whose batteries were almost exhausted), and began wiggling headfirst into a tunnel just large enough to admit me. The flashlight was so dim I could hardly read the numbers on the tape as I squirmed along, descending at a shallow angle. I had gone about eight feet, with sand in my mouth and eyes and feeling increasingly claustrophobic, when the tunnel abruptly bent to the left.

I pointed the failing beam from the torch around the corner and four green-glowing orbs announced that the den was not empty after all. In a millisecond the companionable feeling I had earlier developed for the wolves of Smith House Bay vanished, to be replaced by pure terror inspired by the absolute conviction I was about to be attacked and torn apart.

Angeline, the alpha female of the Wolf Knoll family, and one of her pups of the year were crouched motionless against the back of the nest cavity staring fixedly at what *they* may well have believed was the approach of death.

They did not move.

They did not so much as growl.

Except for the steadfast glow from their eyes, they might have been figments of my imagination.

But I knew they were not, and panic overwhelmed me. I wriggled backwards up the slanting tunnel as if pursued by devils. My mind seethed with imprecations that I may have yelled aloud. I am not certain about that now, but I remember with total clarity what I did when I scrambled out of the tunnel's mouth.

I seized my rifle and began firing point-blank into the tunnel. One – two – three – four roaring explosions to accompany my scream:

"I'll . . . blow . . . your . . . fucking . . . heads off!"

The magazine was empty, and I stepped back to reload. Though the wind was blowing chill, a witless fury boiled within me. I was determined to force the wolves into the open, where I would almost certainly have killed them.

Slinging the rifle over one shoulder, I set about gathering branches, twigs, and leaves that I stuffed into the den mouth until it was stoppered almost full. Then I set the mass on fire. As yellow flames licked upward, I fanned them with my parka to drive roiling black smoke into the depths of the den.

No movement and no sound came from within.

As the flash fire burned down, sanity began returning to me. I put the rifle aside, lit a cigarette, and began considering what I had done. There was no avoiding recognition that in this encounter with creatures for whom I had earlier professed feelings of admiration, empathy, and even affection, I had behaved execrably – in fact, murderously. As the cigarette burned down, I began to see just how viciously I had denied all that my experiences with the Others in this land of theirs had taught me about them. And about myself.

Disgusted by what I had done, I stamped out what remained of the fire and again began waving my parka over the den mouth as a fan – this time driving fresh air into it.

When no more wisps of smoke emerged, I crawled back in myself.

I wasn't afraid anymore. I guess I was too ashamed for that. My poor friends were just where I'd left them but had their noses buried in the sand, I suppose to escape the smoke. The flashlight was about gone but I could see enough to convince myself they were still alive.

I backed out then and left them there. There wasn't anything else I really could have done, though I have to say leaving them made me feel like an absolute shit. A strictly human sort of a shit, because only a human could or would have done what I had done.

As I paddled miserably homeward a wolf howled somewhere to the north – howled lightly, questioningly. I recognized the voice for I had heard it many times before. It was George, the alpha male and pack leader, sounding the Barrens for the absent members of his family.

His was the voice of a lost world. A world and a fellowship that had once been ours.

Until we humans chose the alien role.